AF352709

Enculturation Processes in Primary Language Acquisition

Enculturation Processes in Primary Language Acquisition

Anna Dina L. Joaquin

SHEFFIELD UK   BRISTOL CT

Published by Equinox Publishing Ltd.

UK: Kelham House, 3 Lancaster Street, Sheffield, S3 8AF
USA: ISD, 70 Enterprise Drive, Bristol, CT 06010

www.equinoxpub.com

First published 2013

ISBN 978 1 908049 99 5 (hardback)

British Library Cataloguing-in-Publication Data

A catalogue record for this book is available from the British Library.

Library of Congress Cataloging-in-Publication Data

Joaquin, Anna Dina L., 1975-
 Enculturation processes in primary language acquisition / Anna Dina L. Joaquin.
    pages cm
 Includes bibliographical references and index.
 ISBN 978-1-908049-99-5 (hb)
1. Language acquisition--Cross-cultural studies. 2. Language and culture--Cross-cultural studies. 3. Native language and education--Cross-cultural studies. 4. Psycholingusitics. I. Title.
 P118.J63 2013
 401'.93--dc23
                              2012048804

Typeset by ISB Typesetting, Sheffield, UK

Printed and bound in Great Britain by Lightning Source UK Ltd., Milton Keynes and Lightning Source Inc., La Vergne, TN

For Raphael

Contents

Acknowledgments

This book builds upon the work I began as a doctoral student in Applied Linguistics at UCLA. It would not have been possible without my family and friends, who have provided encouragement and support throughout the many stages of writing and revising of this book. It would also not have been possible without my advisors and colleagues who have provided guidance, many insightful discussions, suggestions, and questions throughout the development of this project, including John H. Schumann, Candy Goodwin, Chuck Goodwin, Alan Fiske, Namhee Lee, Andrea W. Mates, Lisa Mikesell, Michael S. Smith, members of the Neurobiology of Language Research Group (NLRG), and other graduate students in Applied Linguistics at UCLA. Each person stimulated and challenged me with their perspective on how to understand language acquisition and socialization as an interactional, cultural and biological phenomenon.

I am indebted to the FTD patients, their families and caregivers, as well as the researchers who gathered the data. In addition, I am grateful to Fazila Bhimji, Namhee Han and Nadja Reissland, who allowed me to use their data as examples in this book. I am also very thankful for the scholars at various conferences, and the reviewers of this book who provided helpful feedback and comments that have made this book, I believe, better. I am also thankful for the editorial assistance of graduate students at CSUN: Bradley Torti, Christian Leu, and Megan Goetz. Much thanks also goes to Michael S. Smith for his assistance with the illustrations and images that brought the data to life.

Foreword

John H. Schumann

In this book, Anna Joaquin views language as a cultural phenomenon that evolved in phylogenetic time, is acquired in developmental time, and is used by societies in somatic time. Language socialization has been viewed preeminently as a cultural phenomenon, but it depends deeply on biology. Joaquin pursues the Vygotskyan view that it is both. She examines how structures in the human nervous system have developed to respond to cultural practices (and vice versa), allowing experiences at the social level to become incorporated by the brain and body. This blend of neuroscience and social science to address the question of how a child learns to speak, and thus becomes a functioning member of society, constitutes an important contribution to the humanities in this era of post-Chomsky linguistics. Her research recognizes the human as both a biological and a social being in which the biology and the sociality are integrated. Understanding human nature cannot be achieved by studying the two independently. In this volume she achieves a remarkable integration of these two lines of influence on child language acquisition.

Another feature of the book is the concern for language acquisition and cultures in which the intensive face-to-face caregiver child interaction does not seem to occur. She observes that children do acquire language by overhearing it in interaction between and among third parties. She argues that the aspect of the Interactional Instinct that sees infants' desire to bond with and become like conspecifics potentiates language acquisition even with less direct interaction.

Additionally, Joaquin illuminates the social in language acquisition by showing that the prefrontal cortex is involved in mediating the acquisition of language pragmatics. This part of the brain is not ordinarily associated with the neural systems that underlie language. But, by contrasting the loss of social appropriateness in a disease like frontotemporal dementia with the acquisition of social appropriateness by children, she illustrates how this brain region subserves the acquisition of the ability to make appropriate decisions in language pragmatics.

The book reflects the rather unusual training that Joaquin had as a doctoral student as she pursued language acquisition, conversational analysis, and the neurobiology of language. Additionally, in formulating her perspective on socialization, she became a thoroughgoing developmentalist with a deep understanding of the emotional, cognitive, neurobiological and interactional bases for language acquisition.

The book is essential reading for anyone who wants to understand socioneurobiology of language acquisition. It achieves this in a manner that will be informative for developmental psychologists, socio-cultural theorists, and neurobiologists of language. It is written in such a way that all of these audiences will be informed in the area of expertise and will easily grasp the material in the areas in which they are less familiar.

John H. Schumann is a professor of Applied Linguistics and former chair of the Department of Applied Linguistics and TESL at UCLA. His research includes the neurobiology of the language, the neurobiology of learning, language acquisition, and language evolution. He is co-author of *The Interactional Instinct: The Evolution and Acquisition of Language* (Oxford University Press, 2009) and *The Neurobiology of Learning* (Erlbaum, 2004). He is also the author of *The Neurobiology of Affect in Language* (Blackwell, 1997).

1   Introduction and overview

In 1957, in his book *Verbal Behavior,* Skinner suggested that we learn language by making associations through the process of conditioning. In this view, language is learned piecemeal, through the same learning mechanisms as other behaviors, and new instances are generalized and inducted into our existing language repertoires. This notion that we could learn language through simple association and induction processes was challenged by Chomksy (1959), who argued that the individual, piecemeal utterances children are exposed to were insufficient to explain children's understanding, and later on the use of, more complex 'adult' language. This *Poverty of Stimulus Argument* led to the view that human beings have an a priori knowledge of language structure that generally remains the same throughout all stages of language development because it comes from a single universal grammar (UG). This powerful and intuitive theory made way for generative linguistics.

However, since Chomsky's claims, various researchers propose that new findings in research 'suggests a re-evaluation of the situation' (Tomasello *et al.*, 2003: 3). Two basic skills that Tomasello *et al.* (2003) point out are: intention reading and pattern finding skills. Intention reading involves the ability to share and follow the attention of other persons, and to actively direct the attention of others by pointing, showing, and using nonlinguistic gestures. In addition, intention reading involves the ability to imitate communicative acts and intentions (Bates, 1979; Bakeman and Adamson, 1984; Tomasello *et al.*, 1993; Corkum and Moore, 1995). Considering and addressing the symbolic and functional dimension of language acquisition, such skills, according to Tomasello, allow a child to acquire the appropriate use of linguistic symbols, expressions, and constructions. The second skill, pattern finding, includes the ability to perform statistically based distributional analyses on various kinds of perceptual and behavioral sequences and to form categories of similar objects and events (Saffran *et al.*, 1996; Marcus, *et al.* 1999; Rakison and Oakes, 2003; Tomasello, 2003 citing Gomez and Gerken, 1999). Such skills allow children to find patterns in the way adults use linguistic symbols across different utterances, through joint attentional frameworks, and allow them formulate the grammar of a language. Thus, children have at their disposal more powerful learning mechanisms than once thought and language acquisition may be able to occur without a UG.

Others have taken issue with the Chomskyan's data for analysis. As Chomsky's basic concern was to uncover the underlying rules that allow us to generate grammatical sentences, he first distinguished between the ability to produce grammatical sentences (*competence*) and the actual production of sentences (*performance*). Then, because performance data is full of 'noise' or speech errors, Chomsky turned to idealized sentences that are well-formed according to speakers' intuitions to get at our *competence*. Therefore, Chomsky's data set is idealized in the sense that they are: (1) regularized, so that speech errors are removed; (2) standardized and free of pronunciation and speech variation; and (3) decontextualized, or separate from any specific context in which they might be used (Lyons, 1967). By studying speakers' intuitions of such idealized sentences, Chomsky argued that we could get at universal grammar. However, conversation and discourse analysts argue, among other things, that the focus on grammaticality fails to provide a complete explanation of language. They also argue that transcripts of real people having an ordinary conversation reveal that 'utterances are regularly ungrammatical in everyday talk without eliciting comment [from their interlocutors], they cohere into sequential discourse, and they are commonly the joint achievement of two or more people' (Potter and Wetherell, 1987: 13). Language in conversation has been shown to be 'locally managed, party-administered, interactionally controlled, and sensitive to recipient design' (Sacks *et al.*, 1974: 696). Therefore, Sacks (1984) and other conversation analysts (Goodwin, 1979, 1980, 1983; Jefferson, 1973, 1974, 1985; Schegloff *et al.*, 1977) have shown that the 'noise' typically found in natural discourse that is edited out, sanitized by reconstruction and removed in intuition based sentences, is extremely rich and often crucial for interlocutors (Lee *et al.*, 2009). Thus, as Lee *et al.* (2009) point out, 'the ways in which one employs grammar, typically regarded as one's performance, actually demonstrate one's competence' (101). From these perspectives, the primordial site for language is not found in the brain, but is in talk-in-interaction; language is made up of particular utterances deployed by real users in particular contexts to accomplish particular social goals.

In 2009, Lee *et al.* (2009) proposed a perspective on language acquisition based on evolutionary biology and neurobiology. They argued that language is first a cultural artifact that emerges as a complex adaptive system. They proposed that the ubiquity of language acquisition among children is the product of an *Interactional Instinct* that is subserved by the neurobiology of affiliation and supported by pattern finding abilities discussed by Tomasello. This instinct, along with pattern finding abilities, ensures that the language formed and shaped through interaction is passed down to succeeding generations. In some ways this book is an extension of that perspective. It attempts to consider, in greater depth, the social and cultural contexts in which language must be learned. Where context (the social and cultural milieu) from the generative perspective may not be considered and even be onerous to analyze, this book views the contexts that we are exposed to as facilitative and crucial to language acquisition. Furthermore, this book explores how the brain might subserve this learning environment without a UG.

In short, this book explores how language is acquired via enculturation; it asks how one is socialized into becoming a culturally competent member of the society to which he/she belongs and what might be the biology that subserves the socialization. This project will be rooted in the fundamental tenets of Vygotsky's sociocultural theory (Luria, 1976; Vygotsky, 1978), which proposed two general lines of development that are intertwined in the ontogenesis of the individual – the natural line of biological maturation and the cultural line. From the interaction between the two trajectories – the human develops:

> The growth of the normal child into civilization usually involves a fusion with the processes of organic maturation. Both planes of development – the natural and the cultural line – coincide and mingle with one another. The two lines of change interpenetrate one another and essentially form a single line of sociobiological formation of the child's psychology. (Vygotsky, 1960: 47)

Vygotsky, in theory, never discounted the role of biological factors in a complete account of ontogenesis. For Vygotsky, culture can shape our biology and biology can affect our culture as one participates in culturally organized practices, builds social relationships, and learns to use cultural artifacts.

Though, we are, as Rogoff states, 'biologically cultural' (2003: 63), such that our biology exists and perhaps constrains our ability for culture learning, many researchers have 'tended to lose sight of the fact that their ultimate goal is to contribute to some integrated, holistic picture of human nature' (Wertsch, 1986: 1), and many have focused on either the cultural line or the biological line. On the cultural aspect, many researchers have successfully been capturing the practices of socialization among siblings, peers, parents, kin, and teachers to enculturate their youth (Ochs and Schieffelin, 1984; Zukow, 1989; Gutiérrez, 2002; Rogoff, 2003, Paugh, 2005; De Leon, 2008). On the other hand, in the neurosciences, through experimental work, usually done in controlled conditions and not in a natural occurring interactive context, researchers have been trying to understand the neurobiological underpinnings of aspects of social behavior (Grattan and Eslinger, 1991; Damasio, 1994; Nishitani and Hari, 2000; Umiltà *et al.*, 2001; Watkins *et al.*, 2002; Carr *et al.*, 2003; Iacoboni *et al*, 2005; Gallese, 2006). Using technology that allows us to look at the brain, researchers have focused on explaining social behavior as a psychological and/or physiological phenomenon. Though both fields with different methods, foci, and frameworks have been, to some degree, examining the development of human behavior and have been making very important contributions to our understanding, they have generally been separate fields with little discussion between them. Thus, the purpose of this book is to address two fundamental questions: (1) how one is socialized into becoming a competent member of the society to which he/she belongs; and (2) what might be the biology that facilitates, subserves and constrains such learning? In particular, this book explores how language might be acquired via our enculturation, and how that enculturation both fits and forms the brain.

Overview

This book begins with an examination of the practices by which we are enculturated. Indeed, naïve members of a society are given the opportunity to be socialized into their culture, and more specifically how to use language via processes that include eavesdropping, observation, participation, imitation, and language socialization (Fiske, unpublished manuscript; Hogbin, 1970; Ward, 1971; Schieffelin and Ochs, 1986; Ochs and Schieffelin, 2001; Rogoff, 2003; Lancy, 2008). However, ethnographic accounts also overwhelmingly show that children bear great personal responsibility for acquiring their culture. Children become enculturated in large part on their own initiative (Fiske, unpublished manuscript; Lancy, 2008). For example, some societies, such as the Kpelle, rely greatly 'on the child's inherent motivation to imitate adults' and 'rely on the child's curiosity and desire for mastery to propel it forward toward competent practice' (Lancy, 1996: 146). Therefore, in Chapter 3, I argue for a motivation to attune to, seek out, and become like others – or an *Interactional Instinct* (II). This drive is motivated by one's desire for affiliation with others, which facilitates enculturation. Evidence for the interactional instinct comes from studies of human neonate behavior. Infants, shortly after birth have been found to be born with social stimulus feature detectors and perceptual abilities that allow them to be active participants in interaction with caregivers. Thus, very young infants are found to elicit and engage in interaction with those in their social environment. Infants imitate (Meltzoff and Moore, 1997), initiate interaction (Pawlby, 1977), and demonstrate an understanding of emotional expressions (Tronick *et al.*, 1979), 'conversational' practices (i.e. turn-taking) (Beebe *et al.*, 1979), and the relevance of communicative/social cues (Brugger *et al.*, 2007). Such behaviors manifest a drive for interaction and have also been observed in polyadic cultures (Fox Adams, forthcoming; De Leon, 2008) and traditional societies (Hewlett *et al.*, 1998). Moreover, the interactional instinct may also lead to the organization of the bodies of naïve learners and more socially competent beings in an interactive space. The interactional instinct and inter-active social space provide a social framework for the learning of culture through local traditions and practices for the 'teaching' of its naïve members.

As sociocultural theory asserts, cultural learning is intertwined with our biological development. Thus, Chapters 4 and 5 begin the examination of the biology that underlies the interactional instinct. Chapter 4 examines the neurobiology of affiliation and reward as the system that subserves the interactional instinct. Chapter 5, in a way, is an extension of Chapter 3 as it examines how the interactional instinct might be manifested in caregivers as it explores the biology for the 'caregiver's instinct'.

Though direct instruction may occur, the reality is that much of social-ization and learning occurs via listening-in, observation, and imitation (Schieffelin, 1991; Rogoff, 2003; Rogoff *et al.*, 2007). This is also true with language acquisition and use. Though we have seen members of a society scaffold language acquisition, and have seen older members instruct and/or guide naïve members on how to use language, many ethnographic research-ers have also suggested that children in some parts of the world have to learn language mostly, if not exclusively, through eavesdropping. Thus, Chapter 6 explores the extraordinary abilities we have that facilitate language acquisi-tion through exposure and imitation.

The following chapters explore more of our biological readiness and the neurological structures and systems that may have evolved to respond to the input provided by society to facilitate the learning of cultural prac-tices and traditions by its youth. Chapter 7 reports the potential role that mirror neurons may have in the process, and perhaps in language acquisi-tion. Chapter 8 suggests that the trajectory of brain development, particu-larly of the frontal lobes, necessitates the socialization practices that are discussed in Chapter 2, such that society intervenes and acts as an 'external prefrontal cortex' (Joaquin, 2008, 2010b; Schumann, 2010) during one's development. Then, by examining the behaviors of frontotemporal demen-tia patients, who have degenerating frontal lobes, I argue that the prefron-tal cortex mediates one's ability to appraise possible actions and to act as a socially competent member of society. Thus, it is argued that the prefron-tal cortex has a prominent role in the acquisition of cultural schemas, and is central to, if not the target of, the processes of socialization. Chapter 9 more specifically examines the role of the prefrontal cortex in decision-making and pragmatics – what to do/say, how to do/say it, where to do/say it, why to do/say something, and with whom. Finally, Chapter 10 concludes by raising and discussing some challenges to this perspective.

Therefore, this book can be seen as viewing language acquisition through enculturation as the result of three factors. First, we are given the *opportunity* to be exposed to and acquire the language needed to be a socially competent member of society, through societies' social structures and practices of enculturation. Then, we have an innate *motivation* to acquire language; finally, we have the *ability* as supported by our biology to acquire language as a cultural artifact. Such a perspective provides an alternative view to how languages are acquired.

2 Cultural practices for internalization

Though human beings are arguably born with far more than once believed and are more capable than what was once originally thought (Gopnik, 2009), we are not born with an innate knowledge of what are considered to be socially appropriate and inappropriate behaviors. Young children are not born knowing how to do the mundane, the proper ways of speaking to adults, how to address people respectfully, or how to show concern, compassion, and empathy toward others. These are not innate abilities; they must be learned. People's ways of thinking and behaving are not innate traits but are partially a product of the social environment in which they live. Governments, organizations, schools, parents, families, siblings, teachers, coaches, friends – society – invest their resources as 'teachers' to train and socialize children to the appropriate behavior and morals that reflect the culture, family, and organizations.

Though many are involved in the socialization process, it is clear that family members play a significant role in children's acquisition of social knowledge and morality. As Ochs and Kremer-Sadlik state, 'the flourishing of these qualities relies upon experiences with (the family)' (Ochs and Kremer-Sadlik, 2007: 5). They further note:

> This is a tall order for families … morality is embedded in and is an outcome of everyday family practices. The flow of interactions involving children is imbued with implicit and explicit messages about right and wrong, better and worse, rules, norms, obligations, duties, etiquette, moral reasoning, virtue, character, and other dimensions of how to lead a moral life. (Ochs and Kremer-Sadlik, 2007: 5)

Thus, Goodwin (2006), for example, reports directive sequences in which parents vigilantly pursue responses from children in order for them to learn the appropriate next response.

Another important social domain is school. Increasingly, many younger children are spending their most impressionable years in school. For many, preschool may be the first important social community that they encounter beyond the family. Therefore, schools are not just environments for children to gain academic competence, but perhaps even more so – social competence. As Principal Hua, from a Chinese preschool, states 'The work we do here is very important, more important than just caring for children while their parents work. We are not baby-sitters – we are educators. The most important lessons we teach children, in addition to numbers and reading and writing, are moral lessons' (Tobin *et al.*, 1989: 109). School is an environment in which children can receive messages about how society operates and can develop a set of standards for behavior. And, with the large number of dual-career family homes, this responsibility of socialization is increasingly being placed upon substitute caregivers – namely teachers, who model, encourage, and validate prosocial behavior, as well as correct what is considered to be antisocial. Perhaps the critical role that teachers may have is expressed in Chinese theories of development that emphasize that, 'children are not born knowing how to behave correctly … Both Confucius and Mao emphasize that since character is shaped by experience, teachers bear the responsibility of teaching students self-restraint and correct behavior' (Tobin *et al.*, 1989: 96).

Lastly, children spend at least 7–8 hours each day in peer-rich environments. In Western societies, children and adolescents spend most of their days with peers in school, which constitutes another important source of social knowledge for children and adolescents to learn how to act and behave appropriately. Though teachers are often seen as the primary substitute caregivers, peers can also be a very important socializing force. In China, for example, where children are raised without siblings, 'preschools provide single children with the chance to interact with other children and with teachers trained to correct errors' (Tobin *et al.*, 1989: 91).

Thus, though parents have a critical role in the socialization process, caring and providing for the young is also often carried out by others – known as alloparenting. Though often neglected, research on siblings demonstrates that 'siblings act as socializing agents in cultures throughout the world' (Zukow, 1989: 80) and facilitate the 'elaboration of certain values, attitudes, and beliefs that are subsequently critical elements of adult social behavior' (Whittemore and Beverly, 1989: 28). Moreover, a comparison of caretaking practices across traditional hunting and gathering peoples show that 'babies are never left alone and are constantly held by someone, but that someone is not invariably the mother' (Hrdy, 2009: 73). In many traditional societies, shared care is the rule and its significance is indicated in Coontz' statement that 'Children do best in societies where childrearing is considered too important to be left entirely to parents' (Coontz, 1992: 230). For example, Hadza newborns are held by alloparents 85 percent of the time and Efe and Aka mothers pass their babies to other group members immediately after birth, who also nurse the baby (Hrdy, 2009: 76).

Through interactions within these social domains, individuals may be socialized into knowledge of right and wrong, better and worse, appropriate and inappropriate, acceptable and unacceptable behavior and other aspects of what is required to be a socially competent member of society. Researchers from the sociocultural perspective, applied linguists, anthropologists, and psychologists have examined the practices of socialization among multiple caregivers and the methods used to foster learning; siblings, peers, parents, kin and teachers enculturate their young to cultural schemas of the community to which one belongs (Fiske, unpublished manuscript; Weisner, 1982; Schieffelin and Ochs, 1986; Schieffelin, 1991; De Leon, 2008). Such practices may occur within an interactionally constituted space that provides naïve members with opportunities to gain knowledge about cultural beliefs, values, and norms. For example, Nakamura (1996) examined the language and actions of Japanese mothers at home with preverbal infants playing with their infants during dinner. Nakamura found that mothers provided linguistic modeling of polite language in situations in which they were scolding, praising, or requesting from the infants. Mothers also elicited politeness routines from their infants such as waving goodbye, bowing, and gesturing *choodai* 'please give me'. Another example can be seen in the observations of a Kpelle village, where there are designated open spaces, known as 'on the mother-ground'. Such places serve as the locus of adult work that children observe and as a playground where children engage in make-believe play of what they have observed. These open spaces are also places where children can be 'mothered' or watched over, and a place where any adult can rebuke them and has authority over them (LeVine, 1973; Lancy, 1996). The 'motherground' is another example of how cultural practices are made available to naïve members. However, ways of culture learning – transmitting and learning traditions, values, social practices, and the cultural processes involving the use of technologies – vary from community-to-community as 'each society generates routines for the care and enculturation of its children' (Lancy, 1996: 12). Such practices include eavesdropping, observation, participation, imitation and language socialization. These are not the only learning techniques observed in all societies.[1] And though researchers have observed a preference of method or a bias toward a tradition of learning within a community, such techniques may not be mutually exclusive.

Eavesdropping: Listening-in and observation

Consider the following statement made by an adult from a working class African American community:

> You think I kin tell Teegie all he gotta know to get along? He just
> gotta be keen, keep his eyes open, don't he be sorry? Gotta watch

> hisself by watchin' other folks. Ain't no use me telling im: 'Learn
> dis, learn dat. What's dis? What's dat?' (Heath, 1983: 84)

This statement is an example of the perspective of the learning of culture as mediated through 'eavesdropping' or listening-in and observing, and without participating in a relevant activity. Similarly, Ward (1971), in her observations of an African American community in Louisiana, found that learning through overhearing was emphasized. In this community, toddlers silently observe community life as they participated in daily community events and spent hours sitting still and listening in to adults' conversations. Furthermore, children were not encouraged to learn skills in initiating and participating in conversations, nor were they treated as conversational partners. Cultural and social knowledge in such environments, Ingold (1993) notes, may be obtained through an active, practical engagement with other persons and things in the environment, through 'exploratory touching, looking, listening and – of course – speaking' (443).

In a longitudinal ethnographic study of the role of cultural context in the communicative interactions of young Inuit children, Crago (1992) found that children were neither expected to participate nor ask questions of adults who were speaking together. Instead, Inuit men recalled that they learned how to hunt by overhearing conversations in the tents. As one Inuk woman remembered:

> the grown-ups crouched near the stove drinking tea. She remembered lying there listening to their conversations and stories. Not all learning then was done by observation. There was a great deal of information that was learned verbally through listening. However, information was not directed specifically at children nor were children to obtain information by questioning. Instead learning occurred by overhearing the conversations and stories of adults. (Crago, 1992: 498)

Among the Kaluli in Polynesia, Schieffelin (1991) observed that from the beginning, infants are surrounded by adults and older children who spend a great deal of time talking to each other with little speech directed to pre-verbal children. Instead, infants between the ages of 6–12 months are held in caregivers' laps or carried on the shoulders of mothers or older siblings so that they are positioned to overhear and observe all the activities that their mothers participate in. In addition, as 'toddlers become increasingly mobile and develop strong interests in people and activities, their actions are referred to, described, and commented upon by members of the household, especially older children, speaking to one another...[which] is available for the toddlers to hear, though it is not addressed to or formulated for them' (Schieffelin, 1991: 73). For the most part, Kaluli do not provide any explicit instruction or formulate their talk to be directed toward children. In fact, adults claim that children must hear *halaido,* or hard language, if they are to speak correctly. Thus, children must learn, but by listening and observing.

In the Athabascan community in Northern Canada, the preferred way to learn about adult activities is also through eavesdropping. As Scollon and Scollon (1981) report:

> The ideal learning situation for a child or young person is to be able to hear the stories of elders. The ideal situation described is that of elders speaking to each other as narrator and audience with the child in a third, observational role ... Because the child is not directly required to respond to the narratives, his own autonomy is respected at a time in his life when it is likely to be highly vulnerable. While this three-party narrative situation may not always occur, those who are able to learn in this way are regarded as fortunate. (120–121).

Thus, in various communities, cultural practices may be transmitted and learned implicitly as their young listen to and overhear adults' stories, narratives, and conversations.

Observation, participation and imitation

In addition to learning via eavesdropping, in other societies where culture learning involves little explanation and instruction, learning via observation, participation, and imitation is emphasized. Studies have shown that children often repeat an observed action when alone over long periods of time (Aronfreed, 1969). For example, after watching adults who were reading aloud, preschool children have been observed to spontaneously pick up books and imitate adults (Haskett and Lenfestey, 1974).

Nakamura (2000), through audio and videotaped sessions of 14 Japanese preverbal infants with their mothers, observed that mothers sensitize their infants to the use of different levels of politeness in several ways, including modeling, direct instruction, and play routines (3). Thus, by the age of 3, Japanese children are already being socialized in the use of many pragmatic aspects of the Japanese language – namely, the use of polite, formal, honorific and humble language and behavior. Reports also show that by the age of 2, Japanese children adjust their level of politeness according to age, sex, degree of familiarity, context, level of formality, and topic of conversation (Nakamura, 1997, 1999). Another study focused on the learning of a specific form in Japanese – *masu,* typically thought of as a politeness and formal marker (Cook, 2000). Through video and audio data of dinnertime conversations, Cook found that the *masu* form indexed a mode of the self for public presentation, such that the form is used when the caregivers take on a social persona – (i.e. I am speaking as a mother, or as a character in a book). By the age of 3, Cook demonstrated that children had already learned the social meaning and correct use of the *masu* form as a mode of self public presentation.

The practice of 'instruction' in such basic ways of acknowledging people in society, 'greeting and saying goodbye', is also seen in the Japanese preschool observed by Tobin *et al.* (1989) in which the day's activities are bookended with children singing a morning song that greets everybody at the beginning of class (see below) and a goodbye song as the children go outside to the playground where they will be picked up by their parents (14):

> Sensei, Ohayo (Teacher, good morning)
> Minna-San, Ohayo (Everyone, good morning)
> Genki ni asobimasho (Let's play happily)
> Ohayo, Ohayo (Good morning, good morning)

The Kaluli have also been observed to explicitly model tasks by segmenting their performances for the children to make them easier to imitate. For example, '[w]hen a mother is demonstrating how an action is done – as cupping hands to drink water from a stream, peeling a hot cooked banana, or pulling weeds from a garden – (she) will say to the child, ('Do like that') ... demarcates separable actions or simple components of a task ... (it) punctuate(s) each separable point ... and applies to a broad range of actions' (Schieffelin, 1991: 76). Then, after infants have learned to say 'mother' and 'breast', Kaluli believe that infants must be shown how to speak. At this stage, mothers continually request their children to repeat their utterances using a special word ('Say like that') which is used 'to teach the social uses of assertive language (teasing, shaming, requesting, challenging, reporting)' (Ochs and Schieffelin, 1994: 486).

In examining actions that are difficult, if not impossible, to articulate into verbal concepts, Fiske (unpublished manuscript: 3) argues that people acquire most of their culture by observation, imitation, and participation. He claims that 'research on children around the world shows that adults hardly ever tell children how to do anything or explain anything to them' (1). To illustrate, he cites a personal experience with the Moose (pronounced MOH-say) of Burkina Faso in West Africa. The Moose have an annual ritual they call *Kiuugu.* If they are asked the purpose of Kiuugu, Moose reply with a stock phrase: 'It's what we found when we were born – and we'll leave behind when we die.' If the Moose are pressed for more description and explanation, they are unable to. Fiske (unpublished manuscript: 4) notes that Kiuugu is simply a tradition. It is simply what they do. Because, like many other peoples in Africa, they do not do reflective analysis of their own practices, they do not try to explain them. Moose learn many rituals by observing them, then participating in minor roles, and eventually imitating what they have observed with others.

Hogbin (1970) also described dances among the Wogeo of New Guinea in which children are allowed to participate but are not explicitly directed. The children stand alongside more experienced and 'principal dancers, imitating them as best they can, often, as is freely admitted, to the detriment of the general effect. No one ever seems to think of sending them away' (140). Hogbin (1970) also describes occurrences in which he observed children encouraged to work alongside with their parents even if they are likely to be hindrances. For example, when an adult was making a canoe, he allowed his son to take an adze and chip at the dugout. When Hogbin asked why he allowed his son to help, the father agreed that he would be able to work much faster alone. 'But if I send the child away,' he added, 'how can I expect him to know anything? This time he was in the way, but I'm showing him, and when we have to make another canoe he'll be really useful' (143).

McPhee (1955), during her stay in Bali, was surprised by how children learned to play a *gangsa,* a musical instrument, through observation, participation, and imitation:

> Nengah's [music teacher] teaching method in this first lesson seems strangely oblique. He says nothing, does not even look at the children. Without so much as opening a word, he begins by dreamily playing through the melody of the first movement on the *gangsa,* softly, almost to himself. He plays it through again. Then he plays the first phrase only, with more emphasis. He now indicates with a glance at the *gangsa* that they are to begin … Bit by bit the children who are learning the melody are able to extend it, phrase by phrase, forgetting, remembering, gaining assurance (84).

Fiske (unpublished manuscript) notes that the same practice occurs in industrialized societies. For example, in Okinawa, Japan:

> There are no complex systems of training in skills. Adults rely heavily on observation and imitation on the part of children; they seldom 'teach' them to do things systematically. Parents were surprised and amused when questions such as 'How do you teach children to transplant rice, harvest rice, or otherwise help in the fields?' were put to them. 'We don't teach them; why they just learn by themselves,' was the usual answer.

> Children learn by observing and experimenting. Whatever adults
> are doing, children are present to watch their activities and over-
> hear their conversations. (Maretzki and Maretzki, 1966: 144)

Thus, culture learning tends to occur in the context of everyday activities through observation, 'hands-on' practice, and imitation. Indeed, in many cultural communities, observation is encouraged and honed (Kenyatta, 1953; Howard, 1970; Peak, 1986) such that children are *legitimate peripheral participants* (Lave and Wenger, 1992). For example, in a Mayan community in Mexico, children acted as the eyes and ears of mothers for information on village events. The types of questions mothers asked guided children on which events were to be observed (Gaskins and Lucy, 1987). In such communities, Rogoff suggests that *intent participation* is a widely practiced tradition (Rogoff *et al.*, 2003). Key features of the intent participation tradition involves 'keen attention during participation in shared endeavors' and 'learner's access to observe the valued community activity in question, with ongoing or anticipated participation, with learning focused on becoming able to contribute to the endeavor' (Rogoff *et al.*, 2007: 496). In intent participation traditions, children, when able and ready, contribute and pitch-in to activities. Rogoff *et al.* (2007), citing Jordan (1989), describes how Yucatecan Mayan girls who are surrounded by the routines and practices of their mothers who are midwives 'pitch in' as they become able to assist:

> As young children they may be sitting quietly in a corner as their
> mother administers a prenatal massage; they would hear stories
> of difficult cases, of miraculous outcomes, and the like. As they
> grow older, they may be passing massages, running errands, get-
> ting needed supplies. (Jordan, 1989: 932)

Reynolds (2008) examined the discursive practices and participation frameworks of Mayans in Guatemala that enact respect and responsibility within kin and peer relationships. She demonstrates how respect along two dimensions (relational and individual) is embodied. Relational respect is the amount of deference and respect one gives and receives depending on his/her gender and age. Individual respect has to do with a person's right to autonomy and the freedom to choose not to participate in a larger group activity. She shows that 'young children learn the dual notions of respect from adults and their near-peer siblings … in the ebb and flow of everyday activities' (90).

The Inuit is another community in which children are encouraged to be keen observers. Children 'are expected to take initiative in their learning by observing closely, reasoning, and finding solutions independently, with self motivation as the impetus' (Rogoff, 2003: 320). This belief is highlighted in the following account between a white middle-class Canadian child (Anna) and an Inuk mother. The Inuit community is found in northern Quebec. The child requests to be taught a game, but due to the mother's Inuk beliefs, the mother insists that the way for her to learn is through watching (Crago, 1988: 211):

Example 1[2]

> **Anna:** How do you play this game? Tell me what to do. What are the rules?
> **Inuk mother:** (gently) Watch them and you'll see how it goes.
> **Anna:** I don't know how to learn by watching, can't you tell me?
> **Inuk mother:** You'll be able to know by watching.

Thus, some communities in which children have access to observation and participation in mature activities, learning by participation, keen attention and observation – or intent participation – in an activity are encouraged. In these communities, explicit instruction may be rarely observed, however, adults make such activities accessible for observation and participation, and may have practices that facilitate such learning.

Language socialization

Analysts from a language socialization paradigm (Ochs and Schieffelin, 1984; Schieffelin and Ochs, 1986) have shown through ethnographic work the ways in which 'language is used to socialize human beings and how we are socialized to use language' (Shieffelin and Ochs, 1986: 163). The perspective holds that from birth, we are socialized to acquire the beliefs, morals, values, behaviors, and practices of the culture to which one belongs through language. In other words, 'as children acquire language (e.g. words, grammar) they also acquire understanding of the social world including how to use language to index socio-culturally meaningful realities such as social action, activity, stance, and identity' (Burdelski, 2010: 1067). Though other researchers' examples may also demonstrate the use of language in other processes of culture learning, what distinguishes this field is the focus on how *language practices* index sociocultural information. Vygotsky, in his theoretical approach, also acknowledged the mediational power of language to influence others and affect development (Wertsch, 1986: 92). Microanalyses of social interactions within normal everyday contexts reveal that ordinary conversational discourse is a powerful socializing medium through which children learn the ways and worldviews of their culture.

In an example from Bhimji (2002), we can see how family members in South Central Los Angeles use language to socialize younger family members to socially desirable behavior, which in this context is to be patient and inhibit one's immediate desires (99).

Example 2

Two year old Alfredo wants to play with a specific Nintendo game. His older twin cousins (8 years) do not want to play that particular game and attempt to divert his attention.

1	Daniel: →	Vamos a jugar esta.
		Let's play this.
2	Daniel:	Te van a dar horita
		They will give it to you in a little while.
3	Alfredo:	*((Continues to cry))*
4	Daniel:	Que espere.
		Wait.
5	Alfredo:	???
6	Marie: →	Que tienes que esperar poquito.
		You have to wait a little.

Paugh (2005) has examined how children from a middle-class working family in Los Angeles are socialized to work-related values and expectations as they participate and listen to their parents' conversations and narratives about work. Through overhearing their parents, children get a 'glimpse into their parents' perspectives on work … what it takes to be boss … positive qualities of an employee, and that there are parameters for when and how people work' (68).

Goodwin (1990) also notes another way that language is used to affect actions. She demonstrates how the telling of 'instigating stories' among peers about violations of social expectations and the resulting righteous indignation toward such acts, also 'function to suggest future courses of action' for the hearers (267).

Others have focused on the role of teachers and schools (Ahn, 2005; Lowi, 2007). Lowi specifically examined the use of 'deontic,' or social modals such as *should, ought, would, have to, need to, want* and *can*, in adult-child discourse in British and American preschools. Such modals are often used to construct directives and can index social responsibility and moral obligation. Lowi showed how through their deployment, adults socialize children to knowing the next appropriate behavior and how to fulfill social expectations, while He (2000) examined how teachers use disciplinary directives to foster in a child 'the idea that one should show concern for others' (132) in Taiwanese schools.

Ahn (2005), in her qualitative study of the strategies teachers used in three child care centers, found that teachers modeled and encouraged children to empathize and show concern for other children. In this interaction, Ahn observed that a child (Lynn) grabbed a book from another child (Simon) without asking. When the teacher (Ms. K) initially intervenes, she suggests two alternative actions that are acceptable: one is to make a pre-request; the other is to simply make a request to be given the book when Simon is finished. However, the child refuses to comply, leading to a direct reprimand of her actions (57):

Example 3

> [After children had their morning snack, some children started to read books. Lynn and Simon fought over one book. Lynn snatched Simon's book and Simon cried.]
> Ms K approaches them and asks Lynn, 'Lynn, Did you ask Simon? Say gently "Did you finish the book?" Or "Can I have it when you finish?".'
> 'No,' answers Lynn.
> 'You can ask her. Grabbing a book from your friend's hand is not okay. That's not the way you borrow a book. It is Lynn's fault,' says Ms K.

In example 3, as an alternative to snatching the book from Simon, Ms K instructs Lynn on the appropriate action (to ask Simon) and then specifies to Lynn how to do it. She instructs her to make a request from Simon, with the proper affective tone (gently). In doing so, she also employs a prompting directive (say) to instruct Lynn. After Lynn still refuses to change her actions, Ms K explicitly reprimands her and gives sole responsibility for the conflict to Lynn. In this example, we see a child-care teacher instruct the proper formulation/way to borrow a book.

Han (2004) also used the language socialization framework to find the types of verbal and non-verbal behaviors that are encouraged in Korean-American children, and 'what verbal and non-verbal strategies are used by teachers to socialize children into culturally appropriate behaviors' (41–42). Han found that prompting sequences for the use of 'thank you' and 'sorry' were frequently used in teaching table manners or when children broke other codes of conduct. Han also noted that the teacher's prompting was often accompanied with a physical sanction. For instance, if a child did not say 'thank you' after just being served a meal, the teacher would prompt a 'thank you,' while withholding the bowl from the child (60–61). Similarly, Bhimji (2002) also provides an example in which a caregiver uses an implicit directive to teach a child (Vicente; 3) to say 'thank you' (94).

Example 4

((Maria is in her front yard selling tacos. Her friend is sitting next to her. Vicente brings a bottle of apple juice to Maria to be opened))

1	Vicente:	Me lo abra.
		Open it for me
2	Maria:	Ay. Ay. Ay.
3	Sara:	*((Opens the apple bottle juice for Vicente))*
4	Maria: →	Se dice gracias.
		One says thank you.
		Dile gracias.
		Say thank you.

((Vicente walks away with the open bottle.))

As Han (2004) notes, the use of the prompting directives 'illustrate ways in which the teachers at a Korean-American preschool socialize children into culturally appropriate behaviors' (114). Han's dissertation is also useful for understanding how children are socialized into linguistic and cultural norms. Korean culture makes a distinction between honorific and disrespectful terms. Han observed that teachers were correcting the disrespectful use of 'ung' (uh-huh, yeah) and were prompting children to use the honorific form 'ne' (yes). Interestingly, Han also observed that not all teacher directed 'ung' were corrected. The teacher did not prompt its use in informal and casual contexts, which allowed the children to learn to make distinctions between such contexts.

Han's data also showed how children were being taught the system of conversation practices. For example, when a teacher makes a statement with a rising intonation that adds an interrogative force to a sentence, the recipient (child) should follow with either a positive or negative response. However, in some instances the child made an inappropriate next move, such as remaining silent. As a result, the teacher corrected the child by prompting the use of 'ne' to show compliance with the teacher's statement. In this case, because the statement could have been received with either a positive or negative response, Han suggests that the underlying motivation is 'behavioral control' as the child is prompted to say 'ne' against (or regardless of) his own will (84).

In addition, Han observed the use of 'social rules + tag' formula as a tool for stating and reminding children of preferred and dispreferred behaviors. For example, in Korean culture, children are supposed to 'insa' to adults they encounter. The 'insa' often means bowing to lower one's head or upper body before the adult, while saying 'annyongha-si-oyo' (Are you well?). Example 5 shows how the teacher employs the 'social rule + tag' form to remind the child to 'insa' to the researcher.

Example 5

```
3     안녕하세요하고 인사해야지.=
      annyongha-si-oyo-hago   insaha-ya-ji=
      well-S.HON-A.HON-QUOT  greet-should-SUP=
T: →  You should greet like annyounghasioyo, shouldn't you=


4     = 어른보면 인사하라고 그랬잖아. (LHL%)
      = orun  bo-myon  insaha-rago  kure-t-jan-a
      = adult  see-when  greet-QUOT   say.so-PST-EMP-IE
T: →  = I told you to say hello when you see adults, didn't I.
        (LHL%)
```

Conversely, in example 6, the teacher reminds the child of the appropriateness of saying 'goodbye' when leaving school. In fact, the teacher demands that the social rule be enforced.

In line 8, the teacher asserts that Hahyeon needs to say 'goodbye' before she leaves the school, and does so by preparing the girl to 'insa' goodbye by saying 'charyot' (Attention!). After Hahyeon stands in attention and bows to the teacher, the teacher encourages her behavior with 'Right' and then says 'goodbye' to Hahyeon.

How children in a Japanese preschool are socialized into politeness routines with verbal and non-verbal cues has been explored by Burdelski (2010). One verbal strategy used is prompting. The teachers he observed used two types of prompting: (1) leading question (e.g. What do you say?) and performative (e.g. You have to apologize); and (2) elicited imitation (e.g. Say 'thank you'). Another strategy used was reported speech either through repetition and/or glossing an immediately prior utterance and/or non-verbal action of one child to another. Non-verbal strategies that teachers used include enacting the undesirable behavior (e.g. refusal to share) and positioning children to a participation framework for a desirable action (e.g. saying 'sorry') to occur. Burdelski observed that when teachers enact the behavior, they also issue a negative directive toward the behavior. He

Example 6

6   내일 만나 **(LH%)**
     neil   manna-ø
     tomorrow see-zero.IMP
T: See you tomorrow (LH%)

7   ((Hahyeon leaves the room.))

8   어이. 인사하고 가야지.
     uheee insaha-go   **ga-ya-ji**
     hey   greet/bow-VC **go-should-sup**
T: → **Hey, you should say goodbye before you go, shouldn't you.**

9   차렷!
     charyot
     attention
T: Attention!

10   ((Hahyeon stand at attention and bows.))

11   옳지.
     olt-ji
     be.right-IE
T: Right.

12   잘가 하연이?
     Jahl ga-ø   Hahyeon-i
     Well go-zero.IMP Hahyeon-PART
T: Good bye Hahyeon?

noted that children are not expected to perform the routine immediately but rather to recognize a similar situation in which to perform it in the future. In addition, Burdelski observed how peers are powerful agents of socialization, such that after a child's good behavior was acknowledged by a teacher, younger children imitated the behavior.

Howard (2004), in her study of children in a village in Thailand, reported on the socialization of the use of formality marking particles (FMP), which mark the degree of formality of a situation. Howard found that children are explicitly socialized to use FMPs as an important means of displaying respect while they are implicitly being socialized to associating Standard Thai (versus the closely related Kam Muang) with the school setting, formality, and with government institutions. One example is the co-construction by kindergarten students and their teachers of a poster with classroom rules or 'agreements' that are to be observed throughout the year (Howard, 2009). Agreement #3 states that children are instructed to 'show respect' each time they meet a teacher; Agreement #4 reminds the children to 'speak politely' in the classroom by using the Standard Thai particles. In another medium, the textbook, Thai etiquette is also highly valued. In one text that Howard examined, 'Thai etiquette is evaluated as aesthetically superior, or more proper, to the etiquette practiced in other countries, and as something that "should" be followed' (261). As the textbook states: 'Thai manners are more beautiful than any other country's' (254). Speaking politely is bound to Thai identity. However, though FMPs are associated with the classroom, children are not expected to use FMPs in all classroom situations, but in particular forms of participation. In addition, the classroom text focuses on particular embodied displays of text and with whom such displays would be appropriate: the *wai* with adults and teachers (bowing with the hands raised and palms together and the *kraap* with Buddhist icons (prostrating oneself with one's palms together). Howard (2010), contrasted the ideologies of how to teach politeness in Northern Thailand and found that that municipal schoolteachers emphasized their role in 'correcting' children's inappropriate or impolite speech and strictly used Standard Thai. In contrast, the village schoolteacher applied both Kam Muang and Standard Thai in the classroom to foster Muang students' understanding of classroom speech. Despite different teaching philosophies, students learned throughout the school year, when and which types of classroom activities it is necessary to mark respect with politeness particles. Therefore, just as in Han's data (2004), children were not only being taught explicitly the use of formality particles, but also implicitly taught the appropriate situational contexts.

Such language socialization has also been observed in societies that are nearly absent of institutionalized education. One such society is the Tikopia, a Polynesian community of about 1,200 people. At the time of observation, they were a society with minimal European influence, and socialization was largely the role of parents and other kin (Firth, 1970). For example, one area in which considerable attention is paid is the use of speech. According to Firth, there are two main principles of speech. 'The first is to avoid rude and indecent expressions' (82). Children from an early age are taught to distinguish two categories of expressions: good speech (*tarana laui*) and bad speech (*tarana pariki*). When parents heard inappropriate speech, Firth noted them saying, 'Your speech that is made is bad speech, give it up! But use good speech,' and 'These words that you use are evil speech. Abandon them.' (82). Once Firth observed a child babbling 'La-la-la-la' to itself. 'Lala' refers to the clitoris. Therefore, when a group of women overheard the child, they yelled, 'May its father eat filth! It utters evil speech – the lala!'. The second rule is that children must refrain from calling out to passersby, strangers, or people at large, as such an action suggests 'ill-breeding'

(82–83). Thus, socialization of language use in Tikopia in matters of etiquette begins at a very early age.

The Kwoma in New Guinea have also been observed to index appropriate and inappropriate behavior using language. For example, when Whiting (1941) observed an infant defecating on its mother's leg and then proceed to dabble in his feces and put some in his mouth, 'the mother contorted her face and said: "You must not play with feces; they are bad"' (26). The mother then yanked the infant's hand from his mouth and held it to prevent the child from eating it again. Later, when a child is old enough, mothers also gently train their children in proper toilet habits. One mother was observed to tell her child that 'adults go outside near the garbage heap to urinate and that he is big enough to do likewise. Similarly she points out that adults do not defecate in the house but in the household latrine' (Whiting, 1941: 32). If a child is overly demanding and impatient he may be punished as well. For example:

> One morning Kum was calling to his mother, who was a short way down the mountainside gathering firewood: 'Mother, come! I am hungry. Mother, come! I am hungry.' She answered at first that she would be home shortly. Kum kept on shouting until finally his mother stopped answering him. Then he begins to wail. His older brothers, who were playing ball a short distance away, told him to be quiet. His stepmother, who was working in the house, after several times telling him to hush, finally gave him a scolding. (Whiting, 1941: 34–35).

Even in societies in which the burden of learning may rest almost entirely on the learner, such as the Kpelle (Lancy, 1996, 2008), inappropriate behavior is addressed with a directive, such as in this instance:

> The children play with a pan that has a hole in the bottom. The little girl puts empty shells in the pan, then dumps them out, she does this repeatedly. Tiring of this, she bangs the pan on the little boy's head; he takes it from her and wears it as a hat. The little girl starts to scream and one of the women tells him to give it back, which he does. (Lancy, 1996: 74)

In addition, as one parent implies, there is societal pressure and motivation to provide some 'instruction' to children. The parent states, 'If a child doesn't obey you or if you don't advise him, he will cause you shame in front of you friends' (76). Lancy notes that 'teaching' may be rare in Kpelle society as there is 'little need to 'accelerate' development because there is far less information to acquire … (because) the tasks that need to be learned are relatively simple and do not require "schooling"' (79) and 'bad children' are the exception rather than the rule in Kpelle society. Regardless of his observation of a lack of explicit socialization, Lancy also states that parents still 'influence children by example and by setting limits on their behavior' (78) and are willing 'when asked, to serve as a critic' (150).

Thus, each society develops and employs practices to 'parent', 'teach' and 'guide' its members to learn the relevant cultural practices that are central to the lives that one belongs to. Applied social knowledge also serves to maintain social relations (Fiske, 2004). According to Fiske (1991), people in all societies relate to each other in four ways or models (mods): Communal Sharing (CS), Authority Ranking (AR), Equality Matching (EM) and Market Pricing (MP) (Fiske, 1991, 2004). Relating to other members appropriately within these models is culturally specific, and violating the norms of how to conduct oneself within these relationships may have negative effects.

When people focus on what they have in common or if they are of the same kind, they are in a mode of Communal Sharing (CS). The relationship is based on the perception that people within some bounded group are equivalent and undifferentiated. It applies to relationships among family members, spouses, and close friends with very similar interests. In Communal Sharing, partners bond through acts of consubstantial assimilation such as bodily contact, commensalism, and the free sharing of resources. Some examples include being in love, identifying with one's family, or having the all-for-one and one-for-all perspective. When people relate to each on terms of ordered differences, the model is Authority Ranking (AR). This involves perceptions of asymmetry in relationships – whether a person is above or below each person, whether they have differences in status, rights, and/or responsibilities. When people construct relations based on a model of even balance and meaningful differences, such as eye-for-an-eye, tooth-for-tooth, scratch my back and I'll scratch yours, they are in the mode of Equality Matching (EM). They are concerned with, and keep track of, whether the relationship is balanced and labor to keep it balanced. Common examples include turn-taking, one-to-one correspondence practices (e.g., tit for tat, 'one for you, one for me, one for you, one for me'), and maintaining even alignment. And the fourth model is Market Pricing (MP), which organizes interaction with reference to ratio and rates, such as prices, wages, rents and cost-benefit-analysis.

These models are taken to be innate and universal, as they seem to be present across cultures and in early childhood (Fiske, 1991: 401–404). Fiske suggests that CS is probably present at birth, as demonstrated by infants' bonding to parents (Fiske, 2012). He also reports that CS interactions are evident in toddlers and are subtly understood by age six (Greenfield *et al.*, unpublished manuscript; Over and Carpenter, 2009). By 10 months, human infants seem to expect that among novel agents, ABOVE, BIGGER and

EARLIER should be congruent, and therefore have a cognitive representation specific to AR (Thomsen *et al.*, 2011). Also, by age 3, children notice and react negatively to an unfair distribution. For example, when pairs of children, ages 3–5, are given unequal amounts of stickers, children who receive less showed emotional and behavioral signs that they disliked the unfair distribution (LoBue *et al.*, 2009). Although MP is not operative from birth, like walking, talking, or sexuality, the capacity and motivation to engage in symbolic MP interaction emerges naturally as the human brain matures in the social world. Thus, though relational mods are taken to be innate and universal, they are also 'incomplete and indeterminate' (Fiske, 2004: 120). Though these social motives appear to be present in early childhood, they develop into culturally specific forms, which reflect his/her societies' culture and values. People must 'learn how to realize each model according to the paradigm and prototype of their specific culture. No model can be implemented without reference to cultural guidelines' (Fiske, 1997: 387). Thus, people also need to know the cultural paradigms (preos) related to the mod (Fiske, 2008).

A young Mandinko girl's statement may illustrate both AR and EM and how acquiring and learning to implement a relational model is inseparable from experience in the social world. When a young Mandinko girl explains to a younger sibling 'You must (work) for your elders. They will bless you' (Whittemore and Beverly, 1989: 30), implicit in her statement is the acknowledgment of an elder's authority over her; these people have the ability to do something for her if she pleases them. She in turn exercises such authority, both positive and negative, over children younger than she, most notably to her siblings to whom she regularly gives care. Through her instruction, the young girl makes apparent issues of hierarchy and control in relationships between elders in the community and the young, as well as how such a relationship may be balanced. Such a statement brings awareness to what the Mandinko describe as *mandinka silo* or the 'Mandinka Way' (Whittemore and Beverl, 1989: 30).

Childhood is universal, and so is the fact that people are the most significant part of it; they provide the opportunity, serve as models, give direction and guidance on sociocultural knowledge – including language, and through language. These practices vary among cultures, and likely within more localized social domains (i.e. families). Such interactionally constituted spaces provide tremendous opportunity for neonates to be exposed to the language, the social contexts for the use of the language, and the social environment of which one becomes motivated to be a member. But, what motivates such complex sociocultural learning? In the next chapter, I explore the motivation for sociocultural learning and suggest that one learns cultural practices because one is motivated by an innate tendency to seek interaction, or an *Interactional Instinct* (Lee and Schumann, 2005; Lee *et al.*, 2009), which leads to attachment and affiliation with members who are the source of the culture. Once attachment and affiliation is achieved, extrinsic and/or intrinsic rewards – or in cases of misbehavior, punishment – motivate a child to interact, listen-in, observe, and attend to activities, rituals, values, beliefs, and language that are of value in one's society or social domain.

Notes

1. Assembly line instruction and guided participation are part of the process involved in enculturation (Rogoff *et al.*, 2003).
2. All transcripts follow the transcript notations of Conversation Analysis in Appendix A. The exceptions are examples 1–7. These excerpts were created by the original authors and were not altered to follow the conventions of conversation analysis.

3 The interactional instinct for cultural learning[1]

To say that infants are also 'social' is to be banal.

J. Bruner (1983: 26)

This chapter argues that we are born with an *Interactional Instinct* (Lee *et al.*, 2009), which is motivated by the sociostatic value of attachment and affiliation. Human beings are born with an appraisal system to determine the emotional relevance and motivational significance of stimuli received through the sensory systems. The appraisal system determines three kinds of value: homeostatic, sociostatic, and somatic (Schumann, 1997). Depending on the value, the appraisal system directs the appropriate action *vis-à-vis* motor systems. *Homeostatic* regulation guides organisms in ways that maintain homeostasis and ensure survival (i.e. to feed, breathe, to seek light or darkness, to get warmth or coolness). For example, Whiting (1941) describes how a Kwoma infant has learned that 'certainly preliminary behavior is useful in bringing satisfaction more quickly and efficiently. He learns to turn his head to take the nipple in his mouth, to stop sucking from one breast when it becomes dry, and finally even to lift himself from a prone position to a vantage point from which he can suckle' (25). *Somatic value* leads to the development of our preferences and aversions determined by our experiences with our physical and social world. We will discuss the relevance of those values for language acquisition later in Chapters 7 and 8. However, studies of infant communication with persons show that 'from the moment of birth, other processes are active besides those that seek protection and regulation of vital state' (Trevarthen, 2005: 55). Infants take initiative in their learning, and it is proposed that the motivation for such learning begins with the desire for affiliation with another human being. *Sociostatic value* is the innate tendency of a human organism to seek out interaction leading to attachment and social affiliation with conspecifics. Thus, sociostatic value is what underlies the Interactional Instinct, as the instinct motivates human beings to actively pursue and achieve attachment and social affiliation with others.

Early infant abilities

In the 1950s and 1960s, Rene Spitz (1949) and John Bowlby (1969) shocked the world with haunting images of children who were listless, unnaturally passive, developmentally slow, linguistically and expressively deficient because of neglect by their caregivers. Spitz even reported that mortality increased in institutions where children were not exposed to sufficient emotional interchanges. The comparative studies of isolated monkeys with neglected children from orphanages by Harlow *et al.* (1965) further showed that children subjected to these conditions exhibit autistic-like behaviors. Interaction in all its forms, including emotional interchanges, touching, eye gaze, etc., were seen as a central force powerful enough to shape a person while he is still an infant and, in fact, necessary for survival. From this perspective, the child may be perceived as a passive participant who is molded and shaped by his social environment.

However, after researchers closely examined the world of the infant, another story was being told, as Bruner noted that infant 'behavior from early on is guided by *means-end readiness* and by *search*' (emphasis mine: 26), and he argued that infants were endowed with far more abilities than previously thought. This chapter, in part, reflects on what human newborns *do* and explores *why*. It focuses on the phenomena of human neonate behavior with caregivers as behavioral manifestations of the interactional instinct. Throughout the chapter, I specify what researchers have shown to be human endowments, and through behavioral studies I will report how these endowments are deployed to facilitate interaction with conspecifics and achieve social attachment and affiliation in both traditional and Western societies. The second part of this chapter contains what may be considered behavioral manifestations of a human being's innate capacity to interact with conspecifics. The capacity consists of six broad categories: imitation, infant-initiatedness, emotional perception and expression, human-specificity, understanding of communicative signals, and interpersonal organization.

Sensory abilities

Studies have shown that infants are born with social stimulus feature detectors and perceptual abilities that allow them to be active participants in interaction with caregivers. To begin with, they already perceive and remember sounds heard while in the womb in the final weeks of pregnancy. In one study, mothers were instructed to recite a story in the last weeks of gestation. After the infants were born, a recording was played of the mothers reciting two different stories – one they had previously recited and one they had not. The results showed that the newborns had a preference for listening to the one that they had 'heard' in the womb (deCasper and Spence, 1986). It is not surprising, then, that studies have shown that immediately after birth newborns have remarkably developed abilities to see and hear potential interlocutors in their social environment. In his controversial report of 40 newborns with a median age of 9 minutes, Goren *et al.* (1975) observed that neonates turned their heads to follow moving stimuli. Their studies claimed that babies will not only fix on a drawing that resembles a human face, but given that the face is moved at a reasonable speed, newborns will follow the face for 180 degrees with their eyes and will continue to turn their heads to keep it in view. Furthermore, he reported that newborns will follow an adult-like face back and forth; and up and down the delivery room. Fifteen years later, Goren's study was replicated with 24 newborns in the first hour of life (Johnson *et al.*, 1991).

Other studies showed that 2-to-5 day-olds and 4-month-olds have the ability to discriminate between direct and averted gaze, and have a preference for faces that engage them in mutual gaze (Farroni *et al.*, 2002, 2004). In addition, studies show that infants less than six months old can discriminate between normal and abnormal face configurations (Fantz, 1963; Carpenter *et al.*, 1970), and are also able to discriminate between faces of different individuals (Carpenter, 1973; Field, 1985).

Regarding a newborn's capacity to hear stimuli, studies of infant musicality show that six-month-olds discriminate features of tempo, rhythm, melody, and key in the structures of both song and instrumental sound (Trehub *et al.*, 1993). Studies also show that human speech is salient to a neonate among an array of auditory stimuli in its environment (Eisenberg, 1975), and infants seem to make a distinction between human and nonhuman sounds and behave accordingly. For example, when newborns are provided auditory stimuli of various sounds, there is a qualitative difference in their sucking patterns. With nonhuman sounds, the baby stops sucking to attend to them, but then resumes sucking. On the other hand, when they hear a human sound, newborns also stop sucking as if to attend to it, but then resume sucking in a pronounced 'burst-pause pattern' – as if waiting for more human signals (Cairns and Butterfield, 1975). Another method involves the infant turning their heads toward stimuli such as a blinking light. Infants are trained so that when they look toward the blinking lights, a recording of sounds is played. When they turn away, the recording stops. Therefore infants can control and indicate how long and which particular sounds they have a preference for. Such studies show that babies can distinguish between discrete sounds (Karmiloff and Karmiloff-Smith, 2001). The evidence for an infant's auditory abilities is extensive and shows that infants are able to decompose the stream of speech in their environment when they are as young as four days old (Bijeljac-Babic *et al.*, 1991; Kuhl, 2004; Ramus, 2001; Saffran, 2001; Saffran and Thiessen, 2003). They are able to notice the differences between languages that are prosodically different (Mehler *et al.* 1988; Mehler and Christophe, 1995), and even preterms, at around 26–28 weeks gestational age, react to sounds by rotating their heads and trunks in a startled way. Furthermore, studies have shown that the fetus in the last trimester responds to visual, auditory, and kinesthetic stimulation (Tanaka and Arayama, 1969; Brazelton, 1981).

In addition, studies show that just hours after birth, human beings have a well-developed ability to smell. Steiner (1979) held swabs with 'rotten' or 'foul' odors, as well as 'pleasant' odors, under the noses of babies in the first hours of life, before they had any contact with food or odors of food. The odors were first tested with adults. Babies grimaced when they were given the foul swabs and smiled when smelling the pleasant swabs, which was consistent with the adult controls. In another study, MacFarlane (1975) tested to see whether an infant would discriminate between the smell of his mother and her milk, and the smell of another mother and her milk. His study showed that six-day-olds had a preference for their mother's odor and milk, thus having not only the ability to smell but also the ability to discriminate between odors.

Studies have also shown that the capacity to sense touch begins very early in human ontogeny. A preterm in the third month of gestation will respond to the touch of a hair around its mouth. This shows a newborn's remarkable sensitivity to touch, which is greater than an adult's in part due to the infant's thinner skin and greater number of nerve endings (Barlow and Mollon, 1982). Another study by Ellis and Ellingson (1972) tickled 2-to-3 day-olds in the palms of their hands with a weak electrical current. The current was so weak that adults failed to feel it, however, it was felt by neonates.

Facial expressions, gestures and vocalizations

Newborns seem to also be born with an inventory of distinctive expressions and vocalizations that can be interpreted as communicative and can lead to interpersonal communication as well. In many cultures, crying elicits immediate responses from caregivers (Whiting, 1963). For example, among the Kwoma:

> Crying is selected as the most effective response ... it constitutes
> an injunction to the mother to discover the source of the trouble.
> Her first response is to present the breast. If this fails to quiet him,

she tries something else. If she believes that the child is crying because he is too hot, she moves him away from the heat of her body. If she thinks he is cold, she cuddles him. If his crying calls her attention to a mosquito on him, she brushes it off and scratches the bite. If she suspects that sores from yaws are hurting him, she tries to move him to a more comfortable position. If he seems to be crying because he is sick, she tries to distract his attention by crooning to him, rocking him gently, and patting him. (Whiting, 1963: 28)

Among the Kwoma, each time a baby cries, the mother rewards him with a response. Other early infant expressions are cooing and smiling, which seem to be based on a motor pattern formed before birth. Cooing is described as positive, non-crying vocalizations that adults often find pleasurable. And though these sounds are not clear and strong until the second month of life, the appropriate mouth opening and shaping for cooing is often made by infants less than two months old (Trevarthen, 1977). Cooing also develops partly independently of auditory feedback from self and others. In addition, both normal and premature infants display recognizable smiles just minutes after birth. Even infants born blind smile to a voice, a behavior that eventually diminishes because of lack of visual support, and they are able to produce complex emotional expressions. Thus, smiling and other emotional expressions do not seem to simply be imitative responses to seeing the smile of others (Darwin, 1965; Eibl-Eibesfeldt, 1973; Fraiberg, 1974).

Recent research suggests that facial gestalts resembling facial expressions relating to laughter and crying are observed as early as 32.5 weeks in the womb (Reissland *et al.*, 2011). Neonates have also been photographed to display all adult facial expressions with concomitant gestures (Charlesworth and Kreutzer, 1973). Furthermore Izard (1978) has identified facial expressions of interest, joy, disgust, surprise, and distress in young infants. Figure 3.1 is a photographic sample that captures some of a 6 week-old infant's repertoire of facial expressions (Trevarthen, 1979).

Trevarthen also argued that the posturing of the head during many forms of facial expression seems to be systematically related to particular facial expressions and suggested that all the patterns of body expression are present in infants at birth, and the gesticulations of infants (i.e. hand-waving, index-finger pointing, and fingertip-clasping movements near the face when they are vocalizing) are clearly not imitations of adult partners (see Figure 3.2).

Also, though infants are born too prematurely to control and articulate speech and sounds, they show movements that resemble adult articulation, which Trevarthen called *prespeech*. Figure 3.3 shows a comparison of the prespeech of infants to that of adults.

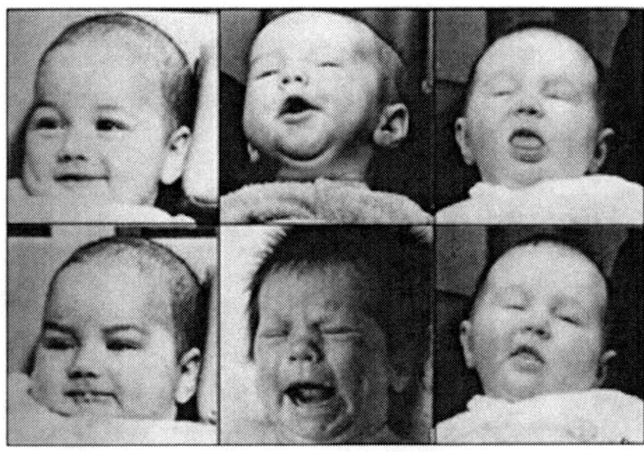

Figure 3.1. Infant expressions. Left smile and jaw set (boy, 12 weeks); centre: above, coo (boy, 6 weeks), below, crying (girl, 6 weeks); right: simulations of disgust and sneer (girl, 6 weeks). (Trevarthen, 1979: 325) © 1979 Cambridge University Press. Reprinted with permission of Cambridge University Press.

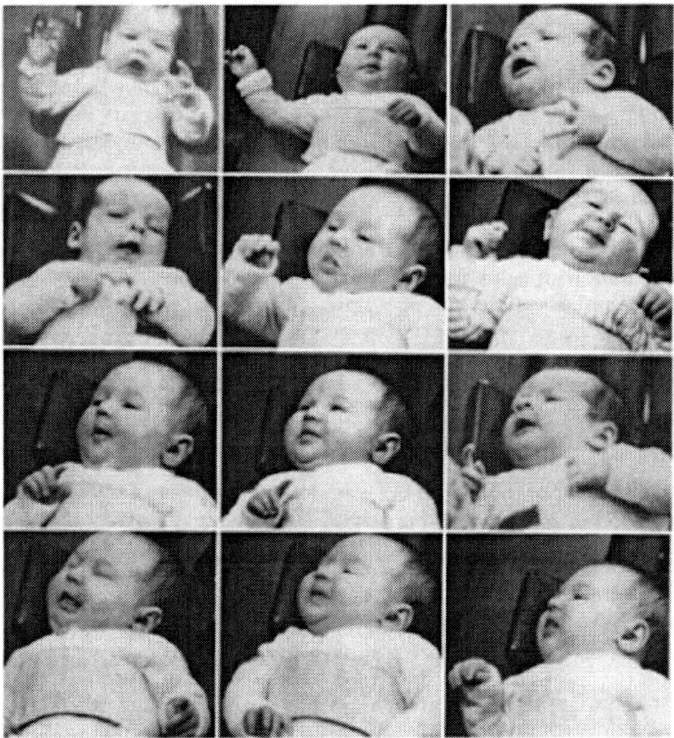

Figure 3.2. Gestures in communication (6–7 weeks). From Trevarthen (1979: 29). © 1979 Cambridge University Press. Reprinted with permission of Cambridge University Press.

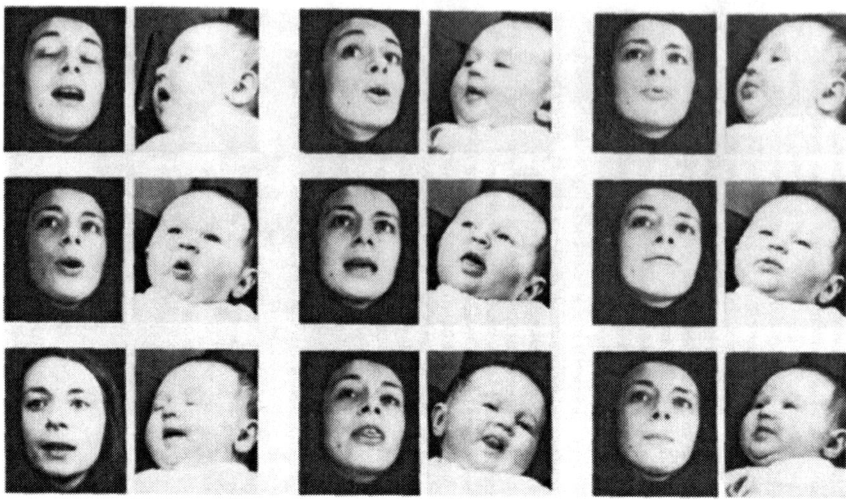

Figure 3.3. Prespeech compared to adult speech. Normal speaking of an adult reading a word list (girl 7 weeks). From Trevarthen (1979: 29). © 1979 Cambridge University Press. Reprinted with permission of Cambridge University Press.

Selective attention

Evidence for an infant's capacity for attunement can be found in a series of studies by Condon and Sander (Condon and Sander, 1974a, 1974b; Condon, 1977), who demonstrated that newborns, ranging in age from 12 hours to 2 days old, respond organizationally to an adult's speech regardless of whether the adult speaker is present or whether the voice comes from a tape recorder. By analyzing the micro-body movements of 16 newborns in response to an adult's speech, they found that infants in the first hours of life synchronize their movements to the rhythm of their mothers' voice. This behavioral attunement with human speech was observed to occur in word stretches of up to 180 words. Eye contact was ruled out as a contributor to the synchronicity because the infant was not looking at the adult. Furthermore, when Chinese was presented to American neonates, there was as clear a correspondence and attunement as there was with American English (Condon, 1980).

Other studies have shown that preterm infants already seem to have the capacity to sustain attention to the sights and sounds of people around them. In one study, preterm babies, at 33 weeks postconceptional age with very low birth weight, if in an awake and nondistressed state, responded to motherese in a way that would resemble what is considered 'attention' in healthy full-term newborns. Even when interacting with strangers, the infants also maintained high levels of attention, particularly exhibiting eye opening and lower limb activity (Eckerman, 1994). In addition, an interesting auditory stimulus, such as a rattle or soft voice, will move infants from a sleepy to an alert state in which their breathing becomes irregular, their faces brighten, and, their eyes become wider. If they are completely awake, their eyes and head will turn toward the sound, which is often followed by a searching look and a scanning motion of eyes, as if they are trying to find the source of the sound. Furthermore, infants seem to orient their gaze and body to attend to social stimuli that arouse interest. In these studies, an experimenter first slowly tries to capture the interest of a newborn by moving a stimulus up and down until the baby becomes alert. Then the examiner moves the stimulus slowly from side to side waiting for the newborn to follow it. Although this shows that a newborn does not visually accommodate to a moving object immediately, it is clear that sight in a newborn is not a passive ability, because an infant actively tries to prolong its attention to an attractive object. When a bright object is brought into a newborn's line of vision and is moved slowly up and down to attract the infant's attention, the baby's pupils contract slightly. Then, when the object is moved from side to side, the baby's eyes begin to widen, her limbs become still, and the baby stares at the object, and begins to slowly to track the object and its movements (Brazelton and Cramer, 1990).

Studies of preterms, newborns, and very young infants provides evidence that they are born with sufficiently developed abilities to experience and engage their social world. They are born with developed sensory systems that allow them to see, hear, smell, and touch social stimuli. They seem to have a repertoire of adult-like facial expressions, gestures, and movements. In addition, newborns have kinesic development to attend and attune to social stimuli in their environment. These seemingly inborn abilities are demonstrated in human newborns long before a child utters her first word. The import of these abilities for the infant and infant-caregiver interaction will be explored in the next section. Though these abilities are not traditionally categorized as 'linguistic', they provide a newborn with communicative equipment and behaviors that are powerful enough to elicit and engage in rewarding interactions with caregivers. Furthermore, they mediate the internalization of the physical, social, and cultural world into which the child is born.

Seeking, interacting, and engaging the sociocultural world

Early in life, tendencies that demonstrate an infant's motivation leading to the satisfaction of the interactional instinct are observable. These behaviors consist of the abilities in the repertoire of the infant described in the previous section and are deployed to communicate desire for social engagement. Furthermore, these behaviors are distinct from those that show an infant's curiosity to explore its social environment and accumulate information (Jones, 1996), such that an infant's behaviors make an interactional response relevant from its interlocutors and can be consequential for the trajectory of the interaction. In this way, an infant's actions can signal desire for communication and have the potential to achieve and prolong interaction with its mother or caregiver(s).

Imitation

Imitation can be roughly defined as the coordination of visually perceived movements of other people with one's own movements. However, recent research seems to strongly suggest that imitation is more than just chance congruence. Researchers propose that neonatal imitation is 'non-reflexive, volitional and intentional' (Meltzoff, 1998). If neonatal imitation is more than just the chance mirroring of actions of another, and is intentional, then we might ask, what do infants intend to achieve through imitation? In this section, I will provide evidence that human neonates do in fact imitate, and that they do so purposively, and I will suggest that one objective may be to achieve attachment and affiliation with conspecifics.

The first observations of infant facial imitation were recorded as early as 1908, when a four-month-old infant was observed to be imitating the tongue protrusions of her parent (McDougall, 1908). Then, in a series of experimental studies, Maratos showed that 4-week-olds were able to imitate tongue protrusion and mouth openings (1973). Meltzoff and Moore (1977; 1983, 1989), in more controlled experiments, supported Maratos' and McDougall's findings, and demonstrated that newborns imitate two facial gestures: mouth opening and tongue protrusion (Figure 3.4). In one study, the mean age of the infants was 32 hours, and the youngest was a mere *42 minutes-old*. Furthermore, the person eliciting the imitation was not the mother, but rather an experimenter.

Similarly, Reissland (1988), who studied the neonatal imitative responses during their *first hour of postpartum* in rural Nepal, observed neonates imitating various mouth gestures (see Figure 3.5). Again, similar to Meltzoff and Moore's study, the experimenter was the first person that the baby saw and the first person with whom the baby interacted.

Further studies reported tendencies to imitate mouth openings and tongue protrusions by infants only 35–68 hours old (Ullstadius, 1998). An infant's ability to imitate tongue movements was further confirmed by research

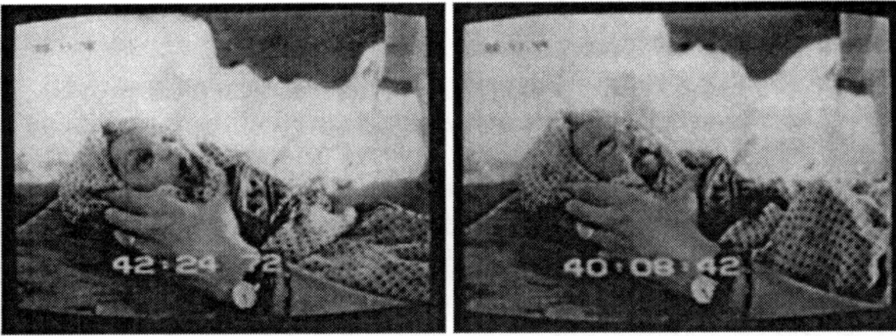

Figure 3.4: Photographs from videotaped recordings of 2-to-3 week-old infants imitating: (a) tongue protrusion; (b) mouth opening; (c) lip protrusion demonstrated by an adult experimenter (Meltzoff and Moore, 1977: 75). Reprinted with permission of the author and AAAS.

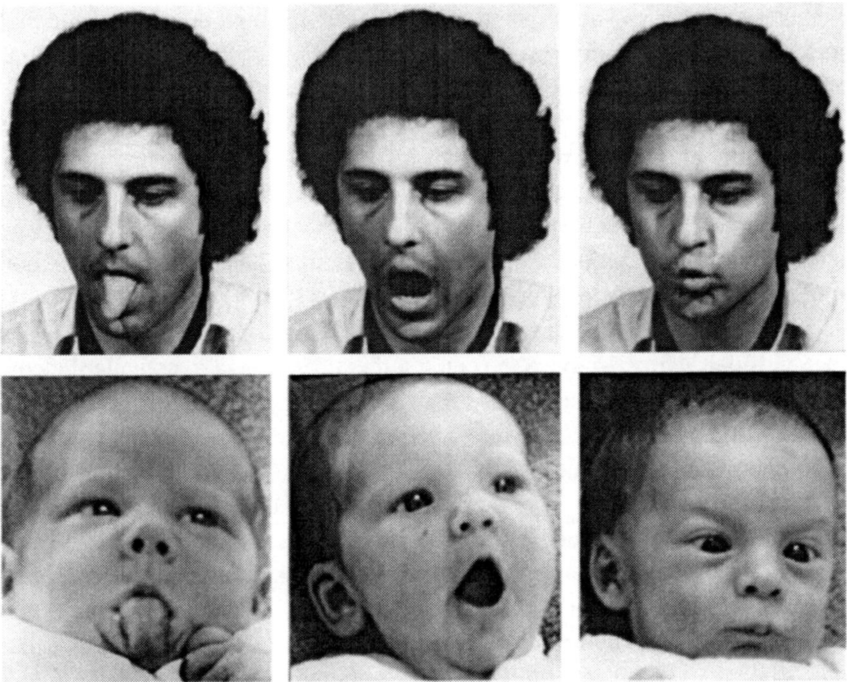

Figure 3.5: Examples of neonatal imitation with vertically pursed lips and lips laterally widened (Reissland, 1988: 4). Reprinted with the permission of the author.

showing that infants differentially imitate two different kinds of movement with the tongue (Meltzoff and Moore, 1994, 1997).

In addition, a series of four other studies by Kugiumutzakis (1998) showed that neonatal imitation occurs right after birth, which eliminates the possibility that imitation is based on learning and socialization. Kugiumutzakis was able to observe 170 newborns immediately after delivery. Thus the mean age of each newborn was approximately *26 minutes*. After a 40–100 second adaptation period until the infant was entirely calm, four models for imitation were presented at a distance of 20–23 cm from the baby's face: tongue protrusion, mouth opening, eye blinking and some vocalizations (/a/, /m/, /ang/). Kugiumutzakis' studies did in fact demonstrate that infants clearly try to imitate and succeed. Seventy-five percent of the newborns imitated with precision on their first attempt, and when they reproduced the model several times, they converged toward a more precise matching each time. With regard to the vocal imitations, which were only presented to infants in the fourth study, the newborns tried –'with clear observable effort – to direct their attention to the mouth part of the experimenter's face. The attention intensifies from a relatively fixed gaze to selective visual exploration' (72). Kugiutmutzakis, Meltzoff, and Moore suggest that these subsequent attempts to match the experimenters demonstrate that imitative behavior is not just a reflex, but shows that infants are intentionally and volitionally trying to imitate their interlocutor.

Some imitation has also been observed in premature babies. One video observation of a preterm (at 29 weeks' gestational age) with her father showed that the preterm mirrored facial expressions and vocalizations (Van Rees and de Leeuw, 1987). Preterm infants, with an average gestational age of approximately 35 weeks, also demonstrate an ability to discriminate and imitate three facial expressions (Field *et al.*, 1983).

Furthermore, the innateness of imitation is also supported by observations that an infant's first response to seeing a facial gesture is to activate the corresponding body part, known as organ identification (Meltzoff and Moore, 1997). For example, when an infant sees an adult protrude his tongue, there is a quieting of other body parts (lips or fingers) and an activation of the tongue in the oral cavity. The infant elevates or moves the tongue. Though the infant may not protrude his tongue at first, he seems to isolate that body part, before even knowing how to move it. Kugiumutzakis (1998) also reported this observation in his study of newborns. Organ identification and observable attempts by newborns to correct their efforts to match an interlocutor's behavior also show that imitation is an intentional activity.

This section has provided evidence that infants have innate facial and gestural imitative tendencies that are observable within the first hours of interaction. Although the evidence is substantial, partial failures by some researchers to replicate the studies of Meltzoff and Moore have raised the possibility that neonatal imitation was not a genuine phenomenon (Koepke *et al.*, 1983; McKenzie and Over, 1983). However, the studies mentioned above are merely a fraction of the research studies on infant imitation, which have been conducted in separate laboratories and research institutions. Numerous studies have demonstrated that there is a broad range of rudimentary behaviors that infants imitate. Infants imitate mouth openings (Fontaine, 1984; Heimann, 1989, 2002; Legerstee, 1991), hand movements (Locke, 1986; Vinter, 1986), emotional expressions (Field, 1983, 1982), head movements (Meltzoff, 1989), lip and cheek movements (Fontaine, 1984; Kugiumutzakis, 1999), and eye blinking (Kugiumutzakis, 1999). Such studies suggest that early infant imitation is a genuine phenomenon because it might be that human beings have an innate propensity to be like other conspecifics and thus have an underlying motivation to engage in imitative interactional activity.

Infant-initiatedness

In studies of infant behavior, there seems to be a number of observations in which interaction is not elicited by a caregiver, but rather by the infant. In fact, Nagy (Nagy, 2004; Nagy and Molnar, 2006) has observed that infants ranging in age from 3 to 54 hours old are not only capable of imitating, but that they also have 'the capacity to provoke an imitative response' (54), called 'provocation' or neonatal initiation (Nagy and Molnar, 2006). They proactively participate in imitative exchanges. Their study showed that infants 'initiated' an interaction with an experimenter who responded, which the baby responded to, and that the experimenter responded to and so on. That is, 'long-lasting "dialogues" were initiated by newborn babies' (229). Such a study demonstrates that an infant actively initiates social engagement through the use of abilities, which are inborn (cooing, vocalizations, gestures, smiling, etc.) or are learned early through experience. These behaviors may collectively display *infant-initiatedness* and provide some evidence for an innate drive for interaction.[2] For example, various studies in industrialized societies show that the major reason babies cry is to reestablish physical contact with caregivers whom they have been separated from (Wolff, 1969). Consider the following narrative of a dyadic interaction:

> F (a newborn) is sitting in her seat holding a rubber toy which is tied to the side of the chair. Mother has her back to F as she reaches for a dish. F squeaks the rubber toy making a noise. As a 'consequence' F kicks her feet and squeals with apparent delight.

> Mother turns toward F smiling. F looks at mother and vocalizes. Mother walks toward F smiling and vocalizing. F quiets, eyes fixed on mother. Mother touches F's face. F vocalizes and moves her hands toward mother. Mother sits in front of F and vocalizes to her. (Talking about the toy which mother now holds.) F watches mother and listens. Mother pauses. F vocalizes. Mother touches F and vocalizes to her. F vocalizes. (Lewis and Freedle, 1973)

In the sequence described above, the newborn was the initiator of the interaction with her mother. By squeaking a rubber toy, squealing, and kicking, the infant successfully got her mother's attention and elicited a smile from her, which was followed by a period of vocal exchange. One study, that observed the interaction between eight mothers and typically developing infants from 17 weeks old, until they were 43 weeks old, revealed that in interaction, the number of infant-initiated sequences was much greater than the number of mother-initiated sequences (Pawlby, 1977). Out of a total 1651 imitative sequences observed for all dyads, 1308 (79%) were reported to be infant-initiated. Also, studies of infant imitation seem to provide evidence for how an infant uses the behaviors in its repertoire to elicit gratifying behaviors from an interlocutor. In one study, infants, while observing an adult, were given a pacifier so that they could not imitate during the adult's demonstration (Meltzoff and Moore, 1977). When the pacifier was withdrawn, the infants initiated their imitative response in the subsequent 2.5-minute response period when they were met with a passive faced interlocutor. In another study, several 6-week-olds performed deferred imitation after a 24-hour delay. On day one, infants, during a play interaction, see a gesture, and then the next day the infant meets the same adult who displays a blank-face. In response to the familiar yet blank-face, the infant initially stares, and then imitates the gesture from long-term memory to initiate interaction with the adult (Meltzoff and Moore, 1994).

Still-face studies also seem to show that infants make repeated attempts to elicit a mother's response (Tronick *et al.*, 1978; Als *et al.* 1980; Als and Brazelton, 1981; Dixon *et al.*, 1981; Adamson and Frick, 2003). In these studies, a mother is instructed to play with her baby (about three months old) for approximately three minutes, just as she would at home, and then to withdraw briefly. After a minute, the mother returns for another three-minute period and maintains an *en face* position with her infant. However, this time the mother is asked to present a perfectly still face and to not respond to her baby. This study was repeated with a number of variations: with mothers, fathers, blind infants with sighted parents, sighted infants with blind parents, brain damaged infants as well as premature infants. A typical observation of a still-face study is as follows. Descriptions of what may be interpreted as infant initiation are highlighted:

> Before the 3-minute period, while still alone, the baby might look contemplatively down at her hands, fingering the fingers of one hand with another. <u>As the mother enters [for the second 3 minute period], her hand movements stop. She looks up at her mother, makes eye-to-eye contact, and smiles.</u> The mother's masklike expression does not change. The baby looks quickly to one side and remains quiet, her facial expression serious. Her gaze remains averted for twenty seconds. <u>Then she looks back at her mother's face, her eyebrows and lids raised, hands and arms stretching slightly out toward the mother.</u> Finding no response, she quickly looks down again at her hands, plays with them for about eight seconds, and then checks her mother's face once more…She turns her face to the side but keeps her mother in peripheral vision. (Brazelton and Cramer, 1990)

When confronted with the still-face, Tronick (1989) reports that most three-month-olds 'initially signal to their mothers using facial expressions, vocalizations, and gestures in an attempt to get their mothers to resume their normal behavior' (114). Throughout experimental periods infants remain intensely fixated on the mother. Similarly, when the mother is not in en-face position but is in profile view, the infant coos, vocalizes, and often leans forward in his seat. The infant may also pretend to cry and intersperse his vocalizations with long periods of looking at his mother. These activities may be interpreted to be eliciting behaviors from his mother. Mothers also report that a similar type of performance often occurs when they are driving their cars and are unable to maintain an en face position with their babies (Tronick *et al.*, 1979).

Other split-screen studies and detailed frame-by-frame analyses' conducted by Trevarthen (1977), show that infants are apparently 'calling the tune,' such that mothers also appear to be carefully imitating the infant's expressions. In another sequence (Figure 3.6), the mother adopts the head postures and expressions of an infant.

In Figure 3.6, the infant is not the one imitating or the one responding, but it is rather the adult that is doing so. In frame A, when the infant gives a social smile, the mother responds. In frame B, the infant modifies her expression and slightly tilts her head backward, which the mother follows. In frame C, the infant shifts her head downward for a more neutral stance, while decreasing her smile, and the mother does so as well. In frame D, The infant has further tilted her head downward to make a facial expression that signals discomfort or slight anger, which the mother also copies.

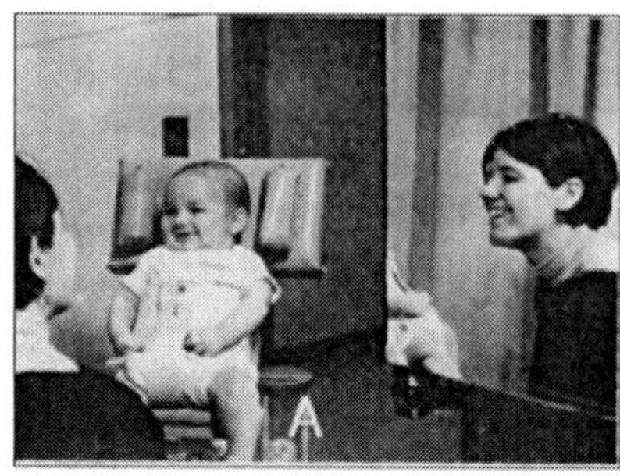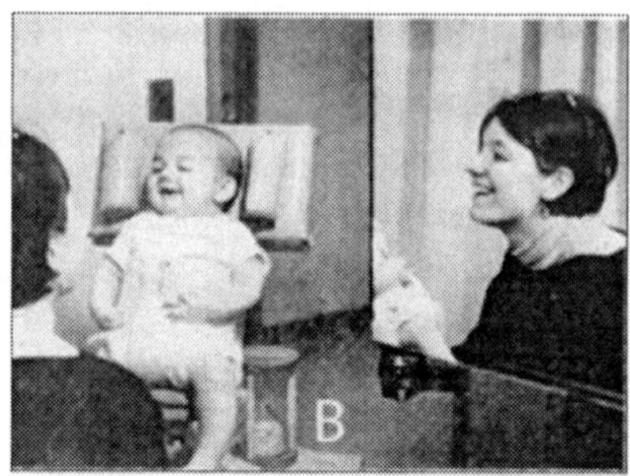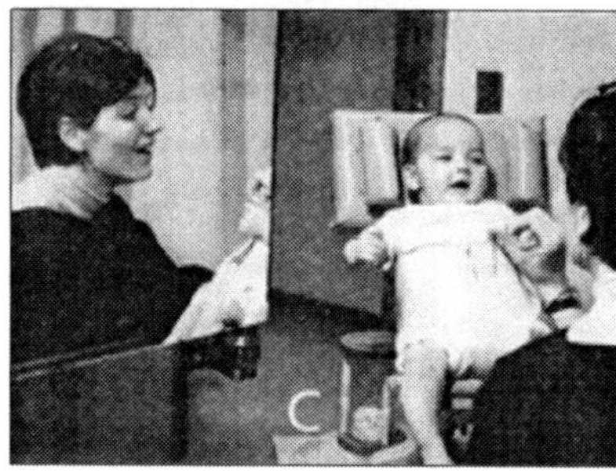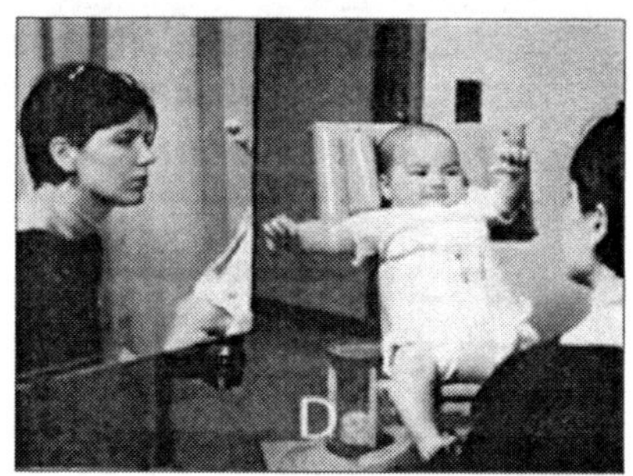

Figure 3.6: Imitation of a baby by a mother who is dependent on the initiative of her nine-week-old boy (Trevarthen, 1977: 244–245). © Elsevier 1977. Reprinted with permission.

Emotional perception and expression

The third type of behavior that deploys the innate abilities of infants and through which the interactional instinct is manifest, consists of those that show an infant's sensitivity to the emotional signals of his interlocutor, the signals value, as well as an infant's ability to communicate his emotional state. Gianino and Tronick (1988) labeled these affective displays made by infants as *other-directed regulatory behaviors.* We must keep in mind that infants are active – not passive – participants in an interaction and in fact are part of an 'active communication system in which the infant's goal directed strivings are aided and supplemented by the capacities of the caretaker'(Tronick, 1989). Within this system, Tronick notes that infants have specific internal goals, which include meeting their homeostatic and sociostatic needs. To accomplish these goals, infants process information about their current state and the state of those in their social environment. They evaluate whether they are succeeding or failing in meeting those goals, at times through 'reading' the messages given by caregivers through their emotional expressions, and they will modify their behaviors, at times communicating their emotional state to reach their goals. Thus, we see infants regulating interaction to achieve a desired interaction.

If we recall the still-faced studies mentioned earlier, when the mother continues to display a blank-face, her infant's response seems to express distress, which increases as the mother walks away. In the example below of an account of a second 3-minute period, we can see the infant displaying her emotional stance when confronted with a still-face through the use of its facial expressions and entire body posture (emotional displays are underlined for emphasis):

> She [the infant] <u>grimaces</u> briefly, and her facial expression becomes more <u>serious, her eyebrows furrowing</u>. Finally the baby completely withdraws, <u>her body curls over</u>, <u>her head falls</u>. She does not look again at her mother…She looks <u>wary</u>, helpless, and withdrawn. As the mother leaves the alcove at the end of the three minutes, she looks halfway up in her direction, but her <u>somber</u> facial expression and <u>curled over body position</u> do not change. (Brazelton and Cramer, 1990: 108)

Figure 3.7 captured a typical still-face response pattern of a 74-day-old infant (Tronick *et al.*, 1979). In the 30-second sequence, the infant begins the sequence with 'greeting' his mother. When he responded to her with a

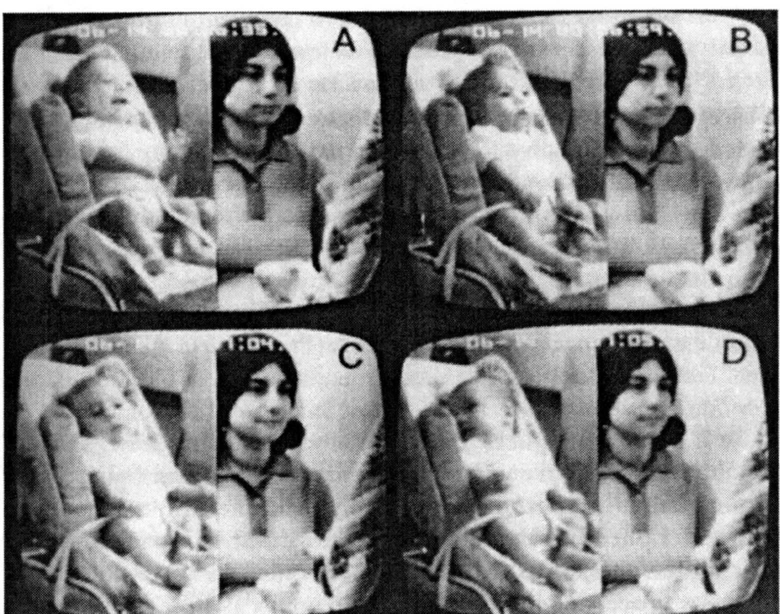

Figure 3.7: A time series of photos taken from the recorded video image of a still face condition. Infant 74 days old (Tronick et al., 1979: 365). © 1979 Cambridge University Press. Reprinted with permission of Cambridge University Press.

still-face, he becomes still and then warily looks away. He then checks back toward his mother again. Finally, he withdraws from the interaction.

In addition to the still face studies, other research has been carried out to examine the sensitivity and expressive capacities of infants under three months old (Murray and Trevarthen, 1985). In one study of 6- to 12-week-olds, infants experienced two different interactional situations. In the first situation, a mother talked to her baby, and then an experimenter entered the room and asked the mother a few questions, causing the mother to turn away and break the interaction between the mother and the infant. Prior to this, the infant displayed behaviors that are typical in positive interactions. He looked at his mother's face most of the time, actively moving his tongue and mouth, and smiling frequently. The expression of the brows was also fairly relaxed with very few frown-like expressions. When the mother was interrupted, the baby's attention to her decreased and the baby turned his attention to the experimenter. Efforts to communicate, such as mouthing and tonguing, decreased, along with the signs of positive affect. Smiling and brow-raising were also no longer sustained. However, the infant did not seem to be withdrawn or distressed, and a relaxed expression was maintained. The second situation was similar to still-face studies in that the mother was directed to become unresponsive and give a blank-expressionless face for 45 seconds while continuing to look at her baby. When the mother posed an emotionless and unresponsive blank-face, within a few seconds the infant showed signs of distress, by grimacing, increased handling of clothes, touching the face, sucking the fingers, and frowning. Efforts to communicate were also intensified at first, mouthing and tonguing postures were maintained and accompanied by active gesturing. The researchers interpreted the infants' actions as the infant's protesting or straining to reinstate interaction with the mother. Eventually, the infant withdrew and averted his gaze downward from the mother's face. The relaxed expression faded and the infant almost never smiled.

Tronick (1989) reports even more evidence of an infant's ability to perceive emotions. He reports a study showing that infants have a preference for facial expressions for joy over anger (Malatesta and Izard, 1984). He also notes studies in which different maternal emotional expressions lead to different infant emotions. If newborns are in a quiet and alert state, looking at and gently talking to them can produce a smile. However, 10-week-old infants react to facial displays of anger with anger and have fewer angry responses when their mothers display sadness (Lelwica and Haviland, 1983).

The responses and actions of infants in these studies seem to indicate that newborns have an inborn ability to communicate their emotional states and perceive emotional states, which they employ to elicit, reinstate, enhance interaction, as well as to communicate evaluations of the interaction. Infants seem to take into account the visible emotional stances of their interlocutor and use that understanding to deploy their next action. Furthermore, infants also seem to have an innate ability to communicate their affective state when the desired and anticipated interaction occurs or fails.

Human specificity

This category of behaviors manifesting the interactional instinct is related to the specificity of the motivation of the instinct, which is to achieve social affiliation and attachment with a *conspecific* and to become like *conspecifics*. In this section, I will demonstrate that infants make a distinction between human and non-human acts; they prefer animate entities to inanimate ones, and they can distinguish between and among conspecifics.

Studies show that by the second week of life, infants are able to use their ability to smile discriminately, such that infants smile more often in the presence of people. In addition, the human voice elicits more smiling in infants than the sound of an inanimate object such as a bell or a rattle (Bower, 1977). Other evidence of human specificity comes from studies of infants' perception of faces. Three studies reported by Maurer and Barrera (1981) suggest that infants have a preference for a human face. In the first study, 24 two-month-olds were shown a naturally drawn face and two faces with selected features deleted. The results showed that infants looked less than half as long at the face in which the features were omitted than at the naturally drawn face. In the second study, the same infants were shown a naturally drawn face, two faces with the mouth and nose deleted, faces with eyes that were either properly or improperly located, and a face in which the eyes and eyebrows were arranged 'unfacelike.' Infants again showed a preference for the naturally drawn face. In the third study, 24 two-month-olds were also shown a naturally drawn face, a face with a design in the bottom half, a face with a single eye, and a face in which the eyes and eyebrows were omitted. As the previous studies reported, infants attended longer to the naturally drawn face than the other 'faces.' Subsequent studies report that four-month-old infants also show a preference for a natural drawing of a human face over distorted drawings of faces (Maurer and Barrera, 1985). Also, if a baby is presented with a flat face after a human-like one, a newborn will look worried and turn away. Although these studies seem to indicate that human beings are born with preference for a human-like face, because the 'unfacelike' faces were distorted, it is unclear as to whether infants were simply showing a preference for something with good form and not faced-ness.

In addition, a series of experiments also demonstrated that neonates ranging in age between 12 and 17 days old have a preference for breast odors from unfamiliar and unrelated lactating females (Makin and Porter, 1989). In the experiment, neonates who have no breast-feeding experience and have only been bottle-fed, were exposed to a gauze pad soiled with an unfamiliar lactating female's breast odor and a clean pad. The experiment showed that infants spent significantly more time turned toward the soiled breast pads than the clean ones. Follow-up experiments demonstrated that the infants were not simply responding to an odor versus no odor at all, or to the strength of the odor.

Other studies seem to support the notion of human specificity such that infants are able to discern between social and nonsocial contexts and respond accordingly. One study shows that when a newborn watches a human's face, the infant's involvement and attention is more prolonged than when it is shown an object (Brazelton and Cramer, 1990). Tronick (1989) also reports Brazelton *et al.*'s (1974) observations that infants show a fundamental distinction between people and objects. When presented with an object:

> [Infants] look intently at it, sit up straight, remain relatively still, and punctuate their fixed gaze with swiping movements and brief glances away. Presented with people, infant's posture is more relaxed, and their movements are smoother. They become active at a slower pace and then look away for longer periods of time than they do with objects. Furthermore, infants give full greeting responses to people but not to objects. Simply stated, infants communicate with people and act instrumentally with objects. (114)

Trevarthen (1974) also observed the distinction in one and two-month-olds' responses to physical objects (i.e. a dangling toy) in comparison to a person. Infants look at, listen to, or touch objects. They also seek and interact with physical objects as sources of interest and as potentially graspable, chewable, and kickable, while human beings are perceived as communicable and are communicated with through expressive movements that are distinct from those with objects. Trevarthen (1977) noted that the 'responses of the infants to persons were different in kind from those to objects, and they were pre-adaptive to reception and reply by persons' (239). Similarly, other researchers showed that 2-month-olds smile, vocalize, and alternate their gazes with an adult, but if presented with an object that moves and sounds contingently, infants will engage intense arm activity while staring at the object (Legerstee *et al.*, 1987).

Neonatal imitation may also seem specific to people, such that inanimate objects that attempt to elicit imitative responses from infants fail. In one study, 27 infants, between 5 and 8 weeks old, were divided into two groups.

Twelve infants were presented with tongue protrusions and mouth openings modeled by an adult, and 15 were presented with these gestures simulated by two objects. Results showed that infants imitated the adults, but not the objects (Legerstee, 1991). In another study, two sets of infants, one with a median age of 5 weeks and another with a median age of 12 weeks, were presented with two inanimate models, one demonstrating tongue movements and another demonstrating mouth openings and closings. Infants were also presented with a human model who performed the same facial gestures. In neither group did the inanimate models elicit imitations. Live human models, however, did increase the tongue protrusions among infants (Abravanel and DeYong, 1991).

The studies of Meltzoff and Moore also suggest that infants attempt to distinguish between individuals and pay attention to unique identity. In their study of delayed imitation (Meltzoff and Moore, 1994), they suggested that the delayed gesture was deployed to see whether the person was the same as the one they had seen the day before. In other words, infants were using gestures to reidentify people, to see if the person was the same one who did that gesture before. In another study, they explored whether infants as young as 6 weeks old could differentiate individuals from each other (Meltzoff and Moore, 1992). In their study, infants were presented with two individuals who appeared and then disappeared. The mother would appear and show one gesture. She then exited and was replaced by a stranger who showed a different gesture. Interestingly, infants were able to switch their actions to play two different gestural games depending on whom they were interacting with. Meltzoff and Moore suggest that 'early interactive behaviour is directed toward *human individuals*' (Meltzoff, 1998: 59).

Understanding of communicative/social cues

Within such fined-tuned interactions, caregivers may provide communicative signals that cue infants to attend to an action. For example, recall the Kaluli that precede or punctuate components of an action with *Elefoma* (Do like this.) to make it easier to imitate (Schieffelin, 1990: 76). In addition to verbal cues, caregivers may use gaze, eye contact, eyebrow raising and pointing as social cues to index relevant information, which infants recognize as signals that the caregiver has communicative intention (Csibra, 2010). Some researchers have shown that infants do in fact read and appreciate such social cues. In one study (Brugger *et al.*, 2007), twenty-one 14- to 16-month old infants observed a novel action with a toy in two conditions. In the first condition, the actions were socially cued. For example, in one trial, the experimenter played with a Fisher Price tape player with a large green start button.

Two colored plastic tubes were attached to one side of the tape player and a thin yellow rod was placed in one of the tubes so that it protruded slightly. The experimenter would look at the infant and say for example, 'Hey, what's this? Watch what I can do'. And then the experimenter would take the rod out of the tube and place it into the other. Then the experimenter again would mark the next action with, 'Did you see that? Now watch this,' and then pressed the start button to make the music play. Of course, moving the rod from one tube to another was an unnecessary action and had nothing to do with turning on the music. Afterwards, the experimenter would make an assessment such as 'Neat, huh'. While making the social cues, the experimenter would also look at the infant, lean in, and go down to the infant's level. In the second condition, the experimenter did not solicit the infant's attention first, at least in a way that was relevant to the toy, nor did her gaze and posture indicate that she was talking to the infant. Instead, the experimenter would look at the wall across the room and say 'Wow! It's nice outside. Spring's almost here.' Only after the action was completed did the experimenter say, 'Did you see that? Now watch what I do next.' Then, as in the first condition, she also provided an assessment. The results showed that almost all the infants looked at the demonstration more and performed the first action after it was socially cued, while less than half of them did so on the un-cued trials. Furthermore, on all trials, most infants did not look at the experimenter while she was talking because they were too busy looking at the toys. The researchers state that 'infants must have sensed that the experimenter was somehow talking to them on the socially cued trials' (819), because they selectively imitated the cued actions.

In another study (Senju and Csibra, 2008), six-month-old infants were observed in two situations. In both situations, the model started with looking down at table and ended with a shift of gaze toward one or two colorful toys placed to her either side. However, there was one crucial difference between both situations – whether a social cue preceded the gaze shift. In the first experiment, infants had eye contact and watched the model look up toward the viewer while raising her eyebrows slightly before turning to one of the toys. In this situation, the infants were more likely to immediately look at the same object as the experimenter after her head turned. Moreover, they made more eye movements toward the gazed object. For another group of infants, instead of a model making eye contact, a colorful cartoon image was overlaid on her head (i.e. a flower) in order to attract infants' attention before the head turn. The researchers found that when eye gaze was removed, infants did not follow the gaze of the model.

In the second experiment, the researchers took away eye contact as well and considered the use of infant directed speech (IDS).[3] In this research design, along with the cartoon image, a female voice would say 'hello' in IDS. Infants in this condition were more likely to look to the gazed direction immediately after the model shifted her gaze. Infants also made more eye movements and looked longer at the gazed toy. Thus, a word uttered in infant-directed speech, not an addressed term (i.e. a name) or a directive, before the head turn, was sufficient to elicit gaze following in infants. Moreover, when 'hello' was not uttered with the qualities of IDS but as adult directed speech (ADS), infants were more likely to follow the model's gaze immediately after her head turn. The researchers also noted that such effects of gaze or IDS cannot be solely explained as 'attention getters' because the non-social attention getter (the cartoon flower) did not facilitate the gaze following behavior.

Also, frequent within infant-caregiver interactions are the use of deictic gestures and referential words, and studies show that infants understand the significance of their use as well, such that when experimenters use both verbal and deictic communicative signals (i.e. pointing), they assume that they refer to the same thing. And if there is any discrepancy, for example, in a condition when the pointing does not index anything, the infants notice and expect that something should be in the area that was pointed to by the experimenter (Gliga and Csibra, 2009).

Understanding of interpersonal organization

In his studies of mother-infant interaction with five two-month-olds, Trevarthen (1974) claimed that 'the foundation for interpersonal communication between humans is "there" when cognitive processes are just beginning' (230) because he observed that the interaction between a mother and infant showed signs of coordination that resembled conversation among adults. He described sequences in which the infant moved its mouth, hands, and eyes in a turn-taking format with an adult (1979). Bateson (1979) similarly looked at newborns 49–105 days old and also noticed mothers and infants 'in a pattern of more or less alternating, non-overlapping vocalization, the mother speaking brief sentences and the infant responding with coos and murmurs, together producing a brief joint performance similar to conversation' (65). Bateson coined this collaboration *protoconversation*. Jaffe *et al.* (2001) also showed that 4-month old infants are highly proficient in vocal turn-taking. Another study (Crown *et al.*, 2002) found that as early as six-weeks of age, coordinated timing occurs between an infant's gaze and adult vocal behavior. Jaffe *et al.* (2001) also found that the way an interaction unfolds between an infant and an adult is akin to the interaction between adults. The rhythms, turn taking, and vocalizations are more tightly coordinated in the beginning, and then the coordination eventually decreases as comfort with a stranger increases, which seems to occur in adult interactions as well (Kendon, 1970).

In another study, Beebe *et al.* (1979) conducted a frame by frame analysis of a continuous interaction between a mother and her 4-month-old infant. They examined two kinds of kinesic patterns: *coactive episodes*, a period in which the mother and infant are simultaneously engaged in kinesic behavior, and *noncoactive episodes*, periods in which behaviors do not overlap. They also looked at behavioral pauses, which end with the initiation of a behavior, and onset-to-onset times, which mark the beginning of a behavior of either mother or infant. The researchers found that their temporal analysis of the kinesic behavior showed patterns that were similar to the temporal patterns of the vocal interactions of mothers and infants. The researchers also found that in noncoactive episodes, infants had a tendency to match the duration of their mother's kinesic rhythms. Furthermore, in their analysis of behavioral patterns and onset times, the authors claim that the infant seems to be predicting maternal initiations of behavior. The protoconversational interactions between infants and mothers may also be seen as precursors to adult conversation patterns. For example, a behavioral pause is comparable to a possible turn-transition or point of recognizable completion, and onset time is similar to uptaking a turn in conversation. These elements are central to the systematic organization in adult conversation (Sacks *et al.*, 1974; Schegloff, 2000). Coactive episodes are similar to overlapping speech and may be a precursor to systematic overlapping in adult dialog, which the field of Conversation Analysis has demonstrated to have an extremely fine order of precision in the organization of interactive speech (Jefferson, 1973, 1983). Using conversation analysis, Filipi (2007) showed that a 10-month-old is able to initiate repair and use interactional resources to communicate to their interlocutor that their talk is inadequate. Berducci (2010) has also suggested that infants' crying and laughing function as incipient turn-taking devices to co-create sequences with caregivers.

Thus, infants on a basic level seem to be born with an understanding of how interpersonal communication is systematically organized. From birth we are already participating in and anticipating dialogic practices in multiple ways. The still-face studies of Tronick *et al.* (1979) mentioned above also demonstrate that infants are attuned to and detect the responses of caregivers. Trevarthen (1979) suggests that the behaviors of infants are manifestations of 'a specifically human system for person-to-person communication' (321) while Csibra and Gergely (2009) have proposed that human infants are sensitive to signals (such as eye gaze) that show that they are being addressed in communication. In 1985, Murray and Trevarthen demonstrated that infants were sensitive to the social behavior that is contingent on their own actions. They had mothers and 6- to 12-month-olds interact via video so that each dyad saw and heard the other on video monitors. Then the researchers rewound the videos of the mothers and played them back for the infants, such that the mother's facial expressions, vocalizations and gaze were exactly the same as they were moments before, except that the mother's actions were not contingent on the infant's behavior. The infants showed a marked sensitivity to the lack of contingency with a loss of positive affect and attention. The same phenomenon occurs with infants of depressed mothers who are less responsive, less spontaneous, and more constrained in their interactions when compared to non-depressed mothers (Field, 1984). In their study of infants' reaction to simulated maternal depression, Cohn and Tronick (1983) suggest that 'infants have a specific, appropriate, negative reaction to simulated depression in their mothers' (185). In another study that was similar to Murray and Trevarthen's (Nadel *et al.*, 1999), with ten infants aged 2-months, researchers used a double teleprompter device that allowed them to offer infants a continuous image and voice of the mother while they alternated 30 seconds of live video with 30 seconds of replay video, then returning to 30 seconds of live video seamlessly. The results produced the same responses from the infants as in Murray and Trevarthen's study, such that only non-contingent interaction induced a negative change in the infant's affect. In addition, the researchers reported that some of the infants recovered a positive state when the video returned to the live contingent interaction. Thus, early in development, infants also demonstrate that they are highly attuned to the actions and responses of interlocutors, and prefer contingent interaction to random stimulation.

Studies such as these suggest that early in life, humans have an inherent expectation and use for communicative signals, which some may call *ostensive signals* (Csibra and Gergely, 2006). Infants are born with an ability to appreciate the communicative significance of social cues, other than emotional facial expressions, crucial to achieving and maintaining social interactions (Goodwin, 1979, 1981). Thus, '[h]uman infants are prepared to be at the receptive side' of learning (Csibra and Gergely, 2009: 148) and seem to facilitate joint attention scenes, which have been argued to be critical for culture learning (Tomasello *et al.*, 1999).

The research in this section demonstrates that infants show imitation, infant-initiatedness, human specificity, an ability to perceive and convey emotional states, an understanding of interpersonal organization and communicative signals. These seem to be inborn abilities – all of which are useful for eliciting and sustaining interaction, the means through which attachment and affiliation are achieved. Although I have classified some behaviors of infants into six general categories through which the interactional instinct is manifest, the categories are not mutually exclusive. Emotional perception may lead to infant-initiatedness, which may lead to sequences of imitation. One example is Meltzoff and Moore's (1997) previously mentioned study, in which infants deployed an act that was imitated 24 hours earlier to initiate an interaction with a familiar conspecific who was showing an expression-less face. Another example from the still-face studies shows that an infant may communicate his emotional distress at the mother's unresponsiveness in an attempt to reinstate or to solicit a positive interaction, or an infant may look distressed and turn away and begin to suck his thumb to signal that he would like the interaction to end.

The interactional instinct in polyadic cultures

Although much of the research reported in this section has been with dyadic interactions, there is evidence that such manifestations seem to also occur in polyadic cultures. Such evidence strengthens the argument for the universality of the interactional instinct. Fox Adams (forthcoming) examined the behaviors of infants in four polyadic cultures, including the Gusii of Kenya (LeVine *et al.*, 1994), the Beng in the Ivory Coast (Gottlieb, 2004), India (Seymour, 1999), and the Chillihuani of Peru (Bolin, 2006). She found that though 'different types of interactions occur in various societies,' infants display behaviors that suggest an innate desire for interaction. For example, LeVine *et al.* (1994) compared Gusii mothers' responses to infant vocalizations, cries, and looks with those of white, middle-class mothers from Boston and found that, 'both Gusii and Bostonian infants use eye contact, crying, and vocalizations to initiate interactions with their caregivers' (10). LeVine *et al.* also reports a statistic that shows that Bostonian infants seek eye contact 8% of the time and Gusii infants seek it 9%. Fox Adams states that the finding is interesting because 'Bostonian mothers look at their infants qualitatively more – 28% of the time compared to 9% of the time for the Gusii mothers' (11). One interpretation of these findings could be that although Gusii infants are not rewarded with the return of eye gaze as much as the Bostonian infants, they still seek eye gaze in similar amounts to Bostonians. Other researchers of polyadic cultures have also demonstrated that infants seek out interaction. For example, 'starting at birth, Zinacantec infants' caregivers establish an intersubjective relation with it, relying on the baby's cries, vocalizations, posture, gaze, facial expressions, and body movements to guide their interactions with it' (De Leon, 2008: 137).

Manifestations of the interactional instinct have also been observed in the West African groups – Aka and Ngandu (Hewlett *et al.*, 1998). The Aka are known to usually hold their infants close, whereas the infant-caregiver interactions among the Ngandu are more distal. Ngandu infants are held about half as frequently as Aka infants. As a result, researchers found that Ngandu infants 'fuss, cry, smile, and vocalize to maintain or attract their parents' attention' (658). The researchers also suggested that they could not conclude that such interactions were rarer or did not happen among the Aka, because 'when infants are held, the body movements, heartbeats, sounds, and smells of infants and adults provide the basis for a subtle 'dance' that is obviously not captured when gross observational methods are used' (658). Perhaps early infant behaviors are less observed in more traditional societies because: (1) in some societies infants spend most of their time in close proximity with the mothers or caregivers, thus there is less 'need' for infants to solicit interaction; and (2) in such societies the methods traditionally used to observe infant-caregiver interactions may be insufficient to capture the subtle behaviors of infants. Therefore, presumably from the known observations, such behavioral manifestations are present in all infants.

The ubiquity of these manifestations in very young typically developing infants, in dyadic and polyadic cultures, with mothers as well as strangers, suggests that they have not been learned, and shows that human beings enter their social world with an 'effective interpersonal intelligence' (Trevarthen, 1979: 15) that instantiates an innate 'drive' for interaction in human beings. Moreover, the interactional instinct ensures opportunity and motivation to attain sociocultural knowledge, including language, through the various practices and ideologies of cultural transmission.

Notes

1. Much of the material in this chapter was previously published in Lee *et al.* (2009). It is reproduced with permission of the author and Oxford University Press, Inc. It has been revised and expanded from the original publication.
2. Provocation is a more specific definition than infant-initatedness as it is related to the use of a previously *imitated* gesture after an experimenter's similar gesture or after an infant's previous imitative response. (Nagy, 2006: 229)
3. Infant directed speech will be discussed more in Chapter 5.

4 Affiliation as motivation for interaction: A neurobiology for the interactional instinct

Thus far, I have suggested that behavioral studies demonstrate that human beings are driven to seek out interaction and to become like others. This then ensures that an infant will have the opportunity to interact with more competent social beings and will be socialized to the culture to which he/she belongs through processes of enculturation. But why? Why do babies as young as 8 minutes old imitate and at times do so as if to initiate and reinstate interaction? Why do infants vocalize, smile, cry, gesticulate, and make facial expressions when they are engaged in positive or negative interactions? Survival instincts will lead to some of the infant behaviors previously mentioned; a baby might cry, vocalize, gesture, and make facial expressions when he is hungry, when he wants to be burped, and when he wants to sleep. However, as I have proposed, there are other processes active besides those that would lead an infant to seek protection or to maintain homeostasis. We have innate tendencies to seek out and sustain interaction with those in our social world leading to attachment and social affiliation. This chapter explores what mediates an infant's ability to engage and what motivates a neonate as young as 8 minutes old to elicit, engage, and prolong interaction.

Behavioral studies show that interaction with another is a rewarding achievement and may be separate from other goals that an infant pursues. Infant vocal behaviors may function to maintain close proximity between a mother and infant before the infant is mobile (Bowlby, 1969). Crying seems to promote close contact by signaling distress and bringing the mother to the infant, and vocalizations, in general, elicit visual attention. Nondistress sounds, such as cooing and grunting also elicit attention and bring the mother to the infant. But during visual attention, infant vocalizations predictably elicit reciprocal vocalizations. Transcriptions of mothers' responses to infants during imitation also show that when an infant imitates an interlocutor, he is automatically rewarded in several ways. First, the interlocutor continues to pay attention to him. Second, the interlocutor will react with excessive pride and pleasure at the infant's abilities. This is seen in the following account of a mother's reaction when imitated (Pawlby, 1977): 'Go …', as mother demonstrates. 'You do that!' Child imitates action. Mother continues, 'ooo! There's a good boy, there's a good boy! That's quite clever' (221).

There is also evidence demonstrating that infants not only orient and prefer direct gaze, but they actually enjoy making eye contact. If an adult breaks eye contact with a 3- to 6-month old, an infant will smile less even though the adult continues to interact vocally with the infant (Hains and Muir, 1996). If an adult, however, does not break eye contact, but averts his/her head while maintaining eye contact, an infant will smile (Caron *et al.*, 1997).

In another study of 24 mother-infant dyads, infants were found to have spent more time vocalizing during maternal absence than while being held, and infants vocalized significantly more when mothers were within arms reach than while they were being held (Anderson *et al.*, 1978). The infants were apparently seeking interaction with the mother because the mother did not provide any other form of reward (i.e. food, ease of discomfort, etc.). Studies such as these show that achieving interaction is separate from other goals that an infant might pursue. Newborn infants, as young as 3 hours old, have been found to not only imitate but to also initiate using previously imitated gestures (Meltzoff, 1988; Nagy, 2006). Thus, neonates proactively participate in imitation exchanges. This book proposes that such behaviors are because of the sociostatic value of interaction, which: (1) increases an infant's chances to benefit from the sustained interaction; and (2) motivates human beings to actively pursue and achieve attachment and social affiliation with others. In this chapter, I discuss two systems involved when an infant encounters social stimuli. These systems motivate an infant to 'seek out' or 'flee' from interactions.

Social engagement theory

The evaluation of whether a social stimulus is safe, dangerous, or life-threatening, which can be derived from the face, voice and movements, is crucial to social engagement or defense. Porges has called this largely unconscious evaluation as *neuroception* (Porges, 2001, 2003, 2005), and has identified specific neural structures that are involved. Functional imaging techniques have shown that the temporal cortex, fusiform gyrus (FG), and superior temporal sulcus (STS) are involved in the detection of face, voice, and movement (Adolphs, 2002; Haxby *et al.*, 1999; McCarthy *et al.*, 1997), which contribute to a social stimulus as being perceived as safe or not. The FG and STS project to the amygdala, an area involved in the processing of emotional experiences and memories of them. The amygdala in turn is connected to the periaqueductal gray (PAG), which regulates fight, flight, or freeze behaviors.

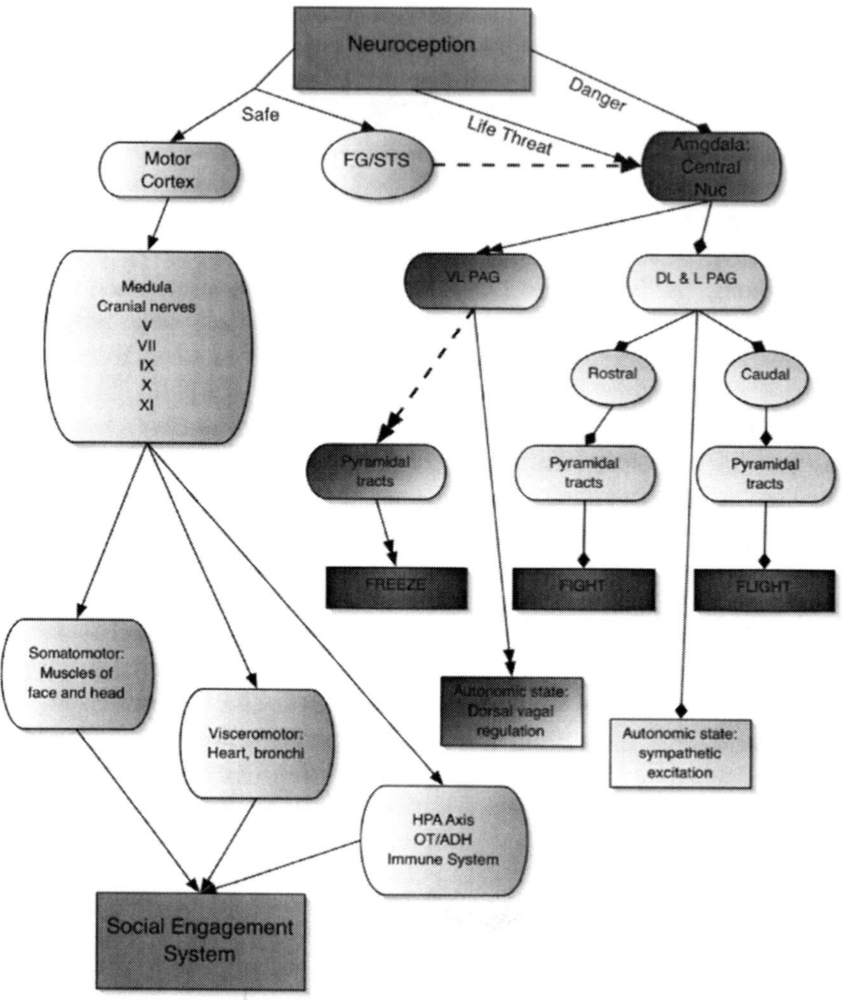

Figure 4.1. Adaptation of Porges' Social Engagement System by Mates from Lee *et al.* (2009). Used with Permission from Oxford University Press, Inc.

Porges reports that stimulating rostrally within the lateral and dorsal PAG produces 'fight' behaviors, whereas stimulating caudally within the lateral PAG and dorsal PAG produces 'flight' or escape behaviors. Furthermore, stimulating the ventrolateral PAG produces 'freeze' behaviors. If no threat or danger is perceived, inhibitory projections from the FG and STS to the central nucleus of the amygdala will inhibit the limbic defense system, providing an opportunity for social behavior to occur (Porges, 2005: 46). This occurs as the cortex exerts control over the brainstem via connections terminating in the cranial nerves, which control visceromotor (e.g. heart beat) and somatomotor (e.g. face muscles) structures. If, however, the social stimulus is appraised as dangerous, the amygdala will be activated, resulting in a fight, flight, or freeze response, dissuading social engagement and therefore affiliation.

Thus, Porges' 'social engagement theory' provides a model for how neural detections in the environment modulate physiological states and behaviors that promote or dissuade interaction seeking (Hardacre, 2009). Another system implicated in the formation of affiliative bonds is one put forth by Depue and Morrone-Strupinksy (2005).

Affiliation and enculturation

Depue and Morrone-Strupinsky (2005), henceforth identified as D&MS, propose that 'behavioral systems are fundamentally emotional systems that incorporate a motivational state and emotional experience that is concordant with the reinforcement properties of critical stimuli' (19). D&MS view our capacity to seek out and experience affiliative rewards,[1] and process the contexts in which rewards are experienced, as a necessary component in acquiring and maintaining affiliative bonds. They propose that this capacity underlies behaviors that lead to the formation of human social relationships – and, I propose, enculturation.

Phases of affiliation

Affiliation, defined by D&MS (2005), involves reflecting on the enjoyment and valuing of close interpersonal bonds, and being warm and affectionate. It also involves *proximity seeking*, which means the child seeks to be near the caregiver because of his/her desire to be near the source of reward or positive feelings. The process of experiencing and maintaining an affiliative reward occurs across two phases of affiliation: an appetitive phase and a consummatory phase.[2]

The appetitive phase of affiliation represents the first step toward attaining interactional reward. Distal stimuli, such as a social smile, vocalizations, and gestures from potential bonding partners are appetitive rewards. Such stimuli have been demonstrated to activate areas in the brain that generate reward. For example, just viewing an attractive female face activates reward areas in heterosexual males (Aharon *et al.*, 2001). Such stimuli are incentives evaluated as positive and powerful in valence, which moves one to pursue and achieve close proximity; behavior analogous to that of a drug addict's (Di Chiara and North, 1992). In humans, the incentive state is associated with subjective feelings of desire, wanting, and enthusiasm (Depue and Morrone-Strupinsky, 2005: 20). Moreover, just the sheer possibility of achieving such a reward is inherently rewarding, such that animals have been shown to work intensively to obtain that reward without evidence of satiety (Depue and Collins, 1999).

When close proximity to a rewarding goal is achieved, incentive motivation approach gives way to the consummatory phase of affiliation. In this phase, behavioral patterns that are specific to such conditions are elicited (e.g. successful engagement and interaction with a conspecific). In contrast to the appetitive phase, the expression of consummatory behavioral patterns elicits feelings of pleasure, gratification, and liking, plus physiological quiescence characterized by rest and sedation, which serve an important feedback status. For instance, the pleasurable experience of an interaction leads to the reinforcement of the production and repetition of such behaviors. Thus, whereas the appetitive approach processes bring an individual to contact with a rewarding stimuli, consummatory processes bring behavior to a gratifying conclusion (Hilliard *et al.*, 1998).

Furthermore, through Pavlovian conditioning, the general context and specific contextual stimuli form an ensemble that is predictive of that reward (Depue and Morrone-Strupinsky, 2005: 22). Studies of mother-infant dyads report that when an infant vocalizes, the mother is most likely to respond with a vocalization of her own. Her next most likely response is to smile at, look at, or touch the infant (Freedle and Lewis, 1977; Stevenson *et al.*, 1986), which are all gratifying responses for the infant. The incentive from seeing a potential interlocutor motivates a neonate to pursue the interaction and to behave in such a way that might elicit a positive response from the potential interlocutor, prolong the action, and repeat the experience of it (Di Chiara and North, 1992). Eventually, a neonate's subsequent perception of a particular contextual ensemble alone might elicit a secondary incentive motivational state powerful enough to arouse goal directed behavior. These processes support acquisition of affiliative memories and the contexts in which they occur, and the pursuit of such interactions.

A neurobiology for the interactional instinct[3]

In a study with infants 3–54 hours old (Nagy and Molnar, 1994), researchers measured the heart rates of infants as they responded to and initiated tongue-protrusion – a behavior that infants have been found to imitate (Meltzoff and Moore, 1977, 1983). The results showed that the imitation of tongue protrusion is accompanied by an accelerated heart rate, while initiating an interaction with a tongue protrusion is accompanied by a significantly decelerated heart rate. Thus, the researchers proposed that heart rate deceleration indexes an infant's orientation or social expectations (Nagy and Molnar, 2004: 61). In contrast, imitation involves tracking a moving and socially significant stimulus, which leads to an accelerated heart rate. What this study demonstrates is that there are psychophysiological differences across imitation and imitation for initiation. Furthermore, the researchers suggest that this study exhibits a clear analogy of the two phases of affiliation: appetitive (approach-initiation) and consummatory (imitation). I will now explore the neurobiology that underlies such processes as proposed by D&MS (2005).

Neural circuit of reward

The positive incentive motivation and experience of reward that underlies the behavioral system of approach is dependent on the functional properties of the ventral tegmental area (VTA) dopamine (DA) projection system, which projects to the nucleus accumbens shell (NAS). These areas have long been identified with the processing of rewarding stimuli (Everitt and Robbins, 1992; Schultz *et al.*, 1992, 1997; Schumann *et al.*, 2004). In rats, neural pathways associated with dopamine neurons are targets for self-stimulation. In these experiments, rats choose to press a bar that will excite neurons at the site of an implanted electrode (Phillips and Fibiger, 1978). Also, if treated with dopamine receptor blockers, rats are not as quick to learn that pressing a bar gives a reward pellet (Wise, 1982). In rats and monkeys, if the VTA DA projection system is blocked, incentive behavior is impaired 'including locomotor activity to novelty and food; exploratory, aggressive, affiliative, and sexual behavior; acquisition and maintenance of approach and active avoidance behavior; food hoarding; and maternal nursing behavior' (Depue and Morrone-Strupinsky, 2005: 323). DA lesions in the NAS or VTA also create a reduction in motivation to work for reward (Depue citing Caine and Foob, 1993; Fibiger and Phillips, 1987). Mirenowicz and Schultz (1996) and Schultz *et al.* (1997) also showed that VTA DA neurons are activated by appetitive incentive stimuli and in the prediction of a reward. These are shown in experiments observing single units of dopamine neurons in monkeys performing behavioral acts and receiving rewards. In the first part of the experiment, monkeys, after doing an action or viewing a stimulus (i.e. a small light) are given access to various appetitive stimuli (i.e. a piece of an apple or a some fruit juice). These stimuli lead to a 'phasic activation' or a burst of activity in VTA DA neurons after the cue. After several days of training and repeated pairings of the stimuli followed by reward, phasic activation occurs to the time of cue onset even before seeing the reward. Then, in trials when reward is not given, at cue onset, phasic activation occurs, but when reward does not come, dopamine neurons are markedly depressed (Schultz, 1986, 2007). Experiments such as these suggest that:

> Dopamine neurons are therefore excellent feature detectors of the 'goodness' of environmental events relative to learned predictions about those events. They emit a positive signal (increased spike production) if an appetitive event occurs as predicted, and a negative signal (decreased spike production) if an appetitive event is worse than predicted. (Schultz, 1997: 1594)

Thus, the VTA DA-NAS pathway is a primary neural circuit for incentive reward.

This may perhaps be analogous to the observations made in the still face studies described in Chapter 3 when infants show pleasure when an expected interaction occurs and show distress when it does not. In the first three minutes a mother plays with her infant in such a way that the infant has a very positive experience throughout. The infant has learned that he will be rewarded with positive stimuli from his mother. Then, during the second three-minute period, the mother returns to the room with a 'still face'. The infant will immediately look at his mother and smile, vocalize, and/or gesture before his mother has displayed any positive affective stimuli, anticipating a positive response from his mother. However, when the infant does not receive any of the expected reward, he demonstrates that the interaction is undesired (Brazelton and Cramer, 1990).

Forming affiliative memories

For the formation of affiliative memories, D&MS focus on the NAS as the area that integrates reward and context because research shows that during periods of focused attention and consummatory events, NAS cells decrease firing. However, NAS cells increase firing with primary and conditioned signals because reward is expected (Apicella *et al.*, 1991; Schultz *et al.*, 1992, 1995). Specifically, the caudomedial shell region of the NAS is a major point of convergence of motivational information from many corticolimbic regions, including the basolateral complex of the amygdala, the extended amygdala, the hippocampus, and the medial orbital prefrontal cortex (MOC 13). The NAS is proposed to be the site of convergence because each NAS spiny neuron dendrite receives 30,000 efferents from the regions mentioned, with each region providing information about stimuli and the contexts in which they are experienced (Depue and Morrone-Strupinsky, 2005). It should be noted that the basolateral amygdala, extended amygdala, and MOC13 receive neural input from regions that process face (fusiform gyrus) and biological motion (anterior and dorsal regions of the temporal lobe) (Adolphs, 2003), which provide information about facial expressions, gaze shifts, arm, and hand movements – cues that are relevant to infants and affiliative interactions.

Information from the amygdala

Studies show that lesions in the basolateral amygdala in primates cause a decline in affiliative behavior, social communication, and emotional responses to other animals (Emery and Amaral, 2000). Studies have also shown that female rats develop increased activity in the basolateral amygdala with increasing interaction with their pups, while lesions in the same area prevents the formation of conditioned place preference with rat pups (Fleming *et al.*, 1999). More specifically, D&MS (2005) cite studies in which bilateral lesions in this area lead to impairments in the conditioning for *explicit, discrete stimuli* (Aggleton, 1999; Everitt and Robbins, 1992; Gaffan, 1992). Discrete stimuli are those that have a close spatial or temporal relationship to the achievement of a particular reward. Gaffan's studies comparing the behaviors of normal and amygdalectomized monkeys demonstrate the specific role of the amygdala (Gaffan, 1992). First, when monkeys are given a series of choices between food items, normal monkeys typically develop an order of preference among the items. Eventually, monkeys develop an association between an item's appearance and its palatability. Thus, the palatability has determined the incentive value of a food item at sight. Monkeys with bilateral amygdalectomies, in contrast, develop weak preferences, which also may reflect a loss of association between the item's appearance and its palatability. Another version of the study associates an arbitrary stimulus with the incentive value of a food reward. In this format, a monkey sees two new stimuli and must learn which to choose. Choosing the correct stimulus produces clicks, while selecting the wrong stimulus produces a white noise. Four correct choices produce a food reward. Thus, hearing clicks mean food and white noise means no food. The association to be learned is based on the clicks or white noise, and not the food, and learning the meanings of the auditory cues is similar to learning what the sight of food means. Normal monkeys are able to learn this association. However, monkeys with bilateral amygdalectomies display a severe impairment in making the associations, though they are still able to perform food-motivated tasks. Amygdalectomized monkeys still know that eating is accomplished by putting things in the mouth, what is lost or impaired is the specific knowledge that a particular

Basolateral amygdala	Explicit, discrete stimuli	Stimuli with a close spatial or temporal relationship to the achievement of a particular reward
Extended amygdala	Non-explicit, non-discrete stimuli	Environmental stimuli (i.e. light conditions, physical features, etc)

Figure 4.2. Information from the basolateral and extended amygdala.

shape and color has a particular value, or that a specific noise or visual stimulus means that food delivery is imminent (474). Thus, the sight of food and the noise predicting the imminent delivery of the reward are explicit, discrete stimuli. This was further specified to the basolateral amygdala in the studies of Everitt and Robbins (1992).

In addition, the basolateral amygdala innervates the extended amygdala, which provides different information to the NAS shell.[4] In contrast, the extended amygdala is highly conditionable for *nonexplicit, nondiscrete stimuli* (i.e. environmental stimuli such as light conditions, physical features, and spatial relations) (Davis *et al.*, 1997; Davis, 1999). The extended amygdala is comprised of the bed nucleus of the stria terminalis (BNST) and its sublenticular extension into the centromedial amygdala, which merge specifically with the caudomedial region of the NAS shell. Lesions to this area 'modify incentive motivation to work for rewards and initiation of locomotor activity as a means of obtaining rewards' (Depue and Morrone-Strupinsky, 2005: 327). Lee *et al.* (2009) explain that the extended amygdala associates environmental stimuli (nondiscrete stimuli) while receiving the discrete features from the basolateral amygdala as it projects to the NAS shell (161).

Spatial and contextual information from the hippocampus

In addition to receiving information from the basolateral and extended amygdala, the NAS shell receives projections from the hippocampus. Lesions in the hippocampal area disrupt associations formed between 'spatial and contextual interrelations of environmental stimuli and reinforcement' (Depue and Morrone-Strupinsky, 2005: 327). Primates seem to be particularly good at attending to and integrating all sensory cues from all modalities in recognizing and bonding with those in their social environment (Leckman *et al.*, 2005). Selden *et al.* (1991) report two experiments that suggest that the hippocampus specifically provides information about the spatial organization of the contextual environment. In one experiment, control rats and rats with bilateral lesions to the basolateral amygdala were pre-exposed to an apparatus with two distinctive chambers (one black and one white) and then received shock pairings in the black chamber. Then contextual conditioning was measured by the relative preference for the 'safe' or 'shock' compartment. Each rat was placed in the apparatus and was allowed to move freely between chambers for 5 minutes, while researchers recorded the number of seconds spent in each chamber. The same format was followed in a second experiment, except rats had bilateral lesions to the hippocampus. The researchers reported that lesions to the basolateral amygdala did not affect conditioning to contextual clues, whereas rats with hippocampal lesions were severely impaired in their ability to select a safe environment based on contextual clues alone.

Sutherland and McDonald (1990) studied the role of the hippocampus in the formation of the associations of stimuli and the context clues. In their study, control rats, rats with hippocampal damage, amygdala damage, and combined damage were placed individually in a box for 10 minutes on two consecutive days. On the third day, rats received two foot shocks each lasting for 10 seconds. On successive days, animals did not receive any shock. All groups showed an increase in defecation and they did not differ significantly in the amount of defecation on either the pre-shock or shock days. During the shock days defecation among the controls and amygdala damaged rats remained high. Previous studies had shown that after experiencing shock, rats defecated more (Vanderwolf, 1962). However, in the Sutherland and McDonald study, the hippocampal and combined damaged rats did not maintain the elevated levels of defecation on post-non-shock days when placed in the same box. This result suggests the role of the hippocampus associating stimuli to its contextual environment. In another study, the same four groups of rats were tested for their ability to find a hidden escape platform in a swimming pool (known as the Morris water task) (Sutherland and McDonald, 1990). This task has been shown to demonstrate a 'rat's ability to learn the topographical relationship among distal cues and the location of the platform' (72). Each rat had eight trials per day for five consecutive days. Though there was very little difference in abilities among rats, in later trials, rats with hippocampal damage took longer to locate the platform, while control and amygdala damaged rats performed normally. D&MS report studies such as these (Annett *et al.*, 1989; Sutherland and McDonald, 1990; Selden *et al.*, 1991) to propose that the hippocampus provides information about the spatial organization of the contextual environment while the amygdala (basolateral and extended) encodes various stimuli associated with the context of the reward.

Role of the medial orbital prefrontal area 13 (MOC 13)

The basolateral and extended amygdala have dense reciprocal connections to the medial orbital prefrontal cortex area 13 (MOC 13), which also has connections to regions that process all 'sensory modalities of contemporaneous and stored information' (Depue and Morrone-Strupinsky, 2005: 328). Its connectivity allows the MOC 13 to form 'higher-level conditional representations of sensory events by associating them with existing or newly developing response-reinforcement contingencies, or more simply, MOC 13 may abstract an integrated structure of appetitive and aversive behavioral contingencies from the environment' (Depue and Morrone-Strupinsky, 2005: 328). In addition, MOC 13 may 'be capable of holding such representations of behavioral-reinforcement contingencies that are relevant to the modification of response programs' (Depue and Morrone-Strupinsky, 2005: 328). The MOC 13, thus, provides higher order context-reward information to the NAS as it encodes and updates behavioral-reinforcement contingencies.

Putting it all together

As the NAS has 30,000 efferents to *each* spiny neuron dendrite from the basolateral and extended amygdala, hippocampus, and MOC13, the NAS thus receives a wealth of contextual information leading to the formation of contextual ensembles, which are encoded for incentive salience and value. The contextual ensemble is then transmitted via the dorsomedial thalamus back to the MOC 13. The result would be a continual updating 'not only of incentive motivational intensity … but also of reinforcement priorities and behavioral outcome expectations constructed' (Depue and Morrone-Srupinsky, 2005: 329).

D&MS then suggest how contextual ensembles are formed (see Figure 4.3). The brain regions, basolateral amygdala, extended amygdala, hippocampus, and MOC 13 carry contextual information and innervate the heads of dendritic spines of the NAS using glutamate as a transmitter. In addition, VTA DA projections also innervate the NAS. DA release to the NAS occurs when stimuli for rewards are unpredicted and unconditioned (Schultz *et al.*, 1995). The effect of DA-glutamate combination is an increased release of each other and facilitates the development of long-term potentiation (LTP). D&MS, in fact, report studies that such DA is essential for glutamate release, which triggers LTP of amygdala and hippocampal afferents to the NAS (Groenewegen *et al.*, 1999; O'Donnell, 1999, 2003; Bissiere *et al.*, 2003; Li *et al.*, 2003). Moreover, if the DA-glutamate interaction occurs at the basolateral amygdala near to the soma of NAS neurons, the interaction

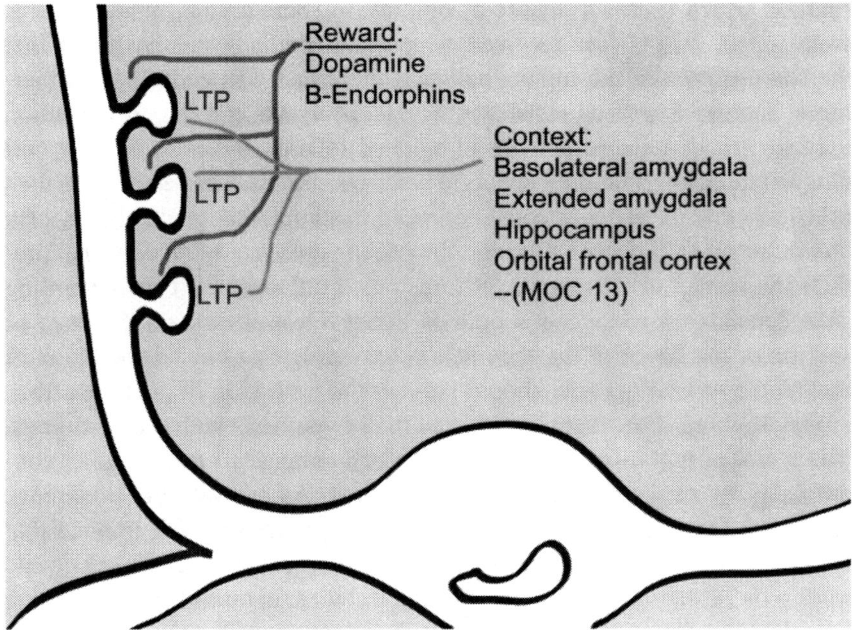

Figure 4.3: Interactional rewards are being tied to the contexts in which those rewards were achieved in the nucleus accumbens shell. (Image provided by Andrea W. Mates).

'has a downstream effect on the synapses from other contextual inputs that are farther from the soma' (Lee *et al.* 2009:162 citing Depue and Morrone-Strupinsky, 2005). In this way, according to D&MS, 'reward magnitude of discrete, contextual stimuli carried by basolateral amygdala afferents to the NAS can facilitate the triggering of LTP in other contextual afferents to the NAS' (330).

Endogenous opiates and neuropeptides

Beta endorphins

D&MS also discuss the significant role beta endorphins and endogenous opiates have in the process of developing affiliative memories, particularly with consummatory reward. These opiates are produced by the pituitary gland and synthesized in the hypothalamus. When beta endorphins bind to mu type opiate receptors, they produce a feeling of '*increased* interpersonal warmth, euphoria, well-being, and peaceful calmness as well as *decreased* elation, energy, and incentive motivation' (italics original, Depue and Morrone-Strupinsky, 2005: 324). In one study (Blass and Shah, 1994), researchers gave sucrose, which causes a release of opioids, to some crying human infants, while other infants just received water. The findings demonstrated that the sucrose calmed the infants and that the effect was enduring. Furthermore, sucrose increased resistance to painful events (i.e. blood collection via heel prick), reduced activity in agitated infants, and reduced tachycardia (increased heart rate) by about 30 beats per minute. The researchers then asked whether the changes could be linked to stimuli that predict them, such that infants would choose to spend time in the presence of an odor that predicts the receipt of sucrose or fat infusions. Furthermore, if the rewarding state depends on endogenous opioids being released through the taste of sucrose or the flavor of fat, then naloxene, a drug that blocks the action of the brain's natural opioids, should prevent the formation of positive affect, or conditioning. The researchers tested their hypothesis with 6-day-old rats. The sucrose or fat infusion was paired with an orange odor. Then after conditioning the rats, naloxene was administered. As a result, the preference for the orange odor was blocked by naloxene. Such a finding implied that the orange odor, which predicted endogenous opioid release, caused opioid release on subsequent occasions, causing a change in motivational state that propelled the pup to maintain proximity with the odor. The researchers have also found that the same effect occurs with human infants 1–2 days old, when the sucrose is paired with either touch to the forehead or a clucking sound. Human infants, after just 10 conditioning pairings, will orient their movements to the source of the sucrose. Moreover, when the stimulus stopped predicting sucrose delivery, 75% of the infants cried. Such research demonstrated that newborns can extract from caretaker interactions certain features that regularly predict the delivery of a substance that causes the release of endogenous opioids and, conversely, the loss of that predictive quality is disturbing (Blass *et al.*, 1984). Thus, opiate release seems to be highly conditionable and such conditioning can take place very early in development, facilitating a positive response to a positive social interaction, which also facilitates the maintenance of affiliative bonds.

In general, naloxene and naltrexone (another opioid receptor antagonist) reduce the reward derived from social interactions. Human females that are administered naltrexone showed an increased amount of time spent alone, a reduced amount of time spent with friends, and a reduced frequency and pleasantness of their interactions (Depue and Morrone-Strupinsky, 2005 citing Jamner and Leigh, 1999). Furthermore, mu opiate receptors have been found in high concentrations in the NAS and VTA, and opiate release in the VTA can increase DA release in the NAS and hence the experience of reward. In sum, 'distal affiliative cues serve as incentive stimuli that activate DA-facilitated incentive-reward motivation, desire, wanting, and approach to affiliative objects. As these objects are reached, more proximal affiliative stimuli strongly activate mu opiate release, which promotes an intense state of pleasant reward, warmth, affection, physiological quiescence, and brings approach to a gratifying conclusion' (Depue and Morrone-Strupinsky, 2005: 326).

Neuropeptides

Oxytocin (OT) and vasopressin (VP), uniquely mammalian neuropeptides, have also been associated with social bonding and social communication. Studies with nonhuman animals show that increases in OT and VP levels are associated with increases in social interactions, which may lead to social bonding. Furthermore, VP appears to be involved in forming the memories of these social interactions (Popik and Van Ree, 1992) and is critical for recognizing familiar individuals (Young and Wang, 2004). Voles have been particularly useful in understanding the role of OT, VP, and DA in social bonding. Prairie voles are socially monogamous, while montane voles typically do not pair bond (Carter *et al.*, 1995). Vasopressin receptors are high in the ventral palladium in the prairie voles but are very low in the same region in the montane voles. In addition, OT receptors are abundant in the NAS in the prairie voles, but not in montane voles. It appears that only those capable of forming selective pair bonds have shown a large number of receptors for both dopamine and either OT or VP in the NAS and ventral palladium (Leckman *et al.*, 2005). Such studies indicate that OT and VP have a role in building affiliation and will be further discussed in the next chapter.

Gonadal steroids

In addition, D&MS suggest that gonadal steroids have a role in whether stimuli are perceived to be affiliative. Gonadal steroids such as estrogen, testosterone, and progesterone are secreted in the gonads (ovaries and testes). In sheep, toward the end of pregnancy, progesterone and estrogen levels rise, which promotes synthesis of oxytocin receptors (Keverne, 2005). For ewes in estrus, but not at other times, male faces and odors result in higher levels of mediobasal hypothalamus activity, where there are both estrogen and progesterone receptors (Fabre-Nys *et al.*, 1997). Though gonadal steroids are primarily associated with sociosexual behaviors, they may have a role in whether social stimuli are affiliative at all.

This chapter attempted to explore how an 8-minute-old infant might appraise an interactional event and what might motivate her to elicit, engage, and prolong interaction. We have a system that appraises facial expressions, vocalizations, and gestures as dangerous or not, and we have a system that appraises and marks our interactions and the contexts in which they occur as pleasurable or not. Early in life, we have a system that allows us to appraise and value cooing, caressing, eyebrow raising, and smiling as pleasurable and rewarding, which involves the expression of endogenous opiates during child-caregiver interactions. This process serves as a hardwired motivational mechanism and entrains a child's attentional mechanisms on caregivers. As the child grows, the rewarding aspect of the attachment bond becomes part of the child's memory, which leads to the approach to and development of affiliative bonds with caregivers and ensures socialization and language acquisition.

Notes

1.   'Reward' is an operational concept for describing the positive value that a creature ascribes to an object, a behavioral act, or an internal physical state (Schultz *et al.*, 1997: 1593).
2.   This two phase model of motivational processes has also been previously discussed by Tinbergen (1951) and Di Chiara and North (1992).
3.   This was first proposed by Lee and Schumann (2005) and was further delineated in Chapter 5 by Mates in Lee *et al.* (2009).
4.   Since the basolateral amygdala innervates the extended amygdala (which projects to the NAS), Lee *et al.* (2009) remind us that the system proposed by Depue and Morrone-Strupinsky (2005) is not linear.

5 The caregiver's instinct

In Chapter 2, I discussed the different cultural beliefs and practices related to making culture accessible to infants. Different as they may be, societies, parents, family members, alloparents, caregivers, siblings, and peers allow infants to observe, imitate, and practice cultural activities that they must acquire to become socially competent beings. I have also suggested that human beings are born with an innate drive to seek out interaction with others. The instinct ensures that infants will be entrained to those in their social environment and thus ensures that an infant will be given the opportunity to interact with more competent social beings and will be socialized to the culture to which he/she belongs. Therefore, it is also important not to overlook the abilities and behaviors of caregivers because their actions are relevant for the infant's learning. Some researchers have suggested that 'humans evolve specialized cognitive resources that form a dedicated interpersonal system of mutual design in which one is predisposed to 'teach' and to 'learn' new and relevant cultural information to (and from) conspecifics' (Gergely and Csibra, 2005: 472). They suggest that humans possessing cultural knowledge are naturally inclined to '*ostensively manifest* their knowledge to (and for the benefit of) naïve conspecifics' (Gergely and Csibra, 2005: 472, italics in original). They call the specific aspects of human communication that allow and facilitate the transfer of generic knowledge to novices 'natural pedagogy'(Csibra and Gergely, 2009: 148).[1] Such a predisposition motivates experts to manifest and prepare novices to receive knowledge, ensures that cultural knowledge is transmitted. In this section, I explore caregiver behaviors toward infants and explore their underlying motivations.

In 1971, Konrad Lorenz argued that infants have a *kindchenschema* (infant schema), or facial features that stimulate feelings of affection and nurturing parental responses. Indeed, in mammals that are characterized by shared care, juveniles and females who have never been pregnant or have never given birth also spontaneously respond to infants, including huddling over pups to keep them warm. In infant sharing primates, females exhibit irrepressible urges to sniff, touch, cuddle, and repeatedly take and carry new babies (Hrdy, 2009). Zahed *et al.* (2007) studied the responses to infant vocalizations of 15 male marmosets with prior caretaking experience. They showed that the males were more eager than those without parental experience to respond to the infant vocalizations. Research, therefore, since Lorenz has shown that infants elicit caregiving behaviors. Caregivers seem to behave differently with infants than they do with non-infants, which may suggest another manifestation of the interactional instinct.

Long before an infant is held by her mother, positive maternal attitudes increase and worries decrease throughout pregnancy (Fleming *et al.*, 1997). Many first time parents report feelings such as: 'No one told me it was like falling in love' (Swain *et al.*, 2007: 264). Such feelings also generally increase during the postpartum period. In addition to an increase in positive emotions, adults behave in characteristic ways toward infants. Despite the repertoire of facial expressions available to caregivers, they rarely, if ever, use the full range of expressions with infants (Stern, 2002). It has been claimed that, in Western societies, only a limited set of expressions is needed in early communication to regulate the general flow of interaction. According to Stern (2002), these 'basic' expressions are the mock-surprise expression, smile, concerned face, frown, and neutral face (27). The mock-surprise expression is the most common expression observed and is typically used to signal a readiness or an invitation to a potential interaction as well as to motivate it. A mother uses this expression nearly every time the infant focuses his vision on her. Stern notes that the smile and expression for concern function to maintain and modulate an ongoing interaction. The smile is a signal that the interaction is going well, while the concerned face is made when the interaction is ongoing but slowing down. It is a clear attempt to refocus, reengage, and thereby maintain the interaction. The frown, when combined with a head aversion and a break of gaze, is a clear signal to stop the interaction momentarily or completely. The neutral or blank face, especially when combined with a gaze aversion, is a clear signal of the mother's intent not to interact. Furthermore, when the caregiver displays these expressions, they are often exaggerated, usually marked by a slow formation and elongated duration.

Studies have also shown that parents are acutely sensitive to their infants' emotional expressions and behavior. Mothers of one-month-old infants have been found to be able to discriminate the discrete emotional expressions of anger, fear, surprise, joy, interest, and sadness. Parents are also attuned to their infant's direction of gaze and modify their behavior accordingly, such that they have a tendency to maintain a certain observational distance (~40 cm) when their infant is looking at something other than them, but they move to a 'dialogic' distance (~22.5 cm) when their infant is focusing on them (Papousek and Papousek, 1987). In addition, when parents give an initial greeting, they usually tilt their head slightly back, raise their eyebrows, and open their eyes and mouth wide.

The caregiver's use of gaze with an infant is also qualitatively different from her gaze transactions with other adults (Papousek and Papousek, 1987: 34). During play interactions, mothers spend up to 70% of playtime gazing at their infant for an average duration of 20 seconds. While feeding, caregivers also gaze at the infant about 70% of the time. Furthermore, mothers have an innate ability that makes them very sensitive to their baby's cry. There are four identifiable types of crying: pain, hunger, boredom, and discomfort, which are apparently distinguishable by the mother by the end of the second week, and by the third day a mother can recognize her baby's cry from that of other newborns (Boukydis, 1979; Lester *et al.*, 1985). Also, an infant's expressions of sadness and anger produce the same affective responses in their mothers (Tronick *et al.*, 1979).

Baby talk, motherese and infant directed speech

In addition to the caregiver's use of gaze, body distancing, and recognition of expressions, there is increasing evidence that motherese is a universal behavior among women, men, and young children. In examining the baby talk of 27 Indo-European, African, and Oceanic languages, Ferguson (1978) found that there were common prosodic features across languages including overall high pitch, exaggerated intonation, and slowed speech. The exaggerated stress and increased pitch appears to assist infants in discriminating phonetic units. In one study, women in three different countries (Russia, United States and Sweden) were recorded while speaking to their 2-month-old infants and to another adult (Kuhl *et al.*, 1997). Mothers used the vowels /i/, /a/, and /u/ in both settings, and their speech was analyzed using a spectograph. The results demonstrated that the phonetic units of infant directed speech (IDS) are exaggerated. The same exaggeration was observed in Mandarin-speaking mother-infant pairs (Liu *et al.*, 2003). Caregivers, when addressing infants, also make other adjustments that aid in learning. For example, Kuhl (2000) reports that parents often repeat the word in stereotyped 'frames' (i.e. Where's the __________, See the __________, That's a __________) (11855), which highlights items in sentence final position. Furthermore, a cross-language study of fathers' speech to preverbal infants in French, Italian, German, Japanese, British English, and American English found that fathers' speech also had modified prosodic features characteristic of motherese, although not as extreme (Fernald *et al.*, 1989). Though it is debatable as to whether IDS has a causal role in language acquisition, it seems to cause an infant to be more receptive to the caregiver and their speech (Cooper and Aslin, 1990; Cooper *et al.*, 1997; Werker and McLeod,

1989). Others have found evidence that IDS exists universally as a species-specific trait. Bryant and Barrett (2007) recorded native-English speaking mothers producing utterances that signal prohibition, approval, comfort, and attention in both IDS and adult directed speech (ADS). The recordings were then played to adult Shuar horticulturalists from Amazonian Ecuador. Bryant and Barrett found that the Shuar were able to reliably distinguish between ID and AD speech and recognize the different categories. This study was the first to demonstrate that 'adult listeners in an indigenous, nonindustrialized, and non-literate culture can accurately infer intentions from both ID and AD speech in a language they do not speak' (Bryant and Barrett, 2007: 746).

Though Ferguson (1978) famously argued that motherese appeared to be universal, listing 17 different features, he also noted that the composition and frequency of its features vary from culture to culture. The constraints of culture are seen in societies that are often cited as ones without motherese. However, when such societies are closely investigated, there is evidence of modified behavior or of special registers used for speaking to their young. Such evidence suggests that what is universal may not be the features, although there may be similarities from culture to culture, but the practice of modifying speech. For example, the Kaluli[2] are reported to not use baby talk, given their belief that infants 'have no understanding' (Schieffelin, 2005: 71) and that doing 'so would result in a child sounding babyish' (Ochs and Schieffelin, 1984: 33). Although there are clear differences in the ways that infants are addressed in other cultures (i.e. Kaluli mothers do not speak directly to their infants), mothers still greet infants by name and use 'expressive vocalizations' in the first few months of babies' lives (Schieffelin, 2005: 71). In fact, Schieffelin (1991) reports that '[w]ithin a week or so after a child is born … Older infants greet and address infants, and in response to this, mothers hold their infants' face outward and, while moving them, speak in a high pitched, nasalized register' (71). Ochs and Schieffelin (1984) also note that during the first six months of life 'language addressed *to* the young infant tends to be in the form of songs or rhythmic vocalizations in a soft, high pitch' (296). Furthermore, when babies begin to babble, '[a]dults and older children occasionally repeat vocalizations back to the young child … reshaping them into the name of persons in the household or into kin terms' (Ochs and Schieffelin, 2001: 485).

Another widely cited argument against the universality of motherese is Pye's (1986a, 1986b) work with the Mayan language Quiché. First, Pye observed that Quiché mothers do not exhibit significant prosodic adjustments when speaking to their children, in comparison to North American mothers. But they do confine exaggerated intonation to infrequent exclamations to both children and adults. Quiché mothers also 'frequently reduced their voice so much that it became a whisper' (Pye, 1986a: 88). With regard to their phonology, Quiché caregivers have a marked tendency to drop word initial syllables and reduce verbs when addressing children (Pye, 1986a: 88–89). With regard to baby talk, Pye listed a 'special lexicon that is unique to baby talk and recognized as such' (Pye, 1986a: 90). The talk has an unusually large number of verb substitutes and an absence of verb compounding. Quiché caregivers also use fewer overt noun phrases and use a fixed word order when speaking to their children, as well as have a tendency to interpret what another has said by repeating to children what the other has said. Quiché caregivers, it seems, do have a special register for their young, though qualitatively different from other infant directed speech.

Like the Kaluli and Quiché, Western Samoans and black working class Americans are often noted as cultures that do not have motherese. However, close examination of reports also indicate that caregivers do use a special register when they direct language toward children. Thus, as Falk (2009) also argues, if we take a cultural perspective of baby talk, it appears that baby talk is a universal *behavior* directed toward infants, though *its distinct features may vary* from culture to culture. And, though it may be unclear as to how the modified speech can facilitate language acquisition, it also appears to be distinct to humans as nonhuman primates do not engage in humanlike motherese.

Motionese/infant directed action

While motherese is specific to the language domain, some researchers have also explored the modifications adults make when processing human actions or 'motionese' (Brand *et al.*, 2002; Brand and Shallcross, 2008; Przednowek, 2009). Researchers of motionese suggest that when adults interact with infants, 'adults modify their movements in ways that simultaneously enhance infants' attention to action and highlight meaningful units within the flow of motion' (Brand *et al.*, 2002: 72). Such modifications have been shown to affect infant behaviors and help them understand the goals of their caregivers (Koterba and Iverson, 2009). Such a notion is worth exploring, as sign language appears to have infant directed modifications as well (Erting *et al.*, 1990; Masataka, 1992; Nonaka, 2004). The following is a transcript from Nonaka (2004) of an interaction using the Thai Ban Khor Sign language between a deaf adult (Mr. Phaiwan) and an infant (Watermelon) (755).

Example 7

1   ((Smiling throughout the interaction, Mrs. Vien repeatedly nods at the child, strokes her nose, playfully slaps her hand, and rubs her face. Meanwhile the other two adults look on smiling and laughing.))

2   Mr. Phaiwan: You're a little-birdie.
I'm gonna feed you.
Your tummy will get big. That's good!
I'm gonna feed you.
Yeah, yeah, yeah.

Nonaka notes that during the interaction, Mr Phaiwan's talk exhibits classic features of motherese:

> His [Mr Phaiwan] initial child-directed utterances (lines 1–5) are made while bending directly over Watermelon. The signs 'you little-birdie' and 'feed you' are articulated very close to the infant's face, maximizing visual acuity. Furthermore, the entire sequence, especially 'feed you', is signed more slowly than in normal adult conversation.
>
> In line 4, Mr. Phaiwan tells the baby ... that as a result of being fed. 'your tummy will get big', and 'That's good!'. While signing 'tummy get big', he actually starts the utterance ... by touching his hand to the girl's abdomen. Signing on an interlocutor's body is rarely used between adults for purposes of normal, everyday conversation, but the strategy is a classic feature of signed baby talk/ motherese. Finally, repetition, a typical feature of both signed and spoken baby talk/motherese, is apparent in line 6, in Phaiwan's repeated non-manual head nod, 'yeah, yeah, yeah'.
>
> (Nonaka, 2004: 756–757)

Overall, characteristics of baby talk in Ban Khor Sign include: '(i) heightened affect, (ii) active physical stimulation of the child, (iii) signing more slowly than usual, (iv) signing close to the child to maximize visual attention, (v) signing on the child's body, and (vi) repetition' (Nonaka, 2004: 754). Similarly, Masataka (1992) explored the use of Japanese Sign Language by eight deaf mothers to their infants and in contrast to their friends. He found that mothers signed at a significantly slower tempo with more exaggerated movements and repetitions with infants than their friends.

To investigate motionese, researchers asked mothers of infants to demonstrate how to use a series of objects to either their infant or to a close friend/partner (Brand *et al.*, 2002). The researchers found that mothers spontaneously modified their actions in a number of ways toward infants that might assist infants' learning about action. 'They demonstrated new objects to infants in closer proximity, with greater enthusiasm, a higher level of interactiveness, greater repetitiveness and movements that were larger in scale but reduced in complexity' (Brand *et al.*, 2002: 78). In addition, mothers that were repeating their actions in succession were also found to punctuate their actions with attempts to lock gaze with the infant before proceeding to the next action. Siblings have also been found to modify their behaviors when interacting with infants as well (Lockman, 2001). While cross-cultural studies on motionese are lacking, such behaviors found among siblings suggests that motionese, like motherese, is not limited to mothers and perhaps not to more traditional cultures.

Furthermore, during adult interaction a listener will often show interpersonal connectedness with a speaker by mirroring the postural configuration of another speaker (Kendon, 1970; Chartrand and Bargh, 1999; Joaquin, 2005). Parents have been observed to do the same with their infants to establish that connectedness (Meltzoff and Decety, 2003). Thus, infants elicit distinct caregiver behaviors, and caregivers demonstrate characteristic behaviors toward infants as well. Such interactions may promote affiliation and attachment between the infant and caregiver. Furthermore, research in neurobiology suggests that interaction with infants from the beginning is inherently rewarding.

Biological motivations

Numerous studies have shown that the interaction between a caregiver and an infant is a powerful interpersonal event that may motivate and facilitate such interactions. Researchers have examined neuroendocrine mechanisms that underlie positive maternal behaviors. One researcher describes the interaction of rats breastfeeding her pups in this way:

> During the actual interactive phase the offspring will start suckling, and as a response to it, the mother ejects milk. She does not, however, only give milk; she also transmits warmth to her young by dilating the blood vessels in the skin overlying the mammary gland, furthermore, she provides protection and care. By offering milk, warmth, protection and care to the offspring the mother is

> interacting in a giving way. But she also is interacting in a receiving way. The suckling, touching and warmth created by the offspring activate maternal somatosensory afferents, which results in milk ejection as well as other 'giving' effects described above.
>
> (Uvnäs-Moberg, 1998: 821–822)

Thus, breastfeeding is more than just meeting the needs of the infant – it promotes interaction and bonding. In fact, women who breastfeed are generally calmer, more interactive, and more social with infants than women who are not breastfeeding or not pregnant (Nissen *et al.*, 1998; Uvnäs-Moberg *et al.*, 1990). Such positive behaviors may also be related to an increase in cortisol, which is found in high concentrations during pregnancy, and peaks at the time of parturition and declines gradually over the first postpartum week. In human females, high levels of cortisol on day 2 or 3 postpartum were correlated with positive maternal approach behaviors and attitudes (Fleming *et al.*, 1987; Corter and Fleming, 1995). Cortisol levels were also related to positive responses to odors from infants, as well as a mother's ability to distinguish the body odor of her own and an unfamiliar infant.

Some researchers have even compared the addictiveness of suckling and other infant cues to the addictiveness of cocaine (Ferris *et al.*, 2005). Researchers implicate the mesocoticolimbic dopamine pathway in the addiction processs (Insel, 2003), which (as discussed in Chapter 4) includes the ventral tegmental area (VTA) that projects directly and indirectly via the amygdala/bed nucleus of the stria terminalis to the nucleus accumbens, which then projects to the ventral pallidum and thalamus, and then projects to the prefrontal and cingulate cortex. Projections from the prefrontal and cingulate cortex ultimately feed back to the VTA. Using fMRI, researchers looking at brain activity of lactating dams and cocaine exposure in females, found that the dopamine reward system was activated in both groups. However, when lactating dams were exposed to cocaine instead of their pups, there was a suppression of brain activity in the reward system. In another study (Mattson *et al.*, 2001), postpartum females were trained to go to one cage for access to three pups and a different cage for access to 10 mg/kg of cocaine. The results showed that dams at postpartum day 8 preferred the pups. Such research suggests that access to pups is more reinforcing than one of the most potently rewarding psychostimulants. In humans, 'non-drug-addicted-mothers' exposure to infant cues appear to be highly reinforcing (or at least invokes motivation to respond and approach behavior as in infant crying)' (Swain *et al.*, 2007: 268). Furthermore, in human mothers, fMRI studies showed activation of similar brain reward regions to cocaine in first-time mothers in response to listening to 30 seconds of infant crying (Lorberbaum *et al.*, 2002) and to face images of infants (Strathearn *et al.*, 2008). Therefore, such caregiving/maternal exchanges, infant behaviors, and characteristics may be rewarding and motivating to caregivers, or simply put, addictive (Insel, 2003). Just as neuropeptides and endogenous opiates, discussed earlier in the previous chapter, contribute to the consummatory reward of affiliative stimuli that encourage proximity seeking, they play a significant role in ensuring and promoting interaction with an infant as well.

Oxytocin, vasopressin, and beta endorphins

Oxytocin (OT) has been suggested to be the hormone of 'mother love' (Klopfer, 1971), as studies show that OT is associated with facilitating the social bond between a mother and child (Insel and Harbaugh, 1989; Pedersen, 1997), beginning in the later stages of pregnancy when OT receptor concentrations rise significantly along with increased maternal behaviors (Pedersen, 1997). As discussed earlier, DA is related to the rewarding and 'addictive' nature of caregiving interactions. Some research with prairie voles suggests that it is the concurrent activation of OT and DA receptors that is essential for social attachment and thus maternal behaviors (Liu and Wang, 2003). Olazabal and Young (2006) have also shown that sexually-naïve female prairie voles with high concentrations of OT receptors demonstrate more spontaneous maternal behaviors. Such voles appeared to lick, groom, and hover more than those with fewer OT receptors. In another study, OT in females rats appeared to shift oral grooming away from themselves and toward their pups (Pedersen and Boccia, 2002). Furthermore, if OT receptors are blocked in mice, deficits in maternal behavior occur as well (Pederson *et al.*, 2006). In contrast, sheep when injected with oxytocin, become attached to an unfamiliar lamb (Carter and Keverne, 2002). Similarly, rhesus monkeys that are injected with oxytocin increase in their frequency of touching, watching, or lip-smacking towards infants, and decrease in the display of facial threats towards observers (Holman and Goy, 1995). In humans, OT has antistress effects and is related to calmness and a desire to interact socially with infants (Uvnas-Moberg and Petersson, 2005; Widstrom *et al.*, 1990). One study showed that following birth, mother-infant contact stimulates OT release by hand movement and suckling (Matthiesen *et al.*, 2001). In another study, oxytocin levels were measured in 62 pregnant women during their first, third, and postpartum month. Initial levels of oxytocin in the first trimester predicted bonding behavior such that mothers with higher levels of OT engaged in more bonding behaviors after birth. Mothers who had higher levels of oxytocin across the pregnancy and the postpartum month also reported more bonding behaviors and attachment-related thoughts (Feldman *et al.*, 2007). In human males, OT has also been found to enhance positive social information so that it is more memorable (Guastella *et al.*, 2008).

Vasopressin (VP) has similar effects on maternal behavior. Injecting a vasopressin receptor antagonist is correlated with less maternal behavior (Pedersen, 1997). Brattleboro rats, which are vasopressin-deficient, show lower levels of parental care (i.e. poor nest building, cannibalistic behavior, etc.) (Wideman and Murphy, 1990), and are more susceptible to the effects of stress (i.e. decreases in body weight, stomach ulcers, etc.) (Wideman and Murphy, 1986). In monogamous prairie voles, vasopressin content is elevated when male parental behavior is particularly likely (De Vries and Villalba, 1997). Though much less is known of the role of vasopressin in caregiver behavior, it is likely to also facilitate parental behavior.

In addition to OT and VP, beta endorphins may contribute to the rewarding experience of caregiving – particularly for the mother. Beta endorphins, as discussed in the previous chapter, are endogenous opiates that are produced by the pituitary gland and synthesized in the hypothalamus. Studies show that beta endorphins increase in mothers during infant-caregiver interaction. In one study, blood samples from women were taken while breast-feeding. After 5 minutes beta endorphins significantly increased, and then reached a peak value after 20 minutes (Franceschini *et al.*, 1989). When released beta endophins produce a feeling of '*increased* interpersonal warmth, euphoria, well-being, and peaceful calmness as well as *decreased* elation, energy, and incentive motivation' (Depue and Morrone-Strupinsky, 2005; Lee *et al.*, 2009 citing Depue and Morrone-Strupinsky, 2005: 324), which may be expressed in the dilation of pupils in both the mother and infant (Hess, 1975). Thus, in addition to dopamine, oxytocin, vasopressin, and beta endorphins facilitate the early interaction experience.

Prolactin and testosterone

Oxytocin and prolactin are the hormones primarily involved in lactation. Oxytocin is responsible for milk ejection, while prolactin is necessary for milk production (Wakerley *et al.*, 1994). Furthermore, sucking increases the levels of a prolactin-release hormone (PRH) known as vasoactive intestinal peptide. However, in addition to producing milk, lactation has also been found to inhibit normal hypothalamic stress responses. For example, in response to infant cries, lactating women had lower levels of skin conductance responses and heart rates when compared to nonlactating mothers (Wiesenfeld *et al.*, 1985). Carter and Altemus (2006) suggest that the 'reduced responsivity to stressful experiences associated with lactation may be viewed as an adaptive response which protects a nursing female from overreacting to stressful stimuli' (167). Furthermore, lactating women have been found to interact more positively with their babies; they touch and smile more toward their infants than do bottle-feeding mothers (Dunn and Richards, 1977). Thus, prolactin has a role in facilitating a positive breast-feeding experience, which also induces the release of other hormones and beta endorphins mentioned above.

Prolactin release has also been examined in men (Storey *et al.*, 2000). Fleming *et al.* (2002) examined prolactin levels when fathers and non-fathers are exposed to four types of infant cries: two hunger cries and two pain cries. Their study showed that fathers with higher prolactin levels were more alert and had more positive responses to the cries. Fathers displayed greater sympathy and a greater need to respond to the infant cries. However, the effects were not specific to nurturance, and the fathers also expressed some negative feelings, such as irritation. Furthermore, experienced fathers had a greater increase in prolactin levels when they heard the cries in comparison to first time fathers. Thus, paternal responses have been linked to increased levels of prolactin.

Other studies have shown that prolactin also inhibits testosterone (T) production, which is a hormone generally linked with aggressiveness and mating effort. Given this relationship, if increased levels of prolactin also increased paternal responses, then T levels in fathers should also be lower. Thus, in their study, Fleming *et al.* (2002) also examined the testosterone (T) levels in saliva samples in father and non-fathers exposed to infant cries. They, in fact, demonstrate that fathers and nonfathers with lower T levels had greater sympathy and/or need to respond to the infant cries than fathers with higher T levels, and when fathers and non-fathers heard the cry stimuli, they showed an increase in T levels. Therefore, the study shows that not only do the cries produce some change in the fathers' testosterone levels, but the levels prior to exposure are also related to how they respond to the cries. Therefore, T seems to be related to male caregiving behavior.

In another study (Gray, 2003), Swahili men were found to have lower testosterone levels in the evening than in the daytime. What is interesting is that men with younger children tended to have marginally lower T levels, but the levels have a U-shape relationship between male evening T levels and the age of the youngest child. So T levels look slightly higher within the first year after a child is born, before subsequently falling, and then increases again when the child is older. Gray suggests that the U-shape could be understood from the standpoint of paternal care. Swahili women nurse their children for approximately two years, and are mostly responsible for direct care. Gray suggests that it may therefore be the case that fathers experience lower T levels once their children are between ages 2–4 because fathers have more contact with their children at these ages. Prior to this, mothers may interact with the child the most, and afterward children begin schooling and play outside the home. Though T may not be directly related to nurturing behaviors, such findings suggest that lower T levels, in response to a young child, can be a part of the system that subserves male caregiving behavior, which in turn facilitates affiliation and attachment.

Neurocognitive substrates

While some researchers examine the role of hormones and neurotransmitters in mediating mother-infant attachment behaviors, others examine how they interact with specific brain circuits particularly relevant to parental behavior. Current research suggests that the main regions of parental behavior include the medial preoptic area (MPOA) and the ventral part of the bed nucleus of the stria terminalis (VBNST), which have outputs to areas rich in dopamine, including the hypothalamus, the ventral tegmental area (VTA), and the substantia nigra (Numan *et al.,* 1988: Numan, 1994; Swain *et al.,* 2007).

In rats, the MPOA is a region where oxytocin receptors increase significantly during late pregnancy (Pedersen, 1997) and lesions of the MPOA/VBNST regions disrupt maternal behavior (Numan, 1974; Numan *et al.* 1988). The VTA and VBNST have also been shown to be areas in which oxytocin activates postpartum maternal behavior (Pedersen *et al.,* 1988; Kendrick, 2000). Furthermore, the VTA and substantia nigra project along the mesocorticolimbic dopamine pathways. Thus, when researchers monitored changes in DA in the nucleus accumbens, they found that infant cues, such as pup grooming and licking, significantly increased dopamine release (Champagne *et al.,* 2004). Furthermore, the magnitude and duration of the increase in the DA signal correlated with the duration of infant cues.

Some researchers have even suggested that infant faces may elicit a very specific pattern of activity in adults (Kringelbach *et al.,* 2008). In one study, adults, both parents and non-parents, are shown multiple faces of infants and adults. Each face has a positive (smiling), neutral or negative (sad) expression. Consistent with other findings, the researchers found that face processing of both adult and infant faces elicit activity in the right face fusiform area (FFA), an area speculated to be specialized for face recognition (McCarthy *et al.,* 1997). However, when viewing infant faces, researchers additionally found more significant activity in the medial orbitofrontal cortex. At around 130 ms after presentation of a face, there was a brief surge of activity in the mOFC in response to infant faces but *not* to adult faces, which was then followed by a response in the FFA. These findings were the same for both parents and non-parents. Researchers were particularly interested as the orbitofrontal cortex is implicated in reward and hedonic processing (Kringelbach, 2005). Furthermore, previous research has shown that prefrontal areas perform a top-down facilitation of activity in the FFA (Bar *et al.*, 2006), thus the research suggests that the mOFC provides a top down amplification of the activity in FFA specifically related to infant faces. The researchers concluded that 'the mOFC appears to exhibit a very early specific neural signature or specific pattern of activity in response to infant faces' (Kringelbach *et al.*, 2008: 3).

In this section, I explored some of the neurobiology that may be involved in facilitating and motivating nurturing behaviors of caregivers even before birth. Though research has mostly been with mothers, there is evidence that the same systems achieve the same nurturing behaviors with non-mothers. It seems that interacting with infants is inherently rewarding – if not addicting. I have also examined behaviors of more competent social actors toward infants, some of which have been argued to be universal. Such behaviors may also serve to facilitate and increase affiliation and attachment with an infant. For example, Werker and McLeod (1989) measured the affective effects of infant directed speech in comparison to adult speech in four- to five-month-olds, as well as seven- to nine-month-olds. They reported that the infant directed speech demonstrated more positive affect and was even greater the younger the infant. Therefore, we may see such behaviors as manifestations of the interactional instinct as well – a caregiver's drive to seek out and achieve interaction with the young. In addition, some have argued that behaviors such as infant directed speech and motionese assist in the acquisition of cultural information, including language and everyday actions. Therefore, the interactional instinct of caregivers may have a role in facilitating the transmission of cultural knowledge.

Notes

1. Gergely and Csibra speculate that Natural Pedagogy was 'selected for during hominid evolution as a consequence of the emergence of recursive tool making practices, which confronted the observational learner with cognitively opaque contents to acquire' (Csibra and Gergely, 2009: 4).
2. Refer to Chapter 2 for more background information on the Kaluli.

6　Learning via eavesdropping

We have seen that societies have different practices to enculturate their youth. Though direct instruction may occur, the reality is that much of socialization occurs via listening-in, observation, and imitation (Schieffelin, 1991; Rogoff, 2003; Rogoff *et al.*, 2007). This is the same with language acquisition and use. Though we have seen members of a society scaffold language acquisition and have seen older members instruct and/or guide naïve members on how to use language, many ethnographic researchers have also suggested that children in some parts of the world have to learn language mostly, if not exclusively, through eavesdropping. This chapter attempts to address some of the issues raised by such learning contexts.

Certainly, what children are faced with does not seem to be an easy task. Children have to extract phonemes, words, and syntactic structure from the connected speech that they overhear, and somehow find their meanings while learning the appropriate contexts in which they are used. One way in which learning is facilitated is through joint attention, when children actively attend to what their interlocutors are most likely referring to, and understand what their social partner wants to call their attention to (Tomasello and Farrar, 1986; Akhtar and Tomasello, 2000; Tomasello, 2003). Such an activity is facilitated by the ability to attend to ostensive cues such as gaze direction, pointing, and social expressions (see Chapter 3), and the view that caregivers are intentional agents (Tomasello, 2008). These abilities might be motivated by our interactional tendencies. However, ethnographic reports of traditional societies and research on persons with Williams syndrome, Down's syndrome, and autism, who display deficits in joint attention behavior, may successfully acquire language (Akhtar and Garnsbacher, 2007). These observations lead to a questioning of the necessity for joint attention and direct instruction for vocabulary development and language development in general. The story I have proposed is that the drive for language acquisition is motivated by an interactional instinct, which provides an attentional and reward mechanism to focus the child on linguistic input and to acquire language, whether engaged or overheard. As I have discussed research that provides evidence for the interactional instinct across cultures (Hewlett, 1991; De Léon, 2008; Fox Adams, forthcoming), the aim of this chapter is to discuss the research suggesting that we have the ability to acquire language through exposure to and eavesdropping on sociocultural interactions, and to explore the biological mechanisms involved.

Discriminating abilities

First, it is widely accepted that infants are born with powerful discriminating abilities. The early studies of Eimas *et al.* (1971), through the use of the high amplitude sucking technique (HAS), demonstrated that infants 1- to 4-months-old are able to discriminate a 20 ms difference in voice onset time (VOT), which is an acoustic difference that is sufficient to distinguish between the voiced /b,d,g/ and the voiceless /p,t,k/ stop consonants in English. Other studies show infants are sensitive to the subtle acoustic differences among vowel sounds (Trehub, 1973; Aldridge *et al.*, 2001). Furthermore, studies show that infants are able to perceive a number of contrasts: stops vs. nasals (Eimas and Miller, 1980); /r/ vs. /l/ contrast (Eimas, 1975); and changes in pitch contour (rising vs. falling) (Morse, 1972).

In addition, 2-month-old infants can perceive the differences between allophones (Hohne and Jusczyk, 1994), and 9-month-olds are sensitive to the phonotactic regularities of their native language, such that they are able to detect language specific restrictions on the sequences of consonants and vowels that occur within words (Friederici and Wessels, 1993; Jusczyk *et al.*, 1994). Another set of studies, in which the high frequencies of speech are eliminated from the stimuli while the prosody is preserved, suggest that newborns are sensitive to the rhythms of languages, such that they can use prosody to discriminate between languages: French-Russian (Mehler *et al.*, 1988); English-Italian (Mehler *et al.*, 1988); English-Japanese (Nazzi *et al.*, 1998); English-Spanish (Moon *et al.*, 1993); Dutch-Japanese (Ramus, 2002).

Other studies demonstrate that infants are sensitive to the prosodic boundaries of a language. In one study, 48 French neonates with an average age of 2.6 days were presented with Spanish stimuli. The experiment showed that French newborns discriminate between bisyllabic stimuli that differ within a sentence whether or not they contain a phonological phrase boundary. The researchers concluded that in Spanish, as in French, newborns can perceive local acoustic correlates of phonological phrase boundaries (Christophe *et al.*, 2001). Another study reported that 13-month-old American infants perceive phonological phrase boundaries as well (Christophe *et al.*, 2003).

Furthermore, the groundbreaking research of Saffran *et al.* (1996) demonstrated that 8-month-old infants can extract word-like strings of phonemes from the statistical properties of the input after only two minutes of exposure. Specifically, the researchers provide evidence that infants can distinguish between syllables that regularly appear together from those that are randomly juxtaposed. Saffran *et al.*'s study was supported by subsequent studies produced by separate researchers with 12-month-olds (Gomez and Gerken, 1999), 8-month-olds (Johnson and Jusczyk, 2001), and 7-month-olds (Marcus *et al.*, 1999). Six-month-olds also use consistent rhythmic patterns to locate word-like units in continuous speech (Goodsitt *et al.*, 1993; Morgan and Saffran, 1995; Morgan, 1996). Though researchers agree that no single word boundary, prosodic, or phonotactic cue is sufficient to support lexical access, they do suggest that taken together, they may allow infants to start acquiring a lexicon. Christophe *et al.* (2003) claim that 'infants recover words by relying on phonological properties of the speech stream, that is readily available in the input' (587). In addition, other cues provide information and mark boundaries for learners, such as pauses at the end of utterances and intonational cues.

Despite such abilities, it is important to note that one source of information is insufficient to perceive boundaries. For example, phonotactic information on its own produces less than 50% accuracy in word segmentation, while utterance boundary and relative stress information produces even less accuracy (Christiansen *et al.*, 1998; Redington and Chater, 1998). However, when the three cues are combined, performance levels exceed 70% accuracy. What this means is that infants seem to be able to utilize all sources and cues simultaneously to make sense of the language around them. Furthermore, given such discriminating abilities, research has shown that with repetition and exposure, very young children also become sensitive to the frequencies of the elements of language.

Frequency effects

Much of children's early social interactions with caregivers are repetitious, such as nursing and feeding. It is through the course of eavesdropping and participating in such interactions that one can be routinely exposed to and can naturally acquire knowledge of the frequencies of the elements of language (Ellis, 2002). This relates to the notion of frequency effects in language processing, which implies that young children are incessantly and unconsciously learning the probabilities and patterns of language. This notion is derived from psycholinguistic and cognitive linguistic theories of language acquisition that hold that the acquisition of language and all of its units is 'the piecemeal learning of many thousand of constructions and the frequency-biased abstraction of regularities within them' (Ellis, 2002: 144). Simply put, learners have to figure language out.

Research, in fact, demonstrates that we are sensitive to the frequency of events in our experiences. One study (Hasher and Chromiak, 1977) tested the abilities of second, fourth, sixth grade, and college-age students to accurately estimate the frequency of word occurrence after shown a list of 96 nouns. The frequencies of the words varied such that some words appeared more frequently than others. In addition, half of the students were given instruction to note the frequency before the presentation and half were not. The results of the study showed that students at all levels were sensitive to the differences of frequency and made accurate estimates on the rates of appearance regardless of whether they received instruction. The researchers concluded that second graders are as prepared to process frequency differences as college students. The same researchers note that students can estimate, with high correlation to actual accounts, the frequency of English words, of single letters, and even pairs of letters (Attneave, 1953; Shapiro, 1969; Underwood, 1971).

Therefore, in the course of routine interactions and socialization, while driven to attend to communication, we can combine our innate abilities to naturally acquire knowledge of the frequencies of the features of language with accuracy. In fact, Chang (2006) synthesized the studies showing how frequency effects can account for the acquisition of constructions from the natural environment, affect and adjust a learner's usage overtime due to exposure to different linguistic forms, and generalize a word's syntactic roles and associate it with other words in the same category (Boyland, 2001; Bybee and Hopper, 2001; Hallan, 2001). Thus, frequency effects can scaffold the understanding, learning, and usage of the elements of the language with minimal 'teaching'.

Priming

Lexical priming

While frequency effects are related to the exposure leading to knowledge, and perhaps learning about a language, priming refers to the facilitative effects of an encounter with a stimulus on subsequent processing of the same or a related stimulus. The effects may be a change in speed, bias, or accuracy of the processing of a stimulus. Studies show that each time we attend to a stimulus (i.e. a word), a lasting representation is created that aids in later identification of the same word. *Priming* can occur as quickly as one encounter and has very long lasting effects. Goldinger (1996) has shown that priming can occur after a one-time auditory presentation of a low-frequency word, as measured after a week's delay. Furthermore, studies show that priming facilitates the later identification of words despite changes in the speech rate, speaker's voice, and adjacent context. Of particular interest to how we learn language through overhearing is research in long-term auditory word priming in very young children.

Church and Fisher (1998) reported three experiments that explored word priming in preschoolers. In the first experiment, they compared long-term auditory priming between English-speaking 2.5- and 3-year-olds and adults. In the study phase, children and college students listened to a list of 16 study words spoken by a robot and chosen to be familiar to young native speakers of English. After a brief distractor task, the children and students listened to a list of 32 words, half of which were in the study phase and half were new. However, during this test phase, the words were filtered so that they were muffled and difficult to identify. The children, after hearing each word, were prompted to repeat what the robot said and to give it a cookie, while the students had to write what they thought each filtered word was. The results showed that all of the age groups performed similarly, regardless of the obvious discrepancies in previous lexical knowledge; all age groups were more likely to identify words that were heard in the study phase, suggesting that all age groups showed equal priming effects. In the second experiment, 2-year-olds were studied and compared to 3-year-olds. The same experimental design was employed, except the study and test lists were half the length of those in the first experiment. As in the first case, the 2-year-olds were just as likely to correctly repeat filtered words that had previously been studied. Therefore, auditory priming is qualitatively similar in 2-year-old preschoolers and college students. The same priming effects in preschoolers were found with non-English words (i.e. yeeg, lell) as well (Hunt *et al.*, 1998; Fisher *et al.*, 2001).

A third experiment examined whether priming in 3-year-old children is affected by whether the study task focuses attention on the word's sound or its meaning. For the study task, participants were divided into two groups: nonsemantic and semantic. The nonsemantic encoding group participated in the same study phase as in experiment 1 (listened to a list of familiar words). The semantic encoding group also listened to a list of study words, however, after each study word, the children were asked to select the matching toy from two choices. Then, in the test phase, the nonsemantic group listened to the robot say filtered words from the study phase and new words as in the previous experiments. The semantic group heard clearly presented words and was asked to decide whether they had heard the robot say each word before. Church and Fisher (1998) report that priming was relatively the same across the two encoding conditions, but the child's ability to discriminate between old and new items was better for the semantic group (the object choice encoding task). Thus, the priming effect did not seem to depend on whether the encoding task encouraged them to access the referent. Follow-up studies (Fisher *et al.*, in prep) with 18-month-olds demonstrated that infants were more likely to identify a familiar spoken word and correctly choose its referent if the word had been heard just twice in a prior listening phase.

While the previous experiments suggest priming effects in children as young as 18 months old, they do not specifically deal with how children deal with variations of previously primed/retained pronunciations of words. For example, word pronunciations vary across speakers and are affected by their contexts; depending on the speaker and context, *potato* may be pronounced with both 't's as /t/, or the second one may be reduced to a tap or flap. Church, Fisher, and Chambers (in prep as cited in Fisher *et al.*, 2004) designed a study to examine how preschoolers deal with such variation. In the first part of the experiment, 2.5- to 3-year-old preschoolers heard 16 study words and were tested on 32 words, half of which were the 16 studied words. In the test phase, all of the study words changed in pronunciation from study to test. The results showed that preschoolers identified and repeated the studied items more accurately than the new items. In a follow-up experiment, half of all the words in the test phase were pronounced the same as in the study phase and the other half were variations of those in the study phase. The preschoolers more accurately identified and repeated words that were pronounced the same way as in the study test. Taken together, such studies suggest that children benefit 'simply from hearing a word repeated, even if that word sounded a little different the next time it was heard' (Fisher *et al.*, 2004: 19), and that the representations formed from priming are sufficiently abstract to support word identification across acceptable variations in pronunciation. Such studies display that children retain quite specific information about how each word is pronounced. Though children are faced with variations of speech in the input, words may be primed in such a way that the representations are abstract enough to deal with the variation but also quite specific enough to identify the words. Further studies, albeit with college students, show that if participants are distracted during the study phase, auditory priming is not disrupted (Mulligan *et al.*, 2007).[1] This would presumably be the same for young children, as they seem to have the same priming capabilities as college students. Therefore, priming plays a central role in the development of the auditory lexicon and perhaps may have a role in the development of syntactic structure as well.

Syntactic priming

Studies of syntactic priming with adults showed that if they heard and produced a particular construction (i.e. dative or transitive construction), they were more likely to use that construction in a subsequent turn or activity (Bock, 1986). The priming effects lasted when up to 10 sentences intervened between the priming sentence and the activity, suggesting that syntactic priming has long lasting effects (Bock and Griffin, 2000). Furthermore, other research with adults demonstrated that repeating a particular construction was not necessary to obtain a priming effect, such that in the course of a dialogue, adults were more likely to produce a particular form (i.e. a dative construction) if their partner used that form in the preceding conversational turn (Branigan *et al.*, 2000).

Syntactic priming has also been observed in young children. In one of the earlier studies (Whitehurst *et al.*, 1974), 4- to 5-year-olds were shown a set of pictures described in the passive form by the experimenter. Interspersed with the pictures were test pictures that the child described. A control group, that did not hear the pictures described using the passive form, was also tested. Afterwards, both groups were tested on their ability to comprehend active and passive sentence forms. The results indicated that children who heard passive forms were more likely to produce and comprehend better than the control group. The priming effects are even more significant when considering that the passive form is rare in children's spontaneous speech. In fact, a 90 minute observation period of 4-year-olds' speech revealed that none of the children ever produced a full passive (Huttenlocher *et al.*, 2002).

Another set of experiments also looked at syntactic priming in 4- to 5-year-olds (Huttenlocher *et al.*, 2004). The first experiment was similar to the study carried out by Whitehurst *et al.* (1974), except that the study involved both transitive (active 'The bunny was eating the flower'/passive 'The flower was eaten by the bunny') and dative (double object 'The girl is throwing the boy a ball'/prepositional phrase 'The girl is throwing a ball to the boy') constructions. The results also showed priming effects as children were more likely to use a transitive or dative form if the experimenter had used it. The second experiment, however, examined whether simply *hearing* speech without repeating a construction is also effective in children. This is particularly interesting as 'most input to young children is heard without being repeated' (Huttenlocher *et al.*, 2004: 187). The design was exactly the same as experiment 1, except that after seeing the experimenter's picture and hearing the sentence, children were not asked to repeat the sentence but were given another picture to describe. The results showed that children were more likely to use the active when the experimenter used active sentences (89%), and children were more likely to use the passive following a passive (23%).

The third experiment was designed to see if the priming effects are long lasting in preschoolers. Experimenters presented and described to children a block of 10 pictures using either transitive or dative forms. The children then described a set of 10 pictures in succession without additional input from the experimenter. The researchers specifically observed whether the priming effect over the course of the 10 trials would decrease, thus they compared the children's production in the first half to the second half of the test trials. They found that the effect does not decrease over at least 10 trials. Such studies demonstrate in experimental conditions that young children are sensitive to syntactic form just through *hearing,* and that form may also be reflected in their subsequent speech. Together with the effects of frequency, such research suggests that infants and very young children attain information about the syntax of a language through hearing.

Listening-in/overhearing/eavesdropping

As ethnographic reports suggest, young children experience very little one-on-one language teaching interactions – much learning occurs without direct instruction. As discussed earlier, studies show that frequency has an effect on word learning. For example in one study, Jusczyk and Hohne (1997) visited 15 8-month-old infants in their homes 10 times each for a two week period. During each visit, the infant would be seated on a chair and would listen to 30 minutes of prerecorded speech consisting of three short stories. In addition to the recording of the three stories, the talker also recorded a list of 72 content words. Thirty-six of the words consisted of the most frequently repeated content words in the stories. The other 30 words were foil words that never occurred in the stories. Two weeks after the last visit, infants listened to lists with the story words and lists without. Infants showed preference for the list with story words. Then, in order to examine whether the preference was the result of the word list simply being more interesting to the infants rather than any prior exposure, the researchers tested an additional group of 15 9-month-old infants with the same method and materials, but without the two-week, 10 visit exposure. The results clearly showed that the infants without prior exposure did not display any preferences for the list of story words. In fact, the infants showed preference for the foil words. The researchers conclude that 8- to 9-month-olds can: 1. segment words from fluent speech; 2. store and access information about the sound patterns of words that occur frequently in fluent speech; and 3. retain words even when there is no contextual support from the surrounding environment.

Other researchers have suggested that children can learn pronouns through overhearing and show that increased exposure also leads to having an advantage in learning personal pronouns (Oshima-Takane, 1988, 1999; Oshima-Takane *et al.* 1996). Researchers have suggested that children make usage errors when using personal pronouns because interlocutors refer to the child as 'you'. Thus, children have to reverse the use of the pronoun's referent correctly, which requires understanding of the relationship between the pronouns and the speech roles. Children, in fact, do learn that 'you' is not a name for them because the researchers suggest that hearing others addressing another as 'you' leads to the inference that 'you' is a word used to refer to whoever is being addressed. In a related study (Oshima-Takane *et al.*, 1996), researchers examined the rate of learning pronouns by second-born children, and they examined the maternal speech in the triadic context (mother, first-born, and second-born). They found that second-borns were more exposed to pronouns in overheard conversations than in speech directed to them and that they are more likely to correctly use personal pronouns. Such results suggest that the second-born advantage in pronoun production is linked to their opportunities to overhear pronouns being used in third party conversations between their sibling and their parents; that is, increased exposure or frequency resulted in more accurate use of personal pronouns.

Two other studies examined whether 2-year-olds can acquire novel words from overheard speech (Akhtar *et al.*, 2001). In both studies children were assigned to either an Addressed or Overhearing condition. In the Addressed condition, the experimenter played a game with the child and introduced a novel word (i.e. toma) for one of four unfamiliar objects/actions. On the other hand, in the Overhearing condition, the child was positioned as an onlooker to an identical interaction between the experimenter and an assistant. The experimenter would then ignore the child and introduce the novel word to the assistant instead of the child. A comprehension trial then followed in which children were asked to show or hand to the experimenter the object requested ('Can you give me the spoon/toma?'). The results showed that children from both conditions were able to give the novel labeled object to the experimenter. The same results were found in a similar study with 18-month-old infants (Floor and Akhtar, 2006).

As the first study examined 2-year-olds' ability to learn labels for nouns, the second study assessed the ability to learn a novel *verb* through overhearing. They were addressed by or overheard the experimenter say 'Now I'm going to meek [character's name]. Let's meek [character's name]. I'll show you how to meek [character's name]'. After the addressed or overheard periods, the child was then asked to *meek* a character. These results showed that both sets of children learned the meaning of a novel verb. Skolnick and Fernald (2003) also report that 28-month-olds are able to learn novel words when they are being referred to indirectly.

Other studies were aimed at examining whether vocabulary can be learned through eavesdropping as a third party when there are other stimuli vying for our attention (Akhtar, 2005). In the first study, 2-year-olds participated in two conditions: Distractor and No-Distractor. In the distractor condition, a child is given an engaging toy (i.e. dinosaur egg) to play with while the experimenter played with a confederate and introduced a novel word for one of four familiar objects (i.e toma or modi) with a labeling utterance (i.e. This is a toma/modi). The child was also an onlooker of the same interaction in the no-distractor situation except the child did not have a toy to play with. Afterwards, the children were invited to play with the objects with the experimenter. Following the play period, the objects, including the novel object, were placed on a tray. The child was then asked to show or give the toma/modi to the experimenter. The results clearly demonstrated that 2-year-olds were equally good at acquiring a novel object label through overhearing when they are engaged in another activity as when there are no distractors. Morever, experimenters observed that children were more likely to shift their attention to the adults when they heard the use of the novel word.

In the second study, children participated in a similar condition, except the novel object was not used in an utterance that stressed the novel label in the sentence final position. In this study, the label was not stressed and was embedded in a directive. For example the experimenter would say to the confederate, 'Now I want you to put the toma down here. Can you put the toma in here? Put the toma down here.' Then to ensure the contrast of a new label, for the non-target objects the experimenter would say 'Now I want you to put this one down here. Can you put this one in here? Put this one down here.' (Akhtar, 2005: 205). The results showed that though the toma/modi was unstressed and used in a directive utterance, children were still able to learn the novel object label. Children were also observed to shift their attention from the distractor toy when they overheard the novel label used. These studies provide evidence of the 'robustness' of young children's ability to learn novel words through overhearing, even when distracted.

However, such studies only use the novel words within one context. The reality is that children hear any given word in multiple contexts. Thus, another study focused on whether children can learn words across situations and contexts (Akhtar and Montague, 1999) and found that 2-year-olds are 'able to use cross-situational learning to ascertain the meanings of initially ambiguous terms' (355). The study also showed that children get better at this skill as they get older (4 years old). The researchers, in conclusion, proposed that 'we may not need to worry about children facing an infinite number of possible meanings for every word they encounter' (Akhtar and Montague, 1999: 355), as children seem to not only be able to extract words through eavesdropping, but also figure out their meanings. We now explore *how might such learning be neurobiologically supported?*

Neural underpinnings: *repetition suppression* and *repetition enhancement*

Repetition Suppression (RS) is the decreased neural activation in specific areas in response to a repeated stimuli, which is not observed in response to novel stimuli (for a review see Henson, 2003). With regard to the learning of language elements, the implication would be that the processing of a previously or frequently encountered stimulus (i.e. a word) requires fewer mental resources resulting in subjects performing faster and better with frequent stimuli. Indeed, there are a number of studies that correlate the number of repetitions with priming effects (Brown *et al.*, 1996; Lewis and Ellis, 1999). In this way repetition suppression may facilitate processing of the components of language. Studies have already shown that reading time and temporal activation decreases when we read sentences with similar syntactic forms (Frazier *et al.*, 1984; Noppeney and Price, 2004). In addition, the repetition of syllables and pseudowords leads to a decrease in brain activation (Belin and Zatorre, 2003; Dehaene-Lambertz and Gliga, 2004).

In a recent study, Orfanidou *et al.* (2006) used fMRI as adult participants listened to words and pseudowords with different voices. The experimental design included 120 test words and 120 pseudowords, each of which were presented twice. Half of all the repetitions were in a different voice from the first presentations. Repetitions also occurred after approximately 12 intervening filler items. The participants were to make a lexical decision on each item – whether it was a word or a pseudoword, and response times (RTs) were recorded. The behavioral results showed that RTs to second presentations of test items were faster regardless of the voice. Though RTs were faster for words than pseudowords the second time, RTs for pseudowords were still statistically significant, reflecting priming. The imaging results showed several brain regions with neural response changes with repetition, which did not differ for words or pseudowords, and voice. In particular, the researchers observed repetition suppression effects to second presentations in the inferolateral frontal regions of both hemispheres and motor regions – areas involved activated in a range of linguistic and nonlinguistic tasks (Duncan and Owen, 2000 as cited in Orfanidou *et al.*, 2006). In addition, the researchers observed an enhanced response from repetitions in the dorsolateral prefrontal cortex as well as the inferior parietal region, the precuneus, and the right posterior inferior temporal cortex, which are areas observed in the retrieval of episodic memories (or contextual memories). This finding suggests that episodic memories of prior encounters are also retrieved with a repeated stimulus.

Other researchers have examined and found syntactic priming and RS in sentence comprehension (Dehaene-Lambertz *et al.*, 2006). In one experiment, participants passively listened to sentences which were repeated up to four times with a 14.4s intersentence interval. The first presentation involved activations in various brain regions including the superior temporal gyri and sulci, the inferior frontal region and the insula, the thalamus, and the right caudate nucleus. The second presentation led to an activation decrease in both temporal regions and in the left inferior frontal gyrus and insula. Subsequent repetitions led to additional decreases, particularly in the left superior temporal region, such that by the fourth presentation activations were limited to the middle part of the superior temporal gyrus.

The effects of the simplicity or complexity of a sentence on repetition suppression have also been examined (Hasson *et al.*, 2006). In the first experiment, participants heard sentences and were instructed to press a key if a sentence was not sensible. The sensible sentences either included subordinate sentences or not (e.g. It was my mother who baked the cupcakes; The sportscaster observed the events and announced his opinions). The nonsensible sentences were ungrammatical utterances (e.g. The army that shot the old aircraft was with). Unlike the first experiment, participants did not have to make a sensibility judgment and only had to passively listen to sentences. Consistent with other studies, RS occurred in the temporal lobes regardless of whether participants were instructed to judge the sensibility of statements they heard. RS effects in the temporal regions have also been observed across languages (German and English) with similar syntactic structures (Weber and Indefrey, 2009). Such studies demonstrate priming and its effects on the neural level for phonemes, words, pseudowords, syntax, and perhaps the contexts in which they are heard (as episodic memories may be invoked).

Autism and listening-in

Additional, but indirect, evidence for our ability to learn via eavesdropping may come from autistics belonging to the nonverbal phenotype. Such patients are severely autistic, have very little speech, and are often retarded. However, within the nonverbal phenotype there is a subgroup of patients who seem to display a disassociation between cognitive abilities and language abilities. That is, though lacking normal speech and having all the behavioral characteristics of severe autism, such patients demonstrate tremendous linguistic knowledge and are able to communicate with a high degree of sophistication using an augmentative and alternative communication device (AAC) which can be as simple as a spell board. One well-known patient is Tito, who can read, handwrite, and communicate by pointing at letters on an alphabet board, and has an IQ of 185. Yet he is nonverbal and severely autistic. The following is a description of Tito's severe autism, as well as his extraordinary ability to communicate as he enters a friend's home:

> Tito ran back inside the house through the front door and the foraging started all over again. There would be no sitting down, there would be no cookies and tea, there would be no reading of poetry books. It was hard to spend time with Tito. In fact it was exhausting.
>
> 'So, Tito,' I blurted out, breathless when I finally caught up with him. 'Can we talk for a minute?' Suddenly Tito dropped to the floor and sat cross-legged, rocking and flapping his fingers furiously at the sides of his face. Soma [his mother] held the alphabet board in front of him. 'C'mon!' she commanded. Tito's hands dropped to his lap and his rocking ceased and he began to point at one letter, then the next, as she read out each word, alternately regarding the alphabet board and then looked away with a strange half smile, his eyes bulging out of his head. His long, tapered, double-jointed fingers tapped out the words with deliberateness. 'I want to talk about Shakespeare, but instead I will open and close a paper bag. I will laugh and sniff the brick wall.' Just as suddenly as he'd begun to type, he resumed his flapping and rocking, now adding a series of loud guttural clicking sounds.
>
> (Iversen, 2006: 90–91)

Another case is Dov, who, like Tito, is also nonverbal and severely autistic, but at the age of nine learned how to communicate effectively using an alphabet board as well. Such extraordinary individuals, with high communicative abilities, provide insight into autistic minds, and perhaps language acquisition.

Some autistics are reported to be generally very detail-oriented, such that when they look at a room, they do not see a room, they see every detail of the room. This may be because some autistics find it difficult to use all sensory modalities at the same time. For example, some severely low functioning autistics appear to be savants in areas that require highly complex calculations, statistical probabilities, and precision because they have channeled their attentional mechanisms on such phenomena. In fact, many calculating prodigies suffer from autism (Dehaene, 1997). Consider the case of Dave, a 14-year-old autistic, who knows nothing about math, reads at the level of a six year old, hardly speaks, and has an IQ less than 50. In an instant, Dave can give the day of the week corresponding to any past or future date, because he spends hours of his day studying the kitchen calendar. Another example is Jedediah Buxton, who after watching a performance of Richard III, could only comment that the actors took 5,202 steps during the dances and spoke 12,445 words – which was found to be exact. Perhaps it is the same for autistics who have communicative abilities; they may hear and see language, and have focused their attention on a specific aspect of the language and/or patterns and use of language. For example, Tito stated that without narrowing his senses down to one channel, in his case listening, the world 'turns into total chaos.' Tito 'suspects that each autistic individual tends to develop one sense more than the others – because concentrating on one sense is a way to get better information from the environment – a chance to make more sense of the world' (Iversen, 2006: 71). Tito's perceptual abilities were examined in a series of experiments (Bonneh *et al.*, 2008). In the first part of the study, Tito would watch a blank computer screen on which a green patch would flash in the center along with a sound. Three index cards were placed in front of Tito with three choices: *see, hear,* or *both.* When asked whether he saw or heard something Tito would always tap the *hear* card. The researchers discovered that Tito could not see the flash unless it appeared alone without the tone. When researchers expanded the time between the flash and the tone to 2 seconds, Tito could experience *both.* However, Tito stated that to experience both was 'painful' (Iversen, 2006: 233). So, very early in life, Tito started to listen – to the exclusion of using his vision – in order to make sense of the world around him (Iversen, 2007). This strategy may have facilitated his and Dov's acquisition of language. Early on, there were behavioral signs that Tito was intently *listening* just as the infant studies on child auditory abilities demonstrated (Cairns and Butterfield, 1975; Bijeljac-Babic *et al.*, 1991; Ramus, 2001; Saffran, 2001). When he was four months old, his mother noticed Tito 'stiffening and arching his body with displeasure whenever she substituted a wrong word in a familiar song' (Iversen, 2007: 24). Also, during his early years before he could communicate, his mother used to read aloud to Tito all kinds of books because she noticed that though his behavior displayed chaos and lack of attentiveness, his mother noticed that Tito simply did not leave the room, though he could have. Dov displayed the same kind of behavior prior to being able to communicate. Tito and Dov may have focused on listening and consequently learning. As Tito wrote:

> I existed with my ears wide open and wide alert
> With all the sounds happening around
> Sounds of songs and all the words.
>
> (Iversen, 2007: 99–100)

Considering the reported talents of such autistics, perhaps some autistics may be able to acquire some language, its lexicon, structure, and meaning, to a very sophisticated degree simply from overhearing and listening to the ambient language, through the effects of frequency and the use of other general pattern finding and learning abilities. Dov explained the process of learning via eavesdropping best. When he was able to communicate, one of the first things his father asked him was 'What have you been doing all these years?' Dov simply replied, 'Listening' (Iversen, 2006: 303).

In Western cultures, learning via ostensive cues is considered to be ubiquitous. However, studies show that labeling (e.g. pointing and saying 'cup') and deictic statements (i.e. This is a cup) actually account for fewer than 20% of maternal utterances to children less than 3 years old (Goddard *et al.*, 1985; Newport *et al.*, 1977). In fact, ethnographic research suggests that children in some parts of the world have to learn language mostly, if not exclusively, through 'eavesdropping' as they participate in routine and shared activities with other members of their society (Schieffelin, 1991; Rogoff, 2003; Rogoff *et al.*, 2007). This chapter explored the evidence for acquisition in various sociocultural contexts in relation to the interactional instinct theory. Certainly, the simplified speech from caregivers (i.e. IDS and motherese) as well as ostensive cues such as eye gaze, pointing, and stress are resources that are provided to learn a language. In addition, we are socialized to use language through language and the process may be facilitated through joint attention. However, research also shows that we are eavesdropping from the womb, and when we become participants in our social world, we can learn aspects of language through frequent exposure via eavesdropping because of our abilities to: 1. discriminate linguistic features in fluent speech; 2. segment words from fluent speech; 3. store and access information about the sound patterns of words and syntactic patterns that occur frequently; and 4. learn via overhearing.

The research in this chapter also raises several issues. First, much of the experimental research cited in this chapter may be interpreted to suggest that frequency and exposure is the process by which language is accessed and by which we are primed to use a particular word, apply a particular construction or syntax, and therefore, is independent of interaction and the sociocultural context. However, faster recognition, word preference, and even knowledge of its syntactic position may not equal understanding and meaning. Thus, another way to view such research is that we are born with a powerful general ability to find patterns. This ability is used to figure out ambient language, and therefore, ensures that the language around us is not simply noise. Second, some of the studies cited also suggest the interaction and context one observes or participates in also serve to index the referent or meaning of some words. For example, while discriminating abilities that note stress may help children access 'you', and pattern finding and priming abilities facilitate the learning of its syntactic position, it is the frequency of use in interaction and context that ensures the accurate deployment of such personal pronouns. Third, research shows that overhearing and being directly addressed may be equally effective as long as the child's attention is claimed. However, research also shows that when other activities vie for a child's attention, minimal attention to no attention may not be necessary for implicit learning to occur. Research that clearly defines the extent and limitation of our ability to learn via listening and overhearing with and without interaction is needed. The research on discriminating abilities, frequency effects, and priming thus far, however, does suggest that features of language are not inaccessible and that very early in life we are born with abilities suitable for learning language in a variety of ways and sociocultural contexts. What the interactional instinct does provide is the motivation to engage in interaction, to attend to the language, and to learn how it is used in the course of routine, everyday interactions. Thus, it is the combination of our innate tendency to attune to and seek out the reward of interaction, practices that provide exposure and opportunity to use language, and powerful abilities discussed in this chapter that allow us to access language in a range of sociocultural contexts with various practices of socialization. So, while I argue that the interactional instinct is necessary but not sufficient to acquire language, I also argue that these abilities alone are not sufficient as it is the interactional instinct that motivates us to attune to the language in our sociocultural environment.

Notes

1.   Although if visual attention is divided, then visual priming and auditory priming are significantly affected.

7 Mirror neurons for the interactional instinct and culture learning

The previous chapters discussed the contexts and opportunities in which language can be acquired and the motivations that stir a neonate to observe, attend to, listen-in, and figure out the language within the opportunities employed by their caregivers that they have affiliated with and with whom they have become attached to. In addition, I have discussed the ways in which caregivers may facilitate learning through ostensive cues, motherese, motionese, and so on. The next chapters explore more of the biology that might be a part of acquiring language within such contexts.

Over a decade ago, neuroscientists discovered premotor neurons in the ventral premotor cortex (vPM) or F5 region of the macaque monkey brain that discharge not only when the monkey executed actions, but when it observed similar actions executed by others. As they were also discovered in humans, these neurons came to be known as the mechanism that subserves how we are able to recognize the actions of others. They were called 'mirror neurons.'

Though their existence in humans is controversial, and even more so is their role in understanding others (Hickok and Poeppel, 2009; Lotto *et al.*, 2009), neuroscientists have provided experimental evidence that they are indeed a characteristic of the human brain. Specifically, support comes from the study of reactivity of the cerebral rhythms during movement observation (Cochin *et al.*, 1998). Traditional EEG studies distinguished two types of rhythms both in the alpha range: a posterior alpha rhythm and central mu rhythm. These two rhythms have different functional significances. The posterior alpha rhythm is present when the sensory systems, the visual one in particular, are not activated, and disappears at the presence of sensory stimuli. The mu rhythm, on the other hand, is present during motor rest and disappears during active movements. Cochin *et al.* (1998) showed that the observation of an action made by a human being blocks the mu rhythm of observers. They demonstrated that during observation of an actor performing leg movements, there was a desynchronization of the mu rhythm as well as of beta rhythms of the central parietal regions. Control experiments in which a non-biological motion, such as a waterfall, was shown to the subjects, the rhythms were not desynchronized. Thus, the rhythms that are blocked or desynchronized by movements are desynchronized by action observation. Another experiment by Cochin *et al.* (1999) involved observing and executing finger movements. The results showed that the mu rhythm was blocked while participants were observing or executing the same movement.

Other neurophysiological studies with humans have supported the idea that action observation causes activation of cortical areas involved in motor control. Fadiga *et al.* (1995) conducted an experiment which showed that when the premotor cortex is stimulated with transcranial magnetic stimulation (TMS) while a subject is observing an action, there are increases in motor evoked potentials (MEPs) in the muscles that are usually used for performing the same action.

However, research on mirror neurons indicates their central role not only in the understanding of actions, but also in understanding the intentions, emotions, and language of others. As we have discussed, infant-caregiver interactions, behaviors, and interpretations are inextricably intertwined. Through vocalizations, gaze, emotional expressions, and other abilities in the infant's and caregiver's repertoire, both interactants are communicating something about their emotional stance and their intention to initiate, engage, and reinstate interaction. Each participant interprets the other's behaviors and assesses the other's intentions. Therefore, I suggest that the mirror neuron system may be another mechanism subserving the interactional instinct and that it facilitates the understanding of intentions, experiences, emotion, interaction, and language between infants and caregivers, in a way that optimizes social interactions to facilitate affiliation.

Understanding intentions and prediction

When individuals start a movement in which they intend to achieve a specific goal, such as picking up a cup, they usually have a clear intention of what to do with the cup. The intent of the action precedes the movement of 'picking up.' However, the observed actions or even the start of actions can actually be interpreted to have a number of intentions, such that picking up a cup can be seen as an intention to drink, to throw it away, to share, etc. Using event-related neuromagnetic recordings, Nishitani and Hari (2000) studied normal human participants under three conditions: grasping an object, observing the same grasping action being performed by an experimenter, and observing while simultaneously imitating the observed action. The results showed that during execution, there was an early activation in the left inferior frontal cortex with a response appearing approximately 250 ms *before* touching the object. The activation was then followed by activation of the left precentral motor area and later in the right one. This study suggests that the participants were anticipating the motor actions before completion.

In another study (Umilta *et al.*, 2001), researchers showed that F5 mirror neurons are also activated when the final critical part of an observed action is hidden, indicating that the goal of the observed action is predicted. In this study, mirror neurons were tested in two conditions. In one test, the monkey saw the hand approaching, grasping, and holding an object. In the following condition, the monkey saw the same action but with the final part (the grasping and holding of an object) hidden behind a screen. The results showed that the neuron discharged during the observation of the full and completed action as well as when only the hand approaching the object was observed without completing the action. Umilta *et al.* concluded that it is the understanding of the intention of an observed action that determined the discharge, and that the monkey predicted the type of action that would follow.

In a more recent study, Fogassi *et al.* (2005) showed that neurons in the rostral sector of the inferior parietal lobule of monkeys code the same motor act differently depending on the intention of the action. In this study two monkeys were tested in three different conditions. In the first condition, a monkey reached for and grasped a piece of food located in front of it and brought the food to its mouth. In the second condition, the monkey reached and grasped an object and placed it in a container. Then in the third condition, the monkey was trained to grasp a piece of food or an object and place it near a container located near its mouth (this condition was to account for the possibility that any differences may be due to the arm flexing). The results of the study showed that all the neurons that discharged more strongly during the grasping-to-eat condition also discharged less in both grasping-to-place conditions. Furthermore, neurons that discharged strongest during the first grasping-to-place condition also discharged when the placing was done in the container located near the mouth. Thus, neurons in the monkey's inferior parietal lobule discriminate between the intentions of actions, and the main factor that determined the discharge intensity was the intention of the action and not the arm flexion. In the same area, some neurons have been found to have mirror properties. The researchers found that though some neurons discharged with the same intensity regardless of the intention of the grasp (for eating or placing), the majority of the neurons were differentially activated depending on the movement following the grasp, such that some neurons discharged with more intensity when the monkey observed an experimenter grasping a piece of food and then placing the food in his mouth. The same neurons also had a weaker activation when the activity following the grasping was placing the food or object in a container. In comparison, other neurons were found to have the opposite behavior, while other neurons did not show any significant difference in discharge. Furthermore, the neurons discharged before the monkey observed the experimenter starting the second motor act (bringing the food to the mouth or placing it in a container). Thus, Fogassi *et al.* found that 75.6% of the neurons in that area were influenced by the final goal of the action. Together, these studies demonstrate that neurons code the same act of grasping in a different way according to the intention.

In another fMRI study (Iacoboni *et al.*, 2005), human subjects watched three kinds of video clips. The first was of a hand grasping a cup without a context. The second was context only without a hand grasping (a scene before tea or a scene after tea). The third type of clip, was a hand grasping embedded in a context such that the context suggested the intention associated with the grasping action (either drinking tea or cleaning up). In this study, the researchers found an increased activity in the right inferior frontal cortex when participants observed hand grasping actions embedded in a context, in comparison to the activity in the same area when observing only hand grasping actions without a context. These findings suggest that mirror neurons in the right inferior frontal cortex participate in understanding the intentions underlying the observed actions.

Though there seems to be evidence for the role mirror neurons in understanding intentions and predicting the actions of others in adults, it still remains to be seen if they are also available in infants. A study by Southgate *et al.* (2009), using EEG machines on nine-month-olds, is among the first. In the study's first phase (reaching), 15 nine-month-olds were seated in front of a puppet stage with the curtains closed. Then, an experimenter passed a mechanical claw holding a graspable toy through the closed curtains. When the infant reached and grasped for the toy, the claw would be withdrawn, and the infant would be allowed to play with the toy. Then, a second experimenter to the right of the infant would take the toy away. This would occur for approximately 20 different toys. In the second phase (observation), a small graspable object would appear on the stage floor. After ~1000 ms a hand reached through a curtain, grasped the object, and removed it from the stage. Trials were repeated for as long as infants were attentive, or until 60 trials had been done. The results showed matching motor activity during action observation and action execution. More significantly, motor activation was evident *prior* to the onset of the observed action after infants could anticipate its occurrence, which demonstrates that infants were predicting the action.

The role of mirror neurons in understanding and predicting intention has led researchers to ask the basic question of how such associations can be formed. How can one know that action X mostly likely leads to Y and not A or B? Gallese (2006) speculates that at present, 'it can be hypothesized that the statistical detection of what actions most frequently follow other actions, as they are habitually performed or observed in the social environment, can constrain preferential paths chaining together different motor schemata' (5). In other words, the ability to pattern-find through experiences of different social contexts and observations may contribute to understanding the intentions of others and constrain the possibilities of what follows next. We know that some actions of caregivers and infants will predictably elicit particular behaviors (e.g. vocalizations elicit visual attention; during visual attention, infant vocalizations elicit reciprocal vocalizations which are most likely followed by a smile, gaze, or touch of the infant). Studies have also shown that neonates 2–48 hours old have the capacity to perceive regularities of social events (Blass *et al.*, 1984; Nadel *et al.*, 2005). The mirror neuron system along with pattern finding abilities may then allow an infant to understand a caregiver's intended trajectory of interactions.

Imitation

The human neonate and infant studies reported in Chapter 3 provided evidence that human beings have a remarkable capacity to imitate conspecifics. In fact, Rizzolatti (2005) suggests that perhaps 'the main purpose of these behaviors [imitation] is to create a link between individuals by facilitating affiliative behaviors and inhibiting aggressive behaviors' (75), which is consistent with the goals of the interactional instinct proposed earlier in Chapter 3. Given the research showing that mirror neurons seem to be involved in understanding actions and directly matching the observed actions to their corresponding motor representations, it is likely that the mirror neuron system may be a human mechanism for imitation, which has prompted researchers to find the specific neural substrates in humans that are activated during imitation.

In one study, researchers (Iacoboni *et al.*, 1999) used fMRI technology to study neural responses of humans under two conditions. The first condition was observation-only, in which the subjects were required to only observe a finger that was lifted (the index or middle), a static hand with a cross on the index or middle finger, or a cross on an empty background. The second condition was observation-execution. The first part involved imitation, in which participants were instructed to lift their index or middle finger on their right hand as fast as possible in response to the stimuli of a hand with a finger lifting. The second part was symbolic instruction during which a static hand was displayed on a screen, and a cross appeared either on the index or the middle finger and the subjects were to lift the corresponding finger of the right hand in response to the cross. The third part was spatial instruction, in which a gray rectangle was presented and a cross randomly appeared on the left or the right side. Participants were instructed to lift the right index finger when a cross appeared in the left side of the rectangle and the right middle finger when a cross appeared in the right side. In this study, the imitation task produced a stronger activation in the left frontal operculum (BA44), the right anterior parietal region, and the right parietal operculum. However, during all observation tasks, there was greater activation in BA44 and the right anterior parietal region. The fact that the activation in these areas was stronger during imitation trials than during the two other observation-execution trials strongly suggested to the researchers that a direct mapping, or a mechanism for imitation, between the observed and the executed act occurs in these areas. They also suggested that BA44 codes the motor goal of the observed action, while the parietal area codes the precise kinesthetic aspects of the movement.

In a follow-up study using the same experimental paradigm as in their first experiment, Iacoboni and colleagues (Iacoboni *et al.*, 2001) studied whether the superior temporal sulcus (STS) region is part of the cortical network for imitation. This seemed to be reasonable as the STS is known to have reciprocal connections with parietal regions and is a visual region where there are a large number of neurons that respond to the observation of biological actions. Similar to the results of the first study, there was greater overall activity in observation-execution conditions than for observation only. Furthermore, there was greater activity in the STS during imitation conditions than other execution conditions.

Taken together these studies suggest that a mirror neuron network, consisting of the STS, BA44 and parietal areas plays a central role in the imitation of actions. The researchers also suggest that the STS may provide the early description of the action to the parietal neurons, which then adds additional somatosensory information to the movement to be imitated, which is then sent to BA44 where the goal of the action to be imitated is coded, which is then sent back to the STS for monitoring purposes.

Speech perception

The speech perception studies mentioned in Chapter 6 demonstrated that human beings are born with remarkable auditory discriminating abilities that do not seem to be specialized for the acquisition of human language. However, mirror neuron studies using a variety of methodologies suggest that the mirror neuron system in humans may, in part, be employed to code some aspects of language. In fact, studies have shown that mirror neurons are activated during the observation of mouth actions and lip reading (Buccino *et al.*, 2001; Santi *et al.*, 2003). The motor theory of speech perception suggests that the objects of speech perception are the speaker's articulatory gestures (Liberman and Mattingly, 1985). The discovery of mouth neurons increases the probability that the mirror neuron system might play a specific role in speech communication by aiding in the recognition of other people's articulatory gestures. From this perspective, observed articulations are coded in the same motor structures that are used during speech production.

Watkins *et al.* (2002), by using TMS techniques, recorded MEPs from a specified lip and hand muscle. Subjects were exposed to four stimuli: continuous prose, nonverbal sounds, speech-related lip movements, and eye and brow movements. Compared to control conditions, listening to speech enhanced the MEPs recorded from the specific lip muscles. Similarly, Sundara *et al.* (2001) found that visual observation of speech movement enhanced the MEP amplitude specifically in muscles involved in the production of the observed speech.

There is also increasing evidence for a system that motorically resonates when the individual listens to specific phonological material. Fadiga *et al.* (2002) recorded the motor evoked potentials (MEPs) from tongue muscles in normal participants who were instructed to listen carefully to verbal and nonverbal stimuli. The stimuli were words, pseudowords, and bitonal sounds. Either a double *f* or a double *r* was embedded in the middle of words and pseudowords. *R*, a linguo-palatal fricative, in contrast to *f*, a labio-dental fricative, requires more tongue muscle movement. During the experiment, the participants' left motor cortices were stimulated. Interestingly, the results showed that listening to words and pseudowords containing double *r* created a significant increase of MEPs recorded from the tongue muscles compared to the stimuli with *f*.

In another fMRI study, subjects passively listened to meaningless monosyllables (i.e. /pa/ and /gi/) and produced the same speech sounds to examine whether motor areas involved in producing speech would be activated (Wilson *et al.*, 2004). The research found that listening to speech bilaterally activated a superior portion of the ventral premotor cortex. Another study used fMRI to observe the premotor cortex (PMC) during three different perceptual tasks (Meister *et al.*, 2007). The first was a speech perception task which involved discriminating between voiceless stop consonants in single syllables (i.e. /pa/, /ta/, /ga/) at baseline. The second task was a color discrimination task. The final task was a tone perception task, which involved recognition of pitch changes. At baseline, the average percentage of correct responses was 78.9% for the speech perception task, 76.6% for the color perception task, and 85.5% for the tone discrimination task. The researchers then disrupted the activity of the PMC with transcranial magnetic stimulation (TMS). When this area was disrupted, the correct responses for the speech task fell to 70.6%. However, participants' color perception abilities were not disrupted and remained at 76.5%, and their tone discrimination abilities also did not decrease significantly. The results suggest that there is a strong trend toward a decrease in performance after TMS is applied to the PMC for the speech condition.

Taking it a step further, Wilson and Iacoboni (2006) asked what happens to this system when speakers have different phonemic inventories and, using fMRI, examined neural responses to non-native (non-English) phonemes. The researchers chose 30 phonemes for the study: 25 non-English phonemes (i.e. postalveolar click, alveolar click, uvular ejective stop, dental click) and five English phonemes (i.e. voiced palatal fricative, voiced bilabial stop, voiced alveolar fricative). Not surprisingly, when native English speakers were asked to produce the phoneme sounds, they were able to easily produce the English-like motor speech areas. However, activity in motor areas differed for native versus non-native phonemes, which suggests that these regions are sensitive to whether or not phonemes are part of the speaker's inventory and that motor areas are actively involved in the speech perception process. But, Wilson and Iacoboni also suggest that our motor mouth neurons do not stop at distinguishing. It is true that when non-natives speak to natives, though their phonemes may not always be accurate, natives may still be able to comprehend what was said and vice versa. Wilson and Iacoboni propose that when perceiving non-native phonemes, the premotor cortex generates forward models of native phonemes to the superior temporal cortex, which matches auditory input to stored templates (Hickok and Poeppel, 2007). Therefore, when the speech is 'not quite native' or a different dialect, the premotor cortex provides top-down information and can facilitate the perception of less intelligible speech if there is a stored template that is similar (Wilson and Iacoboni, 2006: 322). Taken together, these studies indicate that when we listen to others, our motor speech brain areas are activated as if we were talking.

8　Socializing the prefrontal cortex

In Chapter 2, I discussed cultural practices that give members – who are born with a motivation to interact and learn ways of relating to others – the opportunity to be enculturated. Though children of some societies may learn culture without explicit instruction, such societies do not simply raise their children without guidance or discipline. In fact, Quinn (2005) has argued that there are child-rearing universals that effectively turn children into competent adults. As noted by Lancy (1996), 'All societies must deal with the problem of rearing children to become fully human and competent practioners in their own culture' (30). This chapter furthers the discussion of the biological readiness and neurological systems that have evolved to respond to the input provided by society to enculturate its youth. Sociocultural theory and ethnographic studies have successfully led to an understanding of the external cultural basis for behavior. This section will show how our biology exists to encode, subserve, and even constrain our socialization. In short, it will be suggested that the trajectory of brain development, particularly of the frontal lobes, necessitates socialization practices, such that society intervenes and acts as an 'external prefrontal cortex' (Joaquin, 2008, 2010b; Schumann, 2010: 247) during one's development, and later, the brain mediates one's ability to appraise possible actions and act as a socially competent member of society. Thus, it is argued that the prefrontal cortex has a prominent role in the acquisition of cultural schemas and is central, if not the target, of the processes of socialization.

The prefrontal cortex: Structure and connectivity

The prefrontal cortex is the area that covers the anterior section of the frontal lobes (Brodmann's areas 8, 9, 10, 11, 13, 14, 24, 25, 32, 12/47, 44, 45, 46) before premotor and motor areas. In the research and literature, it is often divided into two regions: orbitofrontal (OFC) and dorsolateral (DLPFC). Although researchers also use ventromedial (VM) prefrontal cortex interchangeably with orbitofrontal cortex, the latter refers to the area on the roof of the orbits of the eyes and covers the ventral surface of the frontal lobes (Brodmann's areas 10, 11, 12/47, 13 and 14), whereas the former covers the more central and lateral regions of the ventral prefrontal cortex, including

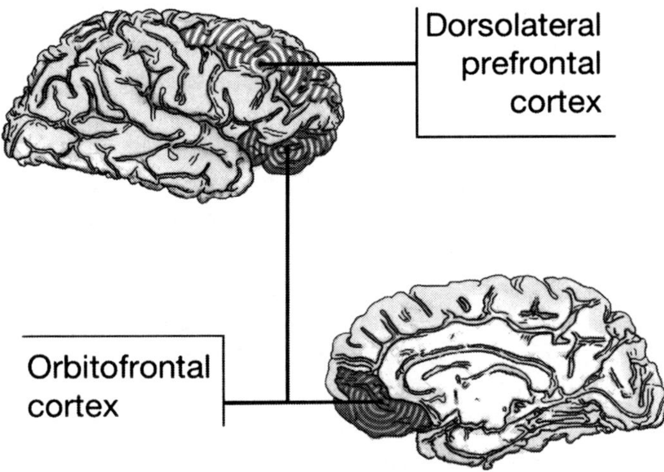

Figure 8.1: The OFC and DLPFC.

Brodmann's areas 25, and lower 24, 32. Thus, the OFC includes both the ventromedial and ventrolateral prefrontal cortex (Krawczyk, 2002).

The orbitofrontal region receives projections from the magnocellular medial nucleus of the mediodorsal thalamus and from the gustatory, olfactory, somatosensory, auditory, and visual areas. It also has direct reciprocal connections to the amygdala, cingulate cortex, insula, hypothalamus, hippocampus, striatum, periaqueductal gray, and dorsolateral prefrontal cortex. It is often thought of as part of a functional network known as the orbital and medial prefrontal cortex (OMPFC) – which includes areas of the orbitofrontal and parts of the anterior cingulate. Brain research suggests that there are medial-lateral and posterior-anterior distinctions in the OFC as well. The medial orbitofrontal region (areas 11, 13, 14 and 47/12) is related to the monitoring, learning, and memory of the reward value of reinforcers, whereas the lateral regions of the OFC are related to the evaluation of punishers, which can lead to a change in ongoing behavior (Kringelbach, 2005). Therefore, the OFC is also important for response inhibition or the ability for humans to change from previously rewarding behavior, when the actions are no longer beneficial (Rolls, 1998) and for decision-making, as such behavior often involves the evaluation of reward.

Its connections to the amygdala and cingulate cortex also involve the OFC in emotional processing, particularly of face and voice expressions (verbal and nonverbal emotional cues) as it receives inputs from the auditory and visual areas (Mah *et al.*, 2005; Baird *et al.*, 2006; Hornak *et al.*, 1996). Emotional processing, of course, is also important in monitoring human behavior, decision-making, as well as engaging in empathic behavior. Furthermore, it is also linked to an ability to infer the likely thoughts or intentions, beliefs, and desires of others (Heatherton *et al.*, 2006; Kelley *et al.*, 2002). In addition, its connections to the basolateral amygdala implicate it in goal-directed behavior.

The dorsolateral area (Brodmann's area 9 and 46) has connections with regions associated with motor control (premotor cortex, supplementary motor area, basal ganglia), performance monitoring (anterior cingulate), and sensory processing (parietal cortex). It appears to be involved in conscious deliberation during decision-making. Much research has also found this area to be implicated in working memory, which is important for maintaining goals, considering options, and therefore, evaluating future outcomes and the probabilities of meeting those goals (Fuster, 1989; Goldman-Rakic, 1992; Krawczyk, 2002).

In addition to the other brain areas already noted, the PFC is highly connected to the basal ganglia, an area that is involved in the control and execution of movement, as well as implicit memory and motor learning. Cummings (1993) identified three frontal subcortical circuits that involve the prefrontal cortex and the basal ganglia. The first is the orbitofrontal-subcortical circuit that is involved in behavioral control, including the selection of appropriate social behavior. Another pathway is the dorsolateral prefrontal-subcortical circuit, which is responsible for mediating executive functions, including inhibition. Another circuit is that of the medial frontal-subcortical circuit, connecting the anterior cingulate to the nucleus accumbens and DLPFC. This circuit is involved in regulating motivation and maintaining activity. Indeed, a distinguishing feature of the prefrontal cortex is that it is very rich in connectivity and feedback loops both with lower brain regions and with virtually all other parts of the cortex. Pathways carrying information about the external environment from posterior areas, information regarding internal and emotional states, and reward values originating from limbic areas, all seem to converge in the frontal areas to make appraisals of what one is observing and experiencing. Thus, the prefrontal cortex has been argued to have a prominent role in the process of socialization (Joaquin, 2010b). Its role is highlighted when one looks at its natural developmental course and the social behaviors observed during maturation and involution, and when one examines the behaviors of patients with suboptimal prefrontal function.

Maturation

Developmentally, the prefrontal cortex and the lateral temporal cortices mature at a protracted rate in comparison to other regions. Though much of the nervous system develops prior to birth, and though the brain has reached its full size between the ages of 5 and 10, subtle developmental changes occur over a longer period of time. In general, in the months after birth, there still is a continuous explosion of connections between neurons (synapses), followed by a period of stable synaptic density, until after puberty when a substantial decline of connections follow (Huttenlocher and Dabholkar, 1997). More recent research even provides evidence that a wave of synaptic proliferation occurs in the frontal lobes around the onset of puberty (McGivern *et al.*, 2002).

Another process involved in neuroanatomical maturation is myelination – the process by which nerve fibers are covered with a white fatty sheath of myelin, leading to improved conduction and communication between cells creating a white appearance (white matter). Therefore, an increase in white matter indicates an increase in myelination. One of the most consistent findings is that there is a steady increase in white matter during childhood and adolescence. In one MRI study (Sowell *et al.*, 1999), a group of children with an average age of 9, and another group of adolescents with an average age of 14, were scanned. The results showed a higher volume of white matter in the frontal and parietal cortex in the older children than in the younger group. In study after study, this linear increase of white matter has been demonstrated by different research groups (see Blakemore and Choudhary, 2006 for references).

Other studies show that there is a cortical gray matter volume increase in the frontal and parietal regions from early childhood into adolescence as well. In one longitudinal study (Giedd *et al.*, 1999) of 145 healthy boys and girls ranging in age between 4 and 22 years old, the volume of gray matter in the frontal lobe increased during pre-adolescence with a peak occurring at around 12 years for males and 11 years for females, followed by a decline in post-adolescence. Research has shown that changes in the frontal regions are especially pronounced and prolonged during adolescence. More specifically, cortical gray matter loss seems to occur earliest in the primary sensorimotor areas and last in the dorsolateral prefrontal cortex (Gogtay *et al.*, 2004). Thus, adolescent years still appear to be a time of continued frontal lobe development. Current research suggests that maturation continues well into the teen years, and even into the 20s, with even some of the greatest developments occurring during puberty and adulthood (Casey *et al.*, 2005). Indeed, such findings have been central to arguments regarding the culpability of adolescents who commit crimes and exhibit generally inappropriate behavior (Bower, 1977, 2004; Scarpa and Raine, 2004).

In general, research reveals that this developmental trajectory likely provides a neural substrate for acquiring the skills necessary for higher cognition (i.e. attention) and social behavior (Grattan and Eslinger, 1991; see Joaquin, 2010b for a review). Such skills are generally a part of the umbrella term 'executive function,' which includes goal setting, working memory, attentional control, behavioral conflict, and response inhibition. Therefore, much experimental research has been aimed at the relationship between the ongoing development of humans in each of these skills and the development of the prefrontal cortex.

For example, Luciana and Nelson (2002) conducted a longitudinal study of children from 4 to 12 years old. They used the computerized neuropsychological testing battery (CANTAB) developed to measure functions attributed to the temporal and frontal lobes in subtypes of dementia in elderly patients, but also to examine cognitive functions in pediatric and adolescent populations. In addition, they gave the test to young adults. In sum, their findings suggest that some behaviors have not reached functional maturity by the age of 12. They conclude executive functions are present in rudimentary forms in middle childhood, but do not fully mature until postpubertal periods.

The Go-no-Go task is a common response inhibition procedure, in which participants are required to inhibit a prepotent response. Participants view a series of letters one by one on a computer screen, and are instructed to press the space bar in response to every letter except 'X' which is programmed to appear only 20% of the time. The fact that non-Xs are used frequently sets up a prepotent tendency to respond on all trials, which then must be inhibited when the X appears. One study using fMRI, compared the performance of nine children (7–12 years old) with nine adults (21–28 years old) (Casey *et al.*, 1997). The results showed that activation in the prefrontal cortex was in the same location, but the activation was significantly greater for children relative to the adults particularly in the dorsolateral regions.

Gerardi-Caulton (2000) used a Task that required 24- to 36-month-old children to respond to the identity of a visual object in a location by pressing a corresponding button. For example, a child is shown a picture of a star or moon on a computer screen, with two buttons in front, with a star on the left and a moon on the right. Regardless of the location of the picture, the child is supposed to press the corresponding button. Therefore, if a child is shown a star on the right side of the screen, the child is still required to press the star button on the left side. If the child presses the correct button, the picture becomes animated for a few seconds. If the child is wrong, then a low beep sound occurs and the screen becomes blank for a few seconds. Thus, the task requires children to, at times, override a prepotent response and substitute it for a conflicting response. As hypothesized, younger children performed slower and with less accuracy than the older children. Therefore, perseveration decreased with age and inhibitory control increased. They noted that younger participants were frequently also more distracted and needed more reminders to stay on task, while the older participants were more engaged. The researchers suggest that the results reflect a general development of attention and self-regulation. A similar test, known as the Simon task, was given to 3- to 4-year-olds (Backen Jones *et al.*, 2003), which showed an increase in reaction times and in the ability to inhibit a response from 22% to 90% between the ages of 3 and 4.

The Stroop Color-Word Task is a classic measure of frontal lobe function (Adleman *et al.*, 2002). In this task, the participant is instructed to name the color of the ink of an incongruent word (i.e. RED printed in yellow ink). In the example case, to say yellow would be the correct response, but the easiest response and incorrect response is RED. Accomplishing this task successfully requires subjects to quickly resolve the cognitive discrepancy and inhibit the incorrect response. Adleman *et al.* (2002) using the Stroop task on three different age groups (7–11, 12–16, and 18–22), found that the strength of activations in the left lateral prefrontal cortex and the anterior cingulate increases linearly with age, which also occurs in conjunction with better performance on some measures (i.e. response time) of the task. Another study using the Stroop task on participants between 6 and 17 years of age focused more on the correlation between demographic variables, including age and behavioral performance (Leon-Carrion *et al.*, 2004), and found that there was an increase in inhibitory control with age.

Other researchers have looked at the relationship between working memory – another frontal lobe function – and development. Conklin *et al.* (2007) recently reported a study in which they hypothesized that the protracted development of the prefrontal cortex may coincide with improvements in working memory in adolescence. They looked at the performance of children and adolescents between the ages of 9 and 17 on several working memory tasks that varied in difficulty and, therefore, required different levels of executive control. They also categorized them into four age groups: 9–10 years, 11–12 years, 13–15 years, and 16–17 years. In the study, recognition tasks required the lowest level of working memory executive control. In the face recognition task, a series of 12 faces was presented one-by-one on a computer monitor. After the 12 faces were viewed, two faces appeared together and the participant was required to indicate which of the two faces was from the previously shown faces. Another type of task involved Span tasks, such as digit, letter and spatial span tasks. For example, in the Digit Span Task, the examiner verbally presents random but specified sequences of digits, and the participants verbally repeat the digits back verbatim in forward or in reverse order. Such tasks were designed to measure immediate recall. The last type of task consisted of self-ordered search tasks (divided into object, verbal, and spatial forms) and required the greatest processing of all three task types. The results showed that there were no significant differences between age groups in the recognition tasks. The digital span tasks, on the other hand, showed significant differences, with each age group performing lower than the next age group (i.e. 9–10 performed worse that 11–12). There was a less clear progression in the self-ordered search tasks, although in general, increased age correlated with better performance. The researchers conclude that the results reveal an improvement in performance on most working memory tasks across the adolescent years. In a previous study, Luciana and Nelson (1998) had also reported that working memory systems develop progressively, with a study showing that 5- to 7-year-olds perform better than 4-year-olds, but have not yet reached adult levels of performance.

Another classic task is the Iowa Gambling Task (Bechara *et al.*, 1994) in which participants are initially given a fixed amount of money and are asked to play so that they lose the least amount of money. They are given four decks (A, B, C, D) which are rigged so that turning each card will give an immediate reward – although some decks give more than others (A, B). However, the turning of some cards also carries some penalty, with some decks having a greater penalty than others (C, D). Of course, playing with the disadvantageous decks leads to an overall loss, while playing from the advantageous decks leads to an overall gain. Some researchers have used such a task, with real money, to look at the development of decision-making by 9- to 17-year-olds (Hooper *et al.*, 2004). In their study, they showed that the older adolescents (ages 14–17) shifted their preference toward the advantageous decks earlier in the task than younger participants, especially the 9- to 10-year-olds who continued to choose disadvantageous cards. Therefore, as the test suggests, younger participants are less sensitive to the future consequences of their decisions. The researchers also suggest that the differences in performance between the 11- to 13-year-olds and 14- to 17-year-olds increases the possibility that performance may continue to improve even after the age of 17. This same performance trajectory has been supported by other researchers using the same task (Crone *et al.*, 2003).

A simpler version of the Iowa Gambling Task designed for children is the Hungry Donkey Task. In this task, the basic format of the gambling task is retained, but the participant is supposed to assist a hungry donkey win as many apples as possible. Crone and van der Molen (2007) used this task while measuring the heart rate and skin conductance changes of participants ranging in age from 8–18 years old. The results demonstrated that children of all age groups process the outcomes of their choices in a similar way. For all ages, when subjects approached making a decision, the heart rate decreased. Conversely, when subjects experienced loss, their skin conductance responses increased. However, despite also having the same reaction to a situation, the older participants (16- to 18-year-olds) still displayed an increase in the number of advantageous choices, although not at the level of adults.

While many studies have focused on the development of executive functions, other researchers have also looked at the development of social cognition (Brothers, 1997), which may include skills such as emotion recognition and perspective taking. For example, one study shows that adolescents process emotions differently than adults. In an MRI study by Yurgulun-Todd (2002) comparing teenagers (11- to 17 years old) to adults on how they interpret facial expressions, found that the adolescents were not able to correctly identify an expression. Thus, when teenagers are shown a picture with a facial expression displaying fear, only 50% are able to accurately identify the emotion. Adolescents typically identified the emotion as sadness, confusion, or shock, while 100% of the adults correctly labeled the expression as fear. Furthermore, brain images reveal that the relative activation of the prefrontal cortex is less than it is in adults. At the same time, the limbic areas (emotional regions) had more activation in the adolescents. Yurgulun-Todd (2002) suggests that this may mean that the emotional regions are not interacting with the prefrontal cortex in the same way as they do in adults.

Other studies have focused on another function subserved by the PFC – the ability to take another's perspective and make inferences about others' intentions – which has been called Theory of Mind, or Mentalizing, and has been shown to have a positive association with social interaction skills (Bosacki and Astington, 1999). Given the continuous development of the PFC and the increased complexity of group interactions that adolescents go through, some studies have also examined the development of perspective taking in adolescence. In one study (Choudhury *et al.*, 2006), researchers asked 30 preadolescents, 40 adolescents, and 37 adults to answer questions that required them to imagine how they would feel in a situation (i.e. You are not allowed to go to your best friend's party. How do you feel?) or how a protagonist would feel in the same scenario (i.e. A girl is not allowed to go to her best friend's party. How does she feel?). The participant was asked to choose as quickly as possible from one of two emotional faces to answer each question from a total of five emotional faces. Reaction time results showed more differences for younger participants and fewer differences among adults. The results suggest that perspective taking in preadolescents and adolescents are developed but are perhaps less efficient than in adults.

I have provided evidence supporting the claim that perhaps the protracted development of the prefrontal cortex is associated with the increased development of skills, which have been suggested to parallel the development of social behavior, and thus necessitates the socialization practices we have observed in caregivers. Incomplete brain maturation in adolescents has been used to explain the impulsive, risky, sensation seeking, aggressive, antisocial behavior that characterizes teenagers. Indeed, such findings have been central to arguments regarding the culpability of adolescents who commit crimes and exhibit generally inappropriate behavior (Bower, 2004; Scarpa and Raine, 2004). Interestingly, the last region of the brain to develop ontogenetically is also the first region of the brain to undergo involution later in life – which also seems to affect some aspects of behavior.

Age-related atrophy

During late adulthood, signs of atrophy begin to appear in the frontal cortex (for a review see Dempster, 1992), which is, as expected, also accompanied by some decrease in executive control. Studies have shown that in most individuals, by the seventh or eighth decade of life, there is some decrease in the size, volume, and density of cells (Uemura and Hartman, 1978), resulting in a decrease of cortical thickness in the frontal regions (Haug *et al.*, 1981; Terry *et al.*, 1987). Most of the decline in cellular size is due to a shrinkage of large neurons (Terry *et al.*, 1987) and to the attrition of horizontal dendrites, which are thought to have inhibitory properties (Scheibel and Schiebel, 1975), and is also often accompanied by a slight decrease in synaptic density (Huttenlocher, 1979). In fact, Dempster (1992) citing Fuster (1989) indicates that 'the prefrontal cortex leads most, if not all other cortical areas in the aging process' (51), and others have also concluded that the prefrontal cortex deteriorates more rapidly with age than other cortical regions (Raz, 2000; Raz *et al.*, 2005). Thus, although not to the extent of children with underdeveloped prefrontal cortices, research using similar, if not the same tasks on individuals in late adulthood also shows a decline in executive control.

One comprehensive study used the Stroop Color-Word Test with over 200 individuals ranging in age from 7–80 years old (Comalli *et al.*, 1962). Consistent with the studies on the development of the prefrontal cortex, the ability to inhibit increased with age from 7 to adulthood, and remained reasonably stable over the young to middle-aged years, but decreased for individuals 65–80 years old. Other studies have also supported Comalli's findings (Cohn *et al.*, 1984; Wise *et al.*, 1975).

To examine the ability of individuals late in adulthood to focus attention, researchers have designed a speeded classification task that requires participants to maintain attention in the face of irrelevant stimuli (Strutt *et al.*, 1975). In this study, subjects have to sort cards according to one or two dimensions. Results showed that sorting times for 6 year olds and older adults (60–81 years) were greater than the older children and middle-aged adults when an irrelevant stimuli was added.

Some researchers have tried to correlate how involution of the prefrontal cortex may affect social behavior. For example, some have suggested that 'excessive and off-target' verbosity, as well as increased stereotyping and prejudice that occurs in older adults, is often the result of inhibitory deficits (Arbuckle and Pushkar-Gold, 1993; von Hippel and Dunlop, 2000; von Hippel, 2007; Henry *et al.*, 2009). In one experimental study, von Hippel and Dunlop (2005), with 80 participants (41 between the ages of 18–25 and 39 between the ages of 65–93), found that older adults were more likely than the younger adults to inquire about private issues in public settings to those with whom they did not have strong relationships. Another study by von Hippel *et al.* (2007) showed that inhibitory deficits also seem to lead to gambling problems among the subset of older adults who already gamble and have an impulsive personality. Thus, for gamblers, the loss of inhibition along with an impulsive personality increases the chances of developing a gambling problem.

Therefore, it seems as if the prefrontal cortex is both the last to develop and the first region of the brain to undergo involution later in life. This developmental trajectory appears to affect the ability to maintain executive control and other aspects of social cognition, which are essential to function in society, and necessitates the intervention of caregivers through socialization practices. The next section of this chapter argues that an impaired 'system' ultimately reverses the efforts and effects of socialization, resulting in behaviors that are similar to those of children and adolescents with ongoing maturation. Prefrontal damage, therefore, produces a regression to more basic tendencies that society worked vigorously to modify through socialization, enculturation, and education. Furthermore, if such damage occurs early enough, attempts to resocialize may not make a significant impact.

Socialization unraveled

Effects of early prefrontal damage on socialization

Powell and Voeller (2004) provide several cases of children with prefrontal damage that illustrate how such damage affects executive function and social behavior. For example, children with dorsolateral prefrontal cortex lesions, an area related to attention, can have difficulty sticking to a task. They can get 'overfocused' on a task and have difficulty shifting, whereas children with orbitofrontal lesions are impulsive, emotionally labile, and often socially inappropriate. Other children have been characterized as having profound memory impairments coupled with a 'lack of insight.' The following is a letter written by the teacher of an 8-year old girl, Mary, who has prefrontal executive function deficits:

> At this point Mary, has few friendships … We have spent a great deal of time talking and practicing social skills in order to build friendships … Mary's lack of awareness – at times – of the people around her and what they are thinking and feeling make [*sic*] it hard for people to be comfortable with her.
>
> (Powell and Voeller, 2004: 793)

In one specific example, Mary found a piece of jewelry and did not grasp the concept that it might belong to another person – despite the teacher's instruction. Her unawareness of social rules was apparent when she proudly wore the jewelry to school. Powell and Voeller (2004) noted that this demonstrated a lack of 'moral understanding,' difficulty in comprehending a situation from another person's point of view. It also demonstrates how the need for immediate gratification overpowers her consideration of the expectations of others and consequences of her behavior (793).

In another case, John, who at 12 months old sustained a prefrontal injury when a car ran over his head. Although he recovered from the accident, and appeared to develop normally, an MRI revealed that he had a large prefrontal lesion in the medial orbitofrontal area. Records of his behavior during adolescence revealed that he was hyperactive and argumentative, and eventually dropped out of school. He then worked a number of blue-collar jobs, but was discharged because of his lack of consistent work and effort. He never had more than one or two friends. He also left home for several years and lived on the street and slept in cars. He ultimately returned home and was able to work at night as a janitor (Powell and Voeller, 2004: 793). His parents felt that his success was entirely due to his mother who supervised him closely and reminded him frequently about what he should do next, when to eat, and not to pilfer. The highly structured environment created by his mother had some positive effects on his behavior. She may have been serving as an 'external' prefrontal cortex.

Ackerly and Benton (1948) provided one the earliest reports of a child with frontal lobe damage. They presented the case of JP, whose frontal damage was congenital. Though he appeared to have the normal developmental milestones and general intelligence, by the age of 3 he showed signs of aberrant behavior. He had a tendency to wander long distances, without fear of being lost or incurring severe punishment from his parents. Sanctions did not cause him to alter his behavior. During his early schooling he exhibited behaviors that made him unpopular and affected his interpersonal relationships such as boastfulness, stealing money, and masturbating in school. He started to receive treatment when he was 20 years old, but his behaviors were intractable. He continued to show a lack of concern for consequences. In addition, perspective taking and theory of mind capacities were practically nonexistent, thus he also did not show anticipation of other people's needs, or attempts to accommodate to others' desires. Interestingly, Ackerly and Benton (1948) remarked that JP seemed to have an excellent sense of right and wrong, which was not reflected in his actions. Their observations led the researchers to characterize JP as having a 'primary social defect,' which was modified insignificantly by experience and consequences.

Russell (1959) also mentioned a boy who at 5 months had frontal lobe damage from a bomb fragment. As he grew older, behavioral problems were obvious – including attacking smaller children, stealing, eating refuse, and deliberately emptying tea on his bed. His deviant behavior was particularly underscored when contrasted to his siblings who behaved normally.

Intriguing evidence of the effects of early prefrontal damage on social behavior also comes from two patients who suffered from bilateral prefrontal damage early in life (Price *et al.*, 1990). The first is G.K., who, because of an increased head circumference during the first seven days of his life, had bilateral ventricular punctures to remove haematoma fluid, resulting in bilateral prefrontal lobe lesions. Records from multiple sources revealed 'that serious behavioral difficulties were first identified by the age of 8 years. He did not respond to parental discipline, always sought gratification of his immediate needs [and] never developed adequate friendships' (Price *et al.*, 1990: 1384). Only under firm guidance and two school transfers was he able to graduate from high school. Records also show that he joined the Marine Corps, but was dishonorably discharged after only six weeks of service. In the next 10 years after graduating from high school, G.K. was imprisoned eight times on charges of assault, forgery, grand larceny, and lewd behavior. He was also charged with arson of two public buildings and masturbating in public. Other examinations showed that he was overly 'impulsive,' and 'showed little insight or empathy' (1384).

The second patient is M.H., who at the age of 4 was hit by an automobile, also resulting in bilateral frontal lobe damage. Over the next year, observers noted that, 'she hit her brother, threw her father over a table, and cut her sister with glass. Family members lived in constant terror and once called the police when she threatened them at knifepoint. She repeated first and second grades, and was only successful with special tutorials' (Price *et al.*, 1990: 1385). When she was 17 years old, she was raped while wandering through a local cemetery, and even returned to the scene on another day only to be raped again by the same man. Though M.H. received individual psychotherapy and medication, her behavior did not significantly change.

G.K. and M.H.'s behavior is even more striking in contrast to their siblings. G.K. was the eldest of six brothers. Though one suffers from mild retardation, the other four siblings are college graduates, and one is a lawyer. His father was a successful landscaper and his mother was a nurse. The family environment was not observed to be particularly stressful or chaotic, as might be expected. As for M.H., she is the fourth of six children. None of her five siblings had similar behavioral problems. Her father was an optician and her mother is employed as a purchasing agent. Neither family had a history of psychiatric disease. In households such as these, G.K. and M.H. would not have been socialized to behave in the ways they did, rather their behavior was the consequence of early frontal damage.

Marlowe (1992) reported the case of PL, who, at three years old, incurred an injury in the right prefrontal cortex from a lawn dart. Though he recovered from the injury, within weeks after his surgery, behaviors that were previously absent became evident. He was aggressive, impulsive, and hyperactive. In pursuit of his own desires, he would act-out and show no remorse for his actions. Eventually PL was given some counseling and efforts were made to teach him strategies to stop and evaluate his behaviors. However, such intervention was ineffective.

Further evidence of the role of the prefrontal cortex in social behavior comes from two young adults who incurred nonprogressive prefrontal damage before 16 months of age (Anderson *et al.*, 1999). The first patient, FD, had been run over by a vehicle at 15 months. There were no apparent behavioral abnormalities until the age of 3, when she appeared to be very unresponsive to verbal or physical punishment. Neither 'slapping her fingers or spanking, nor withholding privileges, appeared to reduce the probability of recurrence of the undesired behaviors' (283). She ran away from home while she was in the fourth grade, and was only brought home after being caught shoplifting. In school, her behavior became progressively disruptive. She lacked focus and was unable to complete assignments. During her teen years, she was reprimanded for theft, bullying, and destruction of property. She showed unacceptable personal hygiene standards. For example, she would hide food in her locker or bedroom and leave it to decay. She exhibited very little or no guilt or remorse. She also exhibited risky behavior and bad judgment, so that as an adult she often put herself in physical and financial risk.

The second patient, ML, had undergone resection of a right frontal tumor at 3 months. This resulted in behavioral abnormalities appearing in early grade school. By age 9, he lacked motivation, had limited social interactions, and displayed a neutral affect, though he had occasional outbursts of anger. Personal hygiene was also poor unless closely supervised. He would often wear soiled clothing and did not dress appropriately for the weather. His living space was described as filthy. ML's eating behavior was also abnormal, in that as an adult he would eat virtually any food item he could find, for example, frozen fish sticks directly out of the freezer, or condiments such as mayonnaise straight from the jar. As an adult, he could not hold a job, and showed reckless financial behavioral patterns. Both patients as adults showed no guilt or remorse for their behavior and could not formulate any realistic plans for their own futures.

In addition to anecdotal reports of their behaviors, Damasio *et al.* (1990) performed a number of tests on these patients, including the Wisconsin Card Sorting Task, Tower of Hanoi, Gambling Task, etc. In the card sorting tasks they continued to select disadvantageously, and persisted in choosing risky options with eventual long term loss. In addition, the patients failed to acquire anticipatory skin conductance responses (SCRs). The patients also demonstrated limited consideration of the social and emotional implications of their decisions, failed to identify the central issues involved in social dilemmas, and generated few response alternatives for interpersonal conflicts.

A slightly different case is JC (Eslinger *et al.*, 1997), who was 7 years old when he had surgical treatment in the right frontal lobe. After surgery he was observed to be impulsive and emotionally labile. He was also noted to talk and fidget excessively, to have a short attention span, to constantly smell items, to be unable to play by himself, and to have a preference for younger playmates. He was noted to call out in class and digress from the subject matter. However, at the 4-year follow up phase, JC was observed to be emotionally and socially connected within family, social, and community settings. Moreover, his inappropriate and problematic behaviors had subsided. His progressive and exceptional improvement was noted at his 8 year follow up, which showed continuing cognitive and social maturation:

> He continues to pursue his high school education with regular attendance and no disruptive or problematic conduct. He is considered a 'good' friend among his peers, and has even been described as sensitive and loyal. His parents continue to report that he shows positive behavior and communication at home, asking about social situations and social behaviors he does not fully understand, expressing his frustrations. JC also participates in family activities and part-time work ... His conduct is not disruptive in school, and he does not appear to stand-out as socially advanced or inadequate.
>
> (Eslinger and Biddle, 2000: 322)

Unlike the other cases, JC showed a significant degree of recovery, to the point of showing typical adolescent maturation and adjustment. Researchers suggest that a key factor may have been the location of his frontal lobe lesion – right lateral prefrontal cortex with spared orbital, polar, and mesial regions in both the right and left frontal lobe. Additional factors may include the age of the onset of damage (7 years), a period in which many aspects of executive functions, social cognition, and self-regulation are already evident, the positive nurturing environment in which he continues to be raised, and JC's own efforts to compensate for and adjust to his neurological limitations.

What can we learn from such reports? For most of the case studies reported above, the effects of early prefrontal damage were lasting and resulted in recurrent and progressively more socially deviant behavior and lack of executive control. The cases showed that affected individuals lack focus, speak at inappropriate times, show impatience, want immediate gratification, and display lack of insight to an other person's perspective and only consider their own. They show a lack of empathy and a lack of concern in matters related to health and personal hygiene. Previous developmental notions suggested that an earlier onset of brain damage had a more likely chance for recovery than brain damage incurred as an adult because an immature brain is more capable of considerable plasticity and reorganization of function (see Benton and Tranel, 2000 for a review). This notion was supported by some studies in which individuals with early damage to language areas seemed to show very little speech and language impairments as an adult. This, however, does not appear to be the case with early onset damage to the prefrontal cortex. In fact, it is suggested that early onset damage may have consequences that are 'considerably more grave than patients with adult-onset lesions' (Tranel and Eslinger, 2000: 274). Early prefrontal damage results in individuals who are unable to be socialized or develop 'systems' that 'guide' them toward socially acceptable, advantageous, and moral behavior. This research is consonant with the theory that the socialization activities discussed in Chapter 2 build prefrontal circuits that support appropriate social and personal reasoning and prosocial behavior.

Adult prefrontal damage

This section adds to the discussion with biographies and experimental studies of adults who have incurred prefrontal damage. What is interesting about such patients is that though they act in ways that are socially deviant, they are unlike children with early damage because they actually possess and can access, under controlled conditions, their 'social knowledge.' Thus, these individuals have internalized the social knowledge and rules to a certain degree, yet prefrontal damage, whether it be the result of frontotemporal dementia, surgery, or a tragic accident, has reversed the force of socialization.

Experimental and anecdotal evidence

As noted earlier, the ventromedial prefrontal cortex is also often associated with impairments in emotional expression and social conduct. Hornak *et al.* (1996) conducted a study comparing 12 subjects with damage restricted only to the ventral part of the frontal lobe to 11 subjects with damage outside the frontal lobes or in the dorsolateral prefrontal region or the posterior lateral surface. They also included normals. In the first part of the study, they showed photographs of facial expressions (i.e. sad, angry, frightened, disgusted, surprised, happy, and neutral) to patients with damage to the ventral part of the frontal lobe. Patients were shown one photograph at a time and asked to choose from a list the adjective that best described the photograph. The second part of the study involved patients listening to a tape with emotional sounds that were chosen to reflect sadness, anger, fear, disgust, puzzlement, satisfaction, and neutral affect, and then they were asked to name each sound from a list. In addition, subjects were asked questions that would reveal their awareness of whether their ability to experience emotion had changed. In general, in both tasks, patients with ventromedial damage were severely impaired in their ability to correctly identify emotional stimuli, whereas the non-ventral groups were very minimally impaired, and were in fact not significantly different than the normals. A follow up test showed that several of the members of the ventral group did not have any problems in either a face-recognition or an environmental sound identification test. Some patients were even able to imitate and produce sounds expressing emotions, though they were not able to identify them.

Some researchers have also used the Interpersonal Perception Task to assess the ability of patients with lesions in the orbitofronal and/or the dorsolateral regions to understand social interactions (Mah *et al.*, 2004). The Interpersonal Perception Task requires subjects to make judgments on different aspects of relationships of the persons depicted in scenes. The scenes are authentic and excerpts from real-life social situations. The researchers modified the task so that participants assessed kinship, intimacy, competition, social status, and deception by perceiving the nonverbal aspects of social exchange (i.e. facial expressions, gesture, and body torque). Social titles (i.e. mother) were omitted from the scenes. In this way, subjects are supposed to 'read between the lines' of verbal dialogue and interpret nonverbal cues (Mah *et al.*, 2004: 1250). For example, in a scene in which two women and a man are shown conversing with one another, the patient is asked, 'Which woman is engaged to be married to the man?' The study found that patients with OFC lesions performed poorly compared to the control subjects. In addition, the study also showed that patients with primarily DLPFC lesions, a region typically ascribed as non-social, performed significantly worse in the task. It was also found that there was a correlation between the extent of the damage in the dorsolateral area and poorer perception ability.[1]

The same researchers (Mah *et al.*, 2005) administered the Test of Social Intelligence to patients with VM and DLPFC lesions and normals. The test includes a series of drawings and cartoons that require subjects to use non-verbal cues to interpret social and emotional situations. The first task presents subjects with drawings of hand gestures, body postures, and facial expressions that show the same thought or expressions. Subjects are then given four alternative drawings, and they must choose one that expresses the same emotion as the preceding drawings. In the second task, subjects are instructed to choose one of four alternative cartoon panels to complete a series of panels depicting a social interaction. The third task requires subjects to interpret the meaning of verbal statements in different social contexts. Lastly, the subjects are shown a cartoon panel with the final panel missing. Subjects must choose the correct panel from three alternatives that depict the event that would follow, based on the characters' emotional reaction to a situation. Thus, this task requires the subject to interpret the intentions and feelings of characters in social situations. As Mah *et al.* (2005) hypothesized, and consistent with their previous research, VM patients had lower scores than the controls. Patients scored particularly lower in the tasks that required them to name an emotion expressed through facial expressions, gestures, or body posture, or to construe the intentions and feelings of characters. These studies are consistent with the vast amount of literature describing deficits in socially relevant behavior following VM lesions.

Impairments in reading social cues are important for inferencing other's mental states and the significance of their actions. This ability may be called Theory of Mind, or an awareness of the mental states of others and the implications for their motives and intentions (Frith and Frith, 1999). Though studies show that Theory of Mind is not diminished in patients with ventromedial damage and that they are still able to comparably complete first and second order false belief tasks as well as normals, they demonstrate difficulty in more difficult tasks (Stone *et al.*, 1998; Torralva *et al.*, 2007). One task is a faux pas test, in which subjects read a story that may or may not contain a social faux pas committed by one of the characters. In order to understand that a faux pas has occurred, subjects have to represent two mental states. First, the person committing the faux pas is unaware that they have said something inappropriate, and second, the person hearing it might feel hurt or offended. Children between the ages of 9 and 11 usually pass this test. In another task, the 'mind in the eyes' task, subjects are shown photographs of the eye region of faces, and are then required to choose a word that best describes what the person in the picture is thinking or feeling (Torralva *et al.*, 2007). In both tasks, patients with frontal lobe damage performed significantly worse than controls.

Rowe *et al.* (2001) also investigated theory of mind in 31 patients with unilateral frontal lobe lesions. Their ability to infer first and second order beliefs were examined. First order beliefs require the patient to know that 'A' thinks 'X'. A second order belief task requires the patient to know that 'A' thinks 'B' thinks 'X'. Subjects were then told stories about characters involved in daily activities with implications for the protagonist's false belief (see Rowe *et al.*, 2001 for examples). They were then asked a theory of mind question followed by three straightforward questions. The results showed that performance on both first and second order theory of mind questions was significantly impaired in comparison to normals. Other studies have also reported that patients with lesions in the orbitofrontal and ventromedial prefrontal cortex show a lack of concern for social and moral rules. J.S. is a notable case, reported by Blair and Cipolloti (2000). He was a 56-year-old electrical engineer, who one day experienced trauma in the right frontal region. After his injury, he had deficits in maintaining social norms. He had episodes where he was violent and destructive even after only a little provocation. He was also reckless regarding others. On one occasion, he continued to push around a wheel-chaired patient despite the patient's screams of terror. He showed a lack of remorse and regret when he hit nurses. He showed impairments in empathy and had 'profoundly disturbing social interactions' (Blair and Cipolloti, 2000: 1124–1125).

Blair and Cipolloti (2000) also gave J.S. a number of cognitive tests and compared the results to five inmates of Wormwood Scrubs Prison who were diagnosed as psychopathic. In comparison to the inmates, J.S. showed a 'profound impairment on expression recognition and emotional responding tasks.' He also showed impairment in attributing fear, anger, and embarrassment to others. He also 'failed to discriminate transgressions which result in victims and those which result in social disorder and to judge inappropriate behaviors likely to induce anger in observers' (Blair and Cipolleti, 2000: 1134).

Other patients with ventral frontal lobe damage have self reported that they have some insight into the social repercussions of their behavior (Hornak *et al.*,1996: 261). As these patients have an awareness of their conduct, and have an ability to reflect and comment on their behaviors as social violations, it becomes evident how damage to this area of the brain mediates social comportment.

Case 2: I've become impulsive since the accident. If I have something to say I can't wait to say it straight away. I am trying to teach myself to be more patient.

Case 7: referring to his tendency to speak his mind (referred to below), said, 'Afterwards I think to myself "Ah, well, I should have kept my bloody big mouth shut … if only I'd approached it in a different way" – and it preys on my mind, and I feel sick and nervy.' He also felt bad about an incident in which he had, in a fit of exuberance, swept a member of the staff off her feet and planted a kiss on her cheek, wrenching her neck painfully.

Case 8: … said that she was much more outspoken and feared that it would get her into trouble one day. She said she was trying hard to control it, and agreed it was part of a general impulsiveness.

Case 10: described how he sometimes swears, shouts, and bangs the table if he misses a shot playing snooker, and people think 'What's going on, why did he swear like that? and I didn't mean it (i.e. to upset people).

(Hornak *et al.*, 1996: 261)

Therefore, anecdotal evidence and experimental studies involving patients with damage to the areas of the prefrontal cortex provide valuable additional information on the role of the prefrontal cortex in aspects relevant to social behavior, which may also be highlighted when one examines the behaviors of frontotemporal dementia patients in naturally occurring interactions.

In frontotemporal dementia patients

Frontotemporal dementia (FTD) is a progressive neurodegenerative disease affecting the frontal and often the temporal lobes of the brain. Its typical onset is between the ages of 50 and 60 years. People with FTD experience drastic behavioral changes. Although the behavioral deficits associated FTD patients have not been fully characterized, FTD patients are known for:

inappropriate social conduct that seems insensitive to the norms governing social interactions and personal behavior in society. [They also] seem to lack empathy for difficulties that others may be encountering. This lack of empathy is not restricted to strangers but also involves spouses and other family members with whom there is great familiarity and intimacy. Comments … may be blurted out without any sensitivity or consideration of context. There is a loss of social graces and a frank rudeness … There appears to be little insight into the intentions of others, and the patients may appear to be entirely self-centered.

(Grossman, 2003: 44)

Thus, common behavioral symptoms include impairments in affect, empathy, social comportment, decision-making, and theory of mind – aspects of behavior that are highly valued and taught in society (Edwards-Lee *et al.*, 1997; Miller *et al.*, 2001).

One study examined the ability to comprehend facial expressions in patients with temporal variant of frontotemporal dementia (tvFTD), a subtype of FTD that involves the amygdala and anterior temporal lobes asymmetrically as well as portions of the OFC (Rosen *et al.*, 2002). Emotional comprehension was evaluated by showing photographs of female faces depicting emotional expressions. Subjects were asked to: 1. discriminate between the identity of two faces; 2. discriminate between two emotions; 3. name emotions depicted; 4. select a photograph displaying an emotion requested by a researcher; and 5. match a depicted emotion with the same emotion. As hypothesized, patients with tvFTD performed poorly compared to controls in all five subtests. Such a deficit in interpersonal skills can have consequences for real world behavioral competencies. Though not FTD patients, there are reports that subjects with ventromedial damage have severe emotional impairments and impairments in real world competencies as well (Anderson *et al.*, 2006).

In another study, Gregory *et al.* (2002) compared the performance among patients with FTD in the ventromedial area, Alzheimer's disease, and normals. Participants were given for first- and second-order beliefs tests, faux pas detection, and reading the 'mind in the eyes' tasks.

First-order false belief tests are designed to assess a subject's ability to infer that someone has a belief that is different from one's own belief. In a typical test, an experimenter describes a story in which two people are in a room together. In the story, Person 1 places an object in a given location, witnessed by Person 2. Something is then spilled or leaves a mark at this location. Person 1 then leaves the room and Person 2 moves the object to a different location. Person 1 then returns to the room. The subject is then asked a series of questions about the story such as where Person 1 believes the object is. This is to find out if the subject understands that others have different mental states from their own – whether Person 1 knows what the subject knows. 3- to 4-year-olds are able to solve these tests.

Second-order false belief tasks are also typically a story between two persons. However, in this version, Person 1 is peeking back in the room and sees the object moved. The subject is then asked questions to find out if the subject will know that Person 2 knows that Person 1 knows where the object is – whether Person 2 knows what Person 1 knows. Six-year-olds are able to understand second order belief.

In *faux pas tests*, a subject is read stories that contain a social faux pas and other stories that contain a minor conflict, but not a faux pas. After each story, subjects are asked about the conduct of the characters. In order to understand that a faux pas has occurred, the subject has to understand that the person making the faux pas does not at that moment know that they should not say something. Subjects also need to understand that the person hearing the faux pas would be upset or hurt. Children 9- to 11 years old have a developed understanding of 'faux pas'.

Finally, the *Reading the Minds' Eyes Test* consists of photos of the eye region of 25 faces. The subject is then required to choose between two words which best describes what the individual in the picture is thinking or feeling. This ability emerges around the time of adolescence. As the researchers hypothesized, FTD patients had significant impairments in theory of mind, while Alzheimer's patients failed only the second-order belief task, which places heavy demands on working memory. In particular, FTD patients performed poorly on the faux pas test and the Reading the Minds' Eyes test. Another interesting finding was that there was a striking concordance between the ranking of patients according to the degree of their impairment on theory of mind tasks and the severity of frontal lobe atrophy. Thus, studies have supported the notion that FTD patients are impaired in their abilities to empathize and take the perspective of another. In the next section, FTD patients in everyday situations are examined to show how this disease affects the comportment, inhibition, decision-making, attention abilities, etc. that society has invested in to develop in its members.

Ethnographic evidence

A general description in FTD literature is that patients act in ways that are comparable to children who have an underdeveloped prefrontal cortex. Indeed, the literature mentioned above describes patients who seem to have regressed in their social skills, while retaining knowledge of the rules of social behavior. Such behavior is also reflected in the attitudes and actions of caregivers with FTD patients (Joaquin, 2010a). This section will show how FTD affects the ability to participate in and carry out social activities that would not be particularly difficult or taxing for a normal adult.

Data and theoretical framework

Data for this study will be derived from visitations, interviews, participant observations, audio and video recordings, and transcription of naturalistic interactions of caregivers, spouses, friends, relatives, and researchers with FTD patients as part of the UCLA FTD Ethnography Project. Led by Dr Alan Fiske, IRB permission was secured from the Office of Research Subjects to visit patients diagnosed with FTD outside of UCLA's FTD and

Neurobehavior Clinic with the aim of characterizing how FTD affects social interaction.

Subjects. Three FTD patients from the FTD ethnography project are included: 'Romeo', 'Kelly', and 'SD'.

Figure 8.2: Romeo, Kelly and SD.

Romeo is a 63-year-old man who has been married to his wife 'Juliet' for over 20 years. They moved to Los Angeles from North Carolina to pursue screenwriting careers. He is a former adult-school teacher. He was diagnosed with FTD early in 2006 with reported behavioral changes beginning several years before. In March 2006, Romeo reportedly went to take the car out to get a smog check. However, he took a wrong turn and went north instead of south. He never turned the car around and ended up in a farmland 2.5 hours away from his home. Fifteen hours later, the police found him inside his car, which was dead on a live train track. The police reported that when they asked where he was going, he said he was going to Charlotte, North Carolina. The incident made the disease very clear to Juliet and demonstrated that he was seriously deteriorating. Romeo and Juliet currently live in North Carolina.

Kelly, at the time of data collection, was 52 years old. She is married to Bron, who described her as 'once a very warm and approachable person … with an uncanny ability to communicate with her students' (Torrisi, 2010: 24). With a Ph.D in piano performance, she made her living as a private piano teacher and a judge for piano competitions. She was also a valued professional among her colleagues. The ethnographer that often researched Kelly noted her 'as someone who made friends easily, was rarely disliked, and on rare occasions when criticism came her way, she was very sensitive to it. Always polite, she did not like confrontation and would not press her point of view or request her desires too boldly' (Torrisi, 2010: 25). In 2003, she began to exhibit behavioral changes and since then has been rapidly declining in her cognitive and emotional abilities. She was first diagnosed with manifestations of FTD in 2005.

SD, at the time of data collection, was living in Los Angeles, California with his wife. He was a composer (for more information on SD see Mikesell, 2010). He passed away in 2010.

Method. The analysis of the data was conducted with the tools proffered by Conversation Analysis. Videotaped data of naturalistic, spontaneous interactions with different participants provides rich resources to study face-to-face interaction, as well as the contextualized settings in which they occur. In addition, video captures information about the engagement and orientation of participants whose actions are built through the simultaneous deployment of available resources. By examining video data of FTD patients with their families, caretakers, and investigators, it is possible to analyze the resources used.

Data was transcribed using transcription conventions from Conversation Analysis (CA) (Sacks *et al.*, 1974; see Appendix A), which looks at speech not as isolated phrases uttered by speakers, but within the sequential organization of that speech in relation to other utterances. Most studies of persons with dementia are experimental and isolated from social contexts, in which everyday communication has taken place, with little examination of the behavior of co-participants who may be intentionally and/or inadvertently influencing the behaviors of patients. The application of CA to patient populations (Wootton, 2002; Goodwin, 2003; Schegloff, 2003; Mates *et al.*, 2010) concerns the ecological validity of the method. Using CA outside of clinical and experimental settings allows a researcher to see subtleties and variations of interactional and pragmatic behavior that are not elicited in experiments or observed by caregivers and researchers not trained to notice.

Inhibition and attention

In the following sequences, FTD patients behave in ways that warrant the deployment of directives and gestures by their spouses, and other participants, to inhibit and control patient behavior. In the first example (extract 1), taken from Joaquin (2010: 186), Romeo and his wife Juliet have been creating a prayer box for Romeo to put all of his prayers in. The activity in itself is suitable for a child, as the prayer box is a shoebox that Juliet wanted Romeo to cover and decorate by taping on some colorful construction paper. Andrea, the graduate researcher, has been helping Romeo, but Juliet is now helping him with the cover of the prayer box.

While Juliet is talking to Andrea, Romeo prematurely tapes a piece of construction paper to the box (line 6). This apparently is premature, according to Juliet, who scolds Romeo, says his name multiple times showing her annoyance, and tells him that he is *jumping ahead* (lines 6–7), because the cover has to be either written or printed on the computer first (line 16–19). Though Romeo acknowledges Juliet's scold (line 8), while Juliet continues to work on the cover, he gets a piece of tape (line 12). Juliet again scolds

Extract 1 Hold off
Romeo 15 February, 2007C

```
01   JLT:   And that's the sort of::: hot pink. But>anyway<
02   ROM:   h
03   JLT:   ugh h
04   AND:   [Well color]s kinda tricky for=
05   ROM:   [Now what  ]
06   JLT:   =Aw Romeo Gaw h Romeo >Romeo Romeo Romeo Romeo:
07          <your jumpin ahea:d.
08   ROM:   Okay.
09          (1.2)((Gets piece of tape from dispenser.))
10   JLT:   Hey lets: just hold off hold off oka:y
11          ((places hands on Romeo's))
12   ROM:   [Okay] ((Gets tape))
13   JLT:   [Hold]off [Hold off]
14   ROM:              [Okay.   ] Now what?
15   ROM:   What?
16   JLT:   Hold off (.) Do you want-Romeo. Do you want Romeo's
17          pra:yer- Romeo stop for a second.
18   JLT:   Do you want Romeo's pra:yer bo:x (.)
19          to be ha:nd printed or from the computer?
20   ROM:   From the computer. ((Places tape on box))
21   JLT:   I guess I ain't gonna be able to stop him (.) He's
22          ready to finish.
```

Romeo, with multiple utterances of the directive to *hold off* (line 10), and she places her hand on Romeo's to indicate to Romeo that he should stop. Again, he acknowledges Juliet's scold as if he was going to listen to her, but against her directions he still gets a piece of tape (line 12). Juliet then begins to ask Romeo what he wants on the cover. However, Romeo anxiously attempts to place the piece of tape that he has in his hand on the box. Juliet then gives him a direct order to *stop for a second*, accompanied with a hand gesture that definitively indicates *no* (line 17). Thus, despite her repeated efforts to control Romeo's behavior, she is unsuccessful. In the end, she concedes and says *I ain't gonna be able to stop him* (line 21–22).

In this sequence, Romeo is provided a range of systematic resources including language structure, prosody, and gesture so that he can participate in an appropriate manner (Goodwin and Goodwin, 2004). However, though showing markers of compliance to Juliet's directions (*okay*), Romeo does not inhibit himself and perseverates against Juliet's instructions.

In the next example, shown in extract 2 (from Joaquin, 2010: 188), the FTD patient is 'Kelly'. The sequence captures her lack of inhibition, which results in social sanctioning from her coparticipants.

Kelly and Bron are eating at a restaurant with two graduate researchers (Andrea and Lisa), sharing their wine tasting adventures. Earlier, Kelly had finished her first glass of red wine and was only drinking her water. At one point, she reached over Bron for his glass of wine. Bron, in response, blocked her arm from getting his wine. Kelly then ordered (and finished) a second glass of wine. Thus, prior to extract 2, Kelly had already drank two glasses of wine, nearly two glasses of water, and had been reprimanded for reaching

```
Extract 2 Reach Over
Kelly 13 March, 2007B


01   KLLY:   California's the wine capital of the U.S.
02   ANDR:   It is: for sure
03   LISA:   France is very upset about that so::
04   ANDR:   Uh h
05   LISA:   The fact that the US is [competitive in wine
06   BRON:                           [>Of course some of those
07           places you have to be um:: sort if a little bit
08           adventurous I: remember that I was at one of the
09           place in Sardinia (.2) d uh:: (.) You know I was
10           just looking at some of the wines and some of the
11           wines were (??) bottles but there I was staying with
12           an Italian fa[mily] and:
13   LISA:                [hhh ]
14   KLLY:   Give me a taste.
15   BRON:   O::: o:: o:: wai::t a mi:nu:ute.
16   LISA:   hhh
17   KLLY:   [??
18   ANDR:   [You've had two already.
19   BRON:   h hhh


20           (5.0)


21   BRON:   And I told them about the wines[that I wanted to buy
22   KLLY:                                  [Give me a little sip.
23   BRON:   and they said that's not the way to do it. And then
24           he took to the bar the local bar and then behind the
25           bar there was this huge bottle of wine.
26   AND:    Ha ha ha ha ha
```

over Bron in an attempt to get his wine. This extract begins with Bron telling Andrea and Lisa about one of his wine adventures in Sardinia prefaced by *I remember* (line 8). As he gives background information, Kelly unexpectedly reaches over him to grab a glass of wine that is to his left. In response to her impulsive behavior, Lisa laughs (line 13 and 16), and Bron reprimands her and gives a directive to control her urge (line 15), while Andrea provides a reason why Kelly should not be reaching over for the wine (she has *had two already*) (line 18). The three different responses, from three different participants, index the social violation, and suggest that Kelly's behavior is, at least within this context, deviant.

In the two interactions discussed in this section, the FTD patients appear to act upon an urge that their co-participants 'work' to inhibit, through directives, statements, and gestures. In the first example, Juliet is unsuccessful, while participants are successful in the second.

Empathy and consideration of others

While other neurodegenerative diseases, such as Alzheimer's, robs patients of their memory, FTD is often labeled as the disease that robs patients of emotions – not only of the ability to display their own, but to understand the feelings of others. This is painfully clear in instances when an intimate is displaying intense emotional pain, and an FTD patient is co-present. In these situations, the patient does not behave or respond in a way that shows any sign of empathy, concern, or attempt to understand, which is shown in extract 3 (from Joaquin, 2010: 190). Prior to this interaction, Juliet has been talking about how she has been coping with her back pains and other difficulties in her life. Co-present are Romeo (who is sitting in the arm chair to her right) and a graduate researcher, Andrea, who is sitting on the floor across from both Romeo and Juliet.

In line 1, Juliet says that she doesn't know *how to run her life* and *what she should do next*, and then starts to cry. At the end of her turn she turns her gaze to Romeo, who is already looking at her, and thus identifies him as the next speaker (line 4). Though they are mutually gazing at one another, Romeo turns away and does not provide a response. Instead, Romeo gets up and walks to the kitchen announcing that he needs *more coffee* (line 6). Though Romeo's gaze and physical orientation on the surface would seem to be a display of mutual orientation and availability as a possible co-participant (Kendon, 1985), his next action and utterance actually indicates otherwise. While Romeo is out of the room, Juliet launches a pre-telling of a story (*the most upsetting thing happened to me on Sunday*), which is going to give an example of one thing that she has had to deal with recently. As Romeo walks

Extract 3 So Much Pain
Romeo 12 December, 2006 (*=crying voice)

```
01   JLT:     I don't know how to run my life.
02              (2.0)
03   JLT:     tch .h*      Sometimes I'm so overwhelmed I don't even
04   JLT:     know (1.0) what I should do ne:xt.
```

```
05              (8.0)
06   ROM:     more coffee
07              (4.2)
```

```
08   JLT:     I'm trying to take it (1.6) one thing at a ti::me
09            (.2) but (6.2) I had (3.2) tch the most upsetting
10            (2.3) thing happen to me on Sunday,
11              (4.0) ((Romeo walks back into the living room))
12   JLT:     *.tch I don't know why it happened.
13   AND:     M:::
14   JLT:     Have you ever had something happen that you wondered
15            theyre happening?
16   AND:     Mhm
17   ROM:     ((clears throat))
18   JLT:     *I was in- (1.2)((sniffles)) I was in s::- I was in
19            so:: much pai:n
20   AND:     Mhm
```

```
21              (2.6)
```

```
22   JLT:     *We went to church tch.
23              (2.2)((Juliet coughs 2X, clears throat, drinks))
24   AND:     You need a tissue?
25   JLT:     ((shakes head 'no.'))
26              (9.0)
```

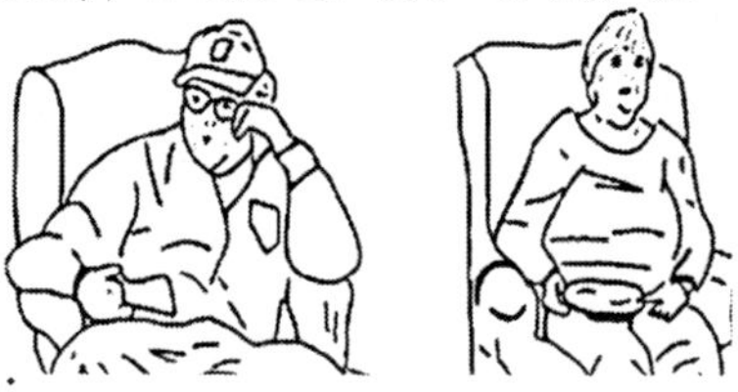

back into the room and prepares to sit, she continues with a crying voice
the pre-telling of an event that happened to her on Sunday. Situated within
her pre-telling is an assessment of the event, which Andrea follows with a
continuer (line 13), showing her collaboration with Juliet in the assessment
(Goodwin and Goodwin, 2004). Juliet still does not go into the story, but continues to build up the story that she is about to tell with a question asked with
a crying voice (line 14–15; *Have you ever have something happen to you that*

you wondered why they were happening?). Andrea, in response to the question, shows agreement (*Mhm*), and displays that she empathizes with Juliet. Juliet then launches her story with background that includes a description of the physical pain she was experiencing at the time (*so:: much pain*). Her facial expression also shows that the pain was excruciating. Along with the sniffles and description, she has also become more emotional. At this point, while Andrea continues to display her participation as a listener (line 20), Romeo shifts his gaze away, reaches for a hat on the couch to his right, puts it on his head, and then reaches for a piece of paper in front of him and starts to read. She then restarts her story by providing more background (line 22). At this point, Romeo's head is completely turned away from Juliet and he continues to read the piece of paper.

Despite Romeo's physical position as a participant in this framework and the multiple displays of Juliet that solicit a collaborating response from her hearers (i.e. crying voice, sniffles, facial expressions, and descriptors), Romeo behaves in a way that seems as if he does not have any concern for his wife. In fact, he seems disinterested and unsympathetic. His behavior is particularly noticeable in contrast to the graduate researcher, who is showing signs of listening, understanding, and empathy, which is also highlighted by the researcher's offer of a tissue (line 24).

In another example, extract 4 (from Joaquin, 2010: 191), Romeo, Juliet, and Andrea have just come from the pharmacy. When Juliet tried to pay for the prescriptions, she was told that her insurance had been terminated. On the drive home, while Juliet is driving, Romeo is in the passenger seat and Andrea is in the backseat, Juliet reacts to the news about her insurance.

Having just heard that her insurance may have been terminated, Juliet is talking about the situation in lines 4–16, and how this is *one thing* she needs as much as *a hole in the head*. Andrea tries to show that she understands Juliet's circumstances; she provides agreement tokens (lines 13 and 17), and even concludes Juliet's turn with an appropriate description of the consequences if Juliet's insurance were terminated (bills would be coming at her *left and right*) (line 19). Juliet confirms Andrea's assessment of the situation by her repetition of *left and right* (line 20), which also shows that Andrea is aligned with Juliet. Beginning with line 20, Juliet's tone changes from angry to emotionally distraught as she begins to cry and says that she does not need *one more thing* to happen to her (lines 24–26). Her repetition of *one more thing* emphasizes her emotion and indicates her view that many things have been happening to her that has made her life very difficult. At a point when Juliet is very emotional, Romeo makes a request *Andrea, can you play this for me on the thing?* Romeo's behavior is striking in comparison to Andrea, whose relationship is more distant in comparison to Romeo, who

```
Extract 4. Can you play this for me?
Romeo 17 January, 2007T (*=crying)

01      JLT:    Andrea
02                 (.8)
03      AND:    Yeah
04      JLT:    They said my insurance was not active.
05                 (1.0)
06      AND:    (You need more help)
07      JLT:    I kno:w that (.4) the owner (.2) of the business
08              (.1) who covers it has been screwing around with it.
09      AND:    m:::
10      JLT:    And I know that heez been tryin to (.) uh:: make a
11              cha::nge in some peoples pla::ns and he assured me
12              mine was no:t affected.
13      AND:    M h[m: ]
14      JLT:       [Now] (.4) heez I need one more thing like I need
15              a hole in th head you know that if it was inactive
16              (.) for that surge[ry (.) that bills are gonna be
17      AND:                      [Ye:ah
18      JLT:    coming at me::
19      AND:    Left and right.
20      JLT:    Left and right so::::: unbelievable you just don't
21              even know.
22      AND:    Yeah
23      JLT:    *I- I- I- just don't know why all this is happening
24              to me I just don't know why:: I get stuck with one
25              more thing and one more thing that is not of the
26              normal (.) Why do things keep coming at me I don't
27              know [(*
28      ROM:         [An- An- can you play this for me on the thing?
29                 (.)
30      JLT:    Nobody's there Romeo
31      ROM:    Kay.
32                 (1.4)
33      JLT:    I don't understand ( ) *Its too much (.) for
34              one person to take.
35      AND:    Yeah.
```

is her husband. Yet Andrea is the one who is actively listening and providing tokens of understanding, and systematically showing that she is a hearer of the talk (Goodwin and Goodwin, 2004), while Romeo remains relatively silent and does not show any sign of concern for or empathy toward Juliet.

The behavior demonstrated in these examples reflects how FTD affects a patient's capacity to understand others and/or to act upon that understanding in a way that is appropriate, which are behaviors that are highly valued and expected of any member of a society.

Social practices and traditions

FTD patients in various situations also show their lack of appropriate social comportment. In the following example, Romeo, Juliet, and a graduate researcher are sitting at the breakfast table ready to eat breakfast. Romeo and

Extract 5 Blessing
Romeo, 12 December, 2006

```
01    JLT    Romeo.
02           (.6)
03    ROM    What?
04           (1.8)
05    ROM    Wha:t? ((Leans toward Juliet))
06           (.8)
07    JLT    Blessing?
08           (.2)
09    JLT    In the name of the Father ((Begins the sign of the cross))
10           (.4) ((Waits for Romeo to join in making the sign))
11    JLT    and of the Son, and of the Holy Spirit Amen.((Romeo joins))
12    JLT    [Bless us oh Lord with these thy gifts from which we are
13    ROM    °[Bless us oh Lord with these thy gifts from which we are
14    JLT    [to receive from they bounty through Christ our Lord Amen]
15    ROM    [to receive from they bounty through Christ our Lord Amen]
16    JLT    And Lord we need your help today. we really need (1.2)
17           s::ome answers  to be going in the right direction (.4)
18           Please help us (.4) Amen.
19    AND    Amen:
20           (.2)
21    JLT    Amen Romeo? ←
22    ROM    Amen. ←
```

Juliet are both quite religious. They begin their day praying together, and Romeo spends much of his morning reading his prayers that he has collected. Therefore, one practice in Romeo and Juliet's home is saying 'grace' before a meal, during which a prayer for blessing is made and closed by an utterance that shows an agreement to the prayer, *Amen*. In this instance, Romeo and Juliet have sat down to eat breakfast, and she reminds him to give the 'blessing.'

As they sit down, Juliet notices that Romeo is looking at the remote control in his hand. Juliet then summons Romeo to mobilize his attention and participation (line 1) (Schegloff, 1968). He looks to Juliet for the answer. Juliet though does not go ahead as expected resulting in a 1.8 silence. Her silence suggests that Romeo's lack of knowledge of what is expected of him is problematic. Without a response, Romeo once again asks Juliet *What* as he sits up, looks, and leans forward toward Juliet, still unaware of the social practice that Juliet has tried to mobilize him to participate in. His answer suggests that he does not know what the appropriate next move is, but still allows for Juliet to go-ahead and make her request. After a .8 pause, she reminds him that they have to say the *blessing*. Juliet begins the introduction to the blessing while making the sign of the cross (line 9). Though she has begun to say it and has begun to make the sign of the cross, Romeo has not yet begun. She watches, which displays that she is waiting for his participation. At the end of the first turn of the prayer introduction (*In the name of the Father*), she waits for .4 seconds, for him to align with her (lines 9–10). When Romeo joins in, she resumes. He is aligned with her, and both are making the sign of the cross simultaneously (line 11). When Juliet concludes the prayer with *Amen*, Andrea also says *Amen,* but Romeo has to be prompted to appropriately participate in the closing of the prayer (line 21).

On another occasion, Romeo, after being prompted to say the blessing before the meal, places his finger on his forehead and does the sign of the cross demonstrating that he is going to participate in the practice of saying the blessing. However, halfway through the prayer, Romeo sits up and begins to eat his cereal, while Juliet and Andrea continue to pray.

Saying the blessing before a meal is an important ritual in this home, which Andrea seems to understand. It occurs before almost every meal observed in the data. It is also a practice that is not found in every home. However, because Romeo and Juliet are religious, it is a part of their mealtime practice, and we can assume it has been for some time, even prior to the onset of his dementia. Romeo appears to know the motions and words. He is able to make the sign of the cross and recite the basic prayer with Juliet. Although he has the social knowledge to participate in the practice, he does not carry it out successfully and needs prompting to do so. Here, we see how FTD breaks down socialized religious practices and leads to inappropriate behaviors.

Personal hygiene

In previous sections, there are reports that the personal hygiene of patients with prefrontal damage appears to be affected (see *Effects of early prefrontal damage on socialization)* one can imagine that basic personal hygiene practices, at least in western cultures, such as brushing one's teeth, washing hands, etc. is imposed and enforced on children. Of course, for normal adults such practices are simple and generally no longer require explicit guidance. However, in these next examples, we see how their knowledge of these socialized practices is impaired. In extract 6, the FTD patient (SD), his caregiver (JEN), and a graduate researcher (TIM), went for a walk at the park. They have now returned home and are getting ready to eat dinner, which Ann (SD's wife) has been preparing. SD is now washing his hands, while Tim and Ann are discussing the food.

Throughout the process, Jen remains close to SD as he washes his hands, and guides him, using directives, beginning with *put soap on,* which he apparently was about to forget (lines 1–2). She directs him and shows him explicitly how to wash his hands thoroughly (lines 9, 11, 14). She helps him accomplish the task by turning the faucet on. She tells him how to wash his hands (*Rub it all off top of your hand*) while modeling for him how to do so (line 11). She even reminds SD to *take all the soap off.* Here, we see

Extract 6 Washing Hands
SD, 28 September, 2006/4

```
01   JEN   No Mr. D put so- [so ]ap on.  Mr. [Da  ]vis (.) put soap
02         on. Put soap on.
03   ANN                    [it's]              [It's]
04   ANN   It's um:::
05   SD    Put soap on. Put soap on.
06   ANN   Um:; Tabouli
07   TIM   Tabouli that's the word.
08   ANN   You knew. (.4) Baba Ganoush I lo:ve.
```

```
09   JEN   Take all the soap off.
10   SD    All the soap.
           All the soap.
```

```
           All the soap.
           All the soap.
           ((singing))
11   JEN   Rub it all off top of your hand. ((Gestures the action))
12   SD    Okay okay okay okay okay ((melodicly))
13   JEN   Okay you take soap off. Take it all off
14         [take all the soap off]
15   SD    [take off all the soap] all the all the soap all the soap
16         okay okay okay ((SD turns off the faucet, dries hands
17         with a towel, Jen walks away))
```

Jen guiding SD through the activity from beginning to end. The practice of washing one's hands before a meal is one that parents and other substitute caregivers in western cultures often teach and guide young children through.

During another activity, Romeo has been given the task of washing the dishes, a more 'adult' activity, while Andrea 'supervises', which is shown in extract 7.

As Romeo washes the dishes, Andrea closely watches him to make sure that he washes them thoroughly. She stands next to him, keeps him on task, and monitors his every move – where he places the dishes, the quality of the washing, and instructs him so that he would do a thorough job (lines 6, 9, 12, 14–15, 18, 20, 22, 24–25, 29). Moreover, she provides him with reasons

Extract 7 Washing Dishes
Romeo, December 5, 2006A

```
01   AND   Hey, where's the thing that stops that uh:: makes the
02         water not go out?
03   ROM   I think th-
04   AND   There
05   ROM   Yeah it's there.
06         (6.8) ((Andrea watches Romeo wash and even follows him as he
           places cleaned dishes to the side))
07   ROM   Now
08         (6.0) ((Romeo dries hands with towel, while faucet is
           running))
09   AND   Okay what about these are these dirty? ((pointing to some
           tupperware by the sink))
10         (2.0)
11   ROM   They might be. ((starts to wash Tupperware))
12   AND   I think they are.
13         (5.6)
14   AND   Oh you haven't quite finished washing it here. Let's get
15         the soap and then this too. ((takes soapy Tupperware and
           places it back on the side of the where he is washing and
           in his field of vision))
16         (1.2)
17   ROM   Okay.
           ------
              | 24 sec. ((Andrea carefully watches Romeo))
           -----
18   AND   Oh↑ that looks a lot better.
19         (4.0) ((Romeo places a cleaned Tupperware on the side,
           Andrea sees some soap and rinses it for him))
20   AND   °Theres some soap there.
21         (5.6)
22   AND   And there's still some soap here. ((points to some soap))
23   ROM   What?
24   AND   There's still soap there you wanna rinse it off real good
25         you don't wanna eat soap.
26   ROM   Yeah.
27   AND   Cause it doesn't taste real good.
28   ROM   Yeah.
29   AND   Okay. That's good. (.2) That box. ((points to another
           Tupperware))
30         (18.0)
```

for doing so (lines 24–25 and 27). She does not leave him alone to carry out the task by himself. She quietly aids him (lines 15 and 19), and provides positive assessments (lines 18 and 29) for doing a good job. Though Andrea has to exert effort throughout the activity, to continue to guide him, Romeo also shows agency (line 3) and perhaps shows understanding of the consequences of not doing the job correctly (lines 26 and 28). Thus, in these two examples, FTD patients are guided to maintain cleaning standards that are taught to and learned by a child.

In this chapter, I have tried to demonstrate that society's child socialization practices and the development of the prefrontal cortex are intertwined. An underdeveloped prefrontal cortex is associated with less executive function and therefore, to some extent, socially undesirable behaviors observed in children and adolescents. Then, as ethnographic studies in Chapter 2 show, socialization practices of parents, caregivers, and peers educate, socialize, and enculturate the prefrontal cortex with the values, behaviors, and cultural schemas that are socially acceptable, and afterwards continues to mediate appropriate social behavior in adults. The prefrontal cortex 'evolved to subserve social experience, incorporating it as knowledge, and then by governing an individual's social behavior via that knowledge' (Schumann, 2010: 246). Although, just as socialization results in learning social knowledge, this chapter also shows that involution, damage to the prefrontal cortex, or having a disease such as Frontotemporal Dementia, results in the opposite – the loss of ability to implement social behavior that was acquired during infancy, childhood, adolescence, and early adulthood. Indeed, the research presented here illustrates 'the exquisite coordination between society and biology' (Schumann, 2010: 246), and that the prefrontal cortex is the target of socialization practices, and is part of a system involved in personal and social decision making. The systems that subserve the ability to apply social knowledge appropriately may also be related to the appropriate use of language – or pragmatics.

Notes

1. Some readers might be surprised as to why the dorsolateral prefrontal cortex, a typically 'non-social' area, was implicated. Mah *et al.* (2004) interpret the deficits in patients with dorsolateral prefrontal damage as a result of deficits in socio-cognitive skills necessary for theory of mind. They noted that patients with DLPFC lesions were particularly impaired in lie detection, a process requiring an intact theory of mind. They also note studies that suggest that problems with working memory, which involves the DLPFC, affect the ability to make decisions (Bechara *et al.*, 1998; Manes *et al.*, 2002).

9 Appraisal, behavior and language pragmatics

Though children of some societies may learn culture without explicit instruction, such societies do not simply raise their children without guidance. As Lancy (1996) states, in communities where 'the role of teacher is assumed far more rarely and children bear greater personal responsibility for acquiring their culture … the society does not just let them flounder but provides a wealth of opportunities for guided and sheltered learning' (18). Even in traditional societies where explicit instruction almost never occurs, some form of action or sign that indexes an appropriate/inappropriate behavior can be observed. Normative behavior by a naïve member may be rewarded or punished either explicitly (i.e. praise), or indirectly (i.e. no punishment), by members of one's sociocultural group, or behavior may have intrinsic reward/punishment (i.e. acceptance/exclusion). Such feedback is emotionally arousing, which makes lessons memorable and can motivate cultural learning (Quinn, 2005), and ultimately informs the individual of future courses of action: what to do, when to do it, how to do it, and with whom to do it. To continue the discussion on the biological readiness and neurological structures and systems that have evolved to respond to input, this section discusses a system that involves prior experiences and learned cultural schemas in appraising a context or situation to make social decisions, to affect behavior, and to use language.

What to do/say, when to do/say it, how to do/say it, why one should do/say it, and with whom

We have briefly examined Porges' social engagement theory (see Chapter 4), which involves a system that modulates one's behavior in interacting with a potential interlocutor, and we have discussed the specific role of the amygdala in the processing of memories and social experiences and the contexts in which they occur through its connections to the thalamus and the hippocampus. Studies in amygdalectomized monkeys and humans with bilateral or partial damage to the amygdala (Adolphs *et al.*, 1994) also demonstrate its relevance for processing social experiences.

Furthermore, the amygdala has direct reciprocal connections to the prefrontal cortex, specifically the orbitofrontal cortex (Kringelbach, 2005), which has been shown to be involved in the process of decision-making through patients who have incurred damage in this region. For example, Elliot, also known as EVR, (Damasio *et al.*, 1990) was a successful professional, happily married, the father of two, and a role model to his younger siblings. However, at the age of 35, EVR had an orbitofrontal meningioma – a tumor affecting the meninges – which required a bilateral excision of orbital and lower mesial cortices. After the surgery, EVR's social conduct was profoundly affected by his brain injury. He entered unwise business ventures that led to bankruptcy, got divorced, and then married a prostitute, whom he divorced 6 months later.

Despite his social failings, EVR demonstrated that he was 'capable of reasoning correctly through subtle hypothetical social problems' (Damasio *et al.*, 1990: 82). In one study, Saver and Damasio (1991) gave EVR five tests that measured his social cognition: 1. An optional thinking test designed to measure the ability to generate alternative solutions to hypothetical social dilemmas; 2. an awareness of consequences test, which measures a subjects' inclination to consider the consequences of actions; 3. a means-ends problem-solving task structured to gauge a subject's ability to conceptualize how to achieve a goal; 4. a cartoon predictions test designed to predict the social consequences of events; and 5. a standard issue moral judgment interview in which participants are given a social situation with a conflict between two moral imperatives, and are then asked to provide a solution to the dilemma and a justification for their responses. In each of the tests, EVR performed either the same or better than the control group. Thus, EVR's social behavior did not reflect his social knowledge, which seemed to be preserved. What was affected was his ability to make socially advantageous decisions.

Through observations of patients like EVR, Damasio (1994) developed the 'somatic marker hypothesis.' He proposed that impairment in a 'somatic marker system' causes socially inappropriate behavior. This system couples internal representations with a somatic marker (body state). He suggests that before we weigh the costs and benefits of a situation, and before we reason toward the solution of a problem, something that guides our behaviors happens: 'When the bad outcome connected with a given response option comes to mind, however fleetingly, you experience an unpleasant gut feeling' (Damasio, 1994: 173). Through experience we gain these somatic markers, which 'force attention on a negative consequence which a given action may lead to, and function as an automated alarm signal which says: Beware of danger ahead if you choose the option which leads to this. The signal may lead you to reject, *immediately*, the negative course of action and thus make you choose among other alternatives. The automated signal protects you against future losses, without further ado, and then allows you *to choose from among other alternatives'* (Damasio, 1994: 173). Damasio states that somatic markers probably increase the accuracy and efficiency of the decision-making process, while their absence reduces them. EVR's 'acquired sociopathy' is the result of an impaired somatic marker system because his damaged OFC cannot process the somatic marker generated in the body (endocrine system, autonomic nervous system, and the musculo-skeletal system) and, therefore, he has an impaired access to emotions that would help him reject some alternatives and select others. Thus, research suggests that the prefrontal cortex, specifically the medial and lateral parts of orbitofrontal region (OFC), may be involved in the evaluation of reward and punishers, respectively, that one has experienced during his or her life-time, thus affecting decision-making (Damasio, 1994; Rolls, 1998; Kringelbach, 2005). Damasio also argues that if rewards and punishers are frequently experienced, representations may be developed in the cortex and appraisals may become automatic (Damasio, 1995). Human beings have a particularly long period of socialization when we learn what is right, wrong, advantageous, disadvantageous, acceptable, unacceptable, rewarding, punishable, conventional, and deviant – forming 'somatic markers' that provide the basis for what we decide (consciously or unconsciously) to do.

Schumann (1999) has suggested that the amygdala, the orbitofrontal cortex, and the body proper are part of the system that subserves our ability to appraise social stimuli. Schumann refers to Scherer's taxonomy of five appraisal categories – the *novelty* and *pleasantness* of a stimulus, whether the situation contributes to one's *goals or needs,* whether he/she has the *coping potential* to deal with the consequences of a situation, and how one's engagement within a situation affects his/her *self and social image* (Scherer, 1984). On the basis of these appraisals, we act. If, however, the stimulus appraisal system is compromised, one might display deficits in social behavior. For example, a deficit in the ability to assess one's coping potential may lead to being easily overwhelmed in a social situation, or may leave one oblivious to his/her social failings. A person with an inability to assess whether actions will contribute to his/her goals or needs may be driven by what they want or need in the moment. A person with deficits in appraising how their actions would enhance their self and social image might act inappropriately and yet be unconcerned with how they are being perceived by others. Persons with deficits may also not attend to novel stimuli, and they may have very different ideas about what is pleasant.

Patients with frontotemporal dementia (FTD) seem to display impairments in social reasoning, leading to social failings. For example, recall the behavior of Kelly during dinner in the previous chapter (extract 2). Kelly had just met the two new researchers a few hours before. During dinner, she finished her first glass of wine, and when she reached over Bron (her husband) for his glass of wine, he blocked her. Then, while Bron was talking about his wine adventures, she interrupts his narrative again by reaching across his body for a glass of wine, despite Bron's earlier reprimand. In response, three different participants mark her behavior as a social violation. Her husband, Bron, expresses his disapproval while holding off her arm; Andrea judges her behavior citing that she had 'had two already'; and, Lisa expresses amusement. Even after Kelly is reprimanded for her behavior she does not inhibit herself and insists on having more wine. The dinner was a part of her first meeting with the two new researchers (Andrea and Lisa), and yet, Kelly does not show concern for her social image, and indeed persists in her inappropriate behavior despite her interlocutors' reactions.

In another example (extract 8), Romeo, the FTD patient, is getting ready to take a walk to the bank with Andrea, who has instructed him to change into his walking shoes. A few minutes later, Andrea finds Romeo in the office, where his wife is working. While he is putting on socks, Andrea notices that Romeo had already put on a pair of socks and was now putting on a second pair on top of the first.

Andrea calls Romeo's attention to his peculiar behavior in line 1, which also raises concern from Juliet (line 2). Romeo's response in line 3 indicates that he is unaware of the implications of his behaviors. As Juliet pursues Romeo for an explanation in line 4, and even more aggressively in line 6, his response of *I don't know* both times in lines 5 and 8, while he continues to put on the second layer of socks, demonstrates that he is oblivious to the negative perceptions of Andrea and Juliet. Then, although Andrea and Juliet continue to discuss Romeo's behavior with obvious confusion (lines 10–12)

Extract 8 Two pairs of socks
Romeo, 17 January, 2007A

```
01   AND   Do you always wear two pairs of socks Romeo?
02   JLT   Honey are you putting on two pairs of socks?
03   ROM   Yeah.
04   JLT   Why?
05   ROM   I don't know.
06   JLT   Romeo? (1.2) Oh Romeo, why do you think you need two pairs
07         of socks?
08   ROM   I don't know.
09         (1.0)
10   JLT   Well I didn't know- I didn't tha:t.
11   AND   I thought he was just changing socks but then he took off
12         his shoe and put on another sock.
13   JLT   ↑ROMEO.
14   ROM   Okay.(.4) Fine. I'll (.) do (.) it.
15   JLT   ((Sighs and turns away and shakes her head))
```

in front of him, he still does not alter his course of action, which leads to Juliet's clear reprimand in line 13, and is even insistent in wearing a second pair of socks (line 14). He is indifferent to the consequences on his social image. In response, Juliet sighs, turns away, and shakes her head, displaying her disapproval.

In another situation, Romeo has decided to watch television. Earlier, Juliet reprimanded him for accidentally turning off the timer on the video recorder. As a result, Juliet was no longer allowing Romeo to touch the television. Now, as Romeo has decided to watch television, Andrea is the one with permission to turn the television on or off. What ensues is a nearly 11 minute interaction in which Romeo repetitively instructs Andrea to turn the television on and off. Extract 9a is from those 11 minutes. It happens after Romeo has returned from the living room and has already asked Andrea to turn on the television.

A few seconds after Andrea prompts Romeo to sit down and watch television (line 2), he requests *Can we turn the TV off?* (line 7). Her agreement token, followed with a partial repeat using the modal *can*, is different from a simple agreement or disagreement token (yes, no), because *we can* marks the activity he requested as one that is not obligatory (line 9). Afterwards, he replies using the inclusive *let's* in line 12 (Wales, 1996), though it is not Andrea's preferred course of action. Thus, as Romeo's back and forth

```
Extract 9a Turn it on, Turn it off
Romeo, 15 February, 2007B


((Romeo returns to the living room from the kitchen.))
   01   ROM   Now what?.h
   02   AND   Wanna sit down and watch?
   03         (1.5)
   04   ROM   Okay. Okay. Alright s: s:it down and watch. ((Romeo sits
   05         Down)) Sit.
   06         (9.0)
   07   ROM   Can can we turn the TV off? ((Looks at Andrea))
   08         (1.0)
   09   AND   Ye:s we can.
   10   ROM   Okay.
   11         (1.0)
   12   ROM   Let's turn it off.
   13         (2.0)
   14   AND   If we turn it off I'm no:t turning it back on.        .
   15   ROM   Okay.
   16   AND   Okay?
   17   ROM   Okay:
   18          (5.0)
            ---
             |
        8 lines omitted
        ((Romeo leaves room and returns))
             |
            ---
```

requesting has been going on for a while, she does not simply agree to his request, but gives Romeo an ultimatum in the form of a conditional statement, that if she turns the television off she will not turn it back on (line 14), with an emphasis on the *not*. In response, Romeo agrees to her ultimatum (line 15). Then, given his prior behavior, Andrea confirms his agreement again in line 16. Nevertheless, 30 seconds later, Romeo asks Andrea if the television can be turned back on (which is transcribed in extract 9b).

Continuing extract 9a, Romeo requests Andrea to turn the TV back on in line 29. In response, Andrea asks Romeo to recall the condition for turning

Extract 9b Turn it on, Turn it off
Romeo, 15 February, 2007B

```
27  ROM  Now what?
28       (13.0)
29  ROM  Can we turn the TV back on?
30       (1.6)
31  AND  What did I say about last time when you asked me to turn it
32       off: ((AND is reading the newspaper and does not look at
         him))
33       (1.6)
34  ROM  You're not gonna turn it back on.
35       (1.0)
36  AND  So why did you ask me to turn it on?
37       (1.0)
38  ROM  I don't know.
39       (3.2)
40  ROM  But I'm asking you to turn it on now. ((Romeo gets up and
         walks out of the living room))
41  AND  Oh::kay I'll turn it o:n.((Andrea puts down newspaper and
         gets up))
42       (2.0)
43  ROM  Uh::
44       (1.0)
45  AND  Are you sure you want it o:n?
46  ROM  Yeah.
47  AND  You su:re you want it on?
48  ROM  Yeah I'm sure I want it on.
49  AND  °Okay
            -----
              |
        11 lines omitted
           24 sec.
              |
            ------
60  ROM  Turn it- uh:: ba-
61       (2.0)
62  ROM  I'm gunna turn it o:ff again.
63       (3.0)
64  ROM  W- Wheres the off button?
65  AND  The furthest right one.
66       (2.0)
67  ROM  Okay.
68       (2.0)
69  ROM  Now,(2.0) Juliet.((Romeo walks out of the room)).
```

----

off the television earlier (lines 31–32). Romeo demonstrates that he does in fact recall the ultimatum that he agreed to (line 34). When she seeks an explanation for his behavior, he does not give a satisfactory answer, and instead of honoring the terms to which he had initially agreed, he continues to break his agreement and asks Andrea to turn on the television (line 40). His request is instantiated in his turn beginning with *But,* which precludes a dispreferred response. Regardless of the agreement he made just seconds earlier, Romeo insists on his way, gets up from his chair and walks away from the argument. As Romeo walks away, Andrea agrees. Her extension of *Okay* displays her reluctance (line 41). Thus, she seeks Romeo's certainty in line 45 and again in line 47. Romeo's emphatic *Yeah* with a full repeat communicates his certainty. As a result, Andrea agrees to turn on the television (line 49). However, just 12 lines later, Romeo decides to turn off the television again. In line 60, Romeo begins the turn with a directive presumably toward Andrea (*Turn it –uh:: ba-*). As Andrea made a clear stance that she would not be pleased to turn on the television again, Romeo cuts himself off and restarts his turn, effectively replacing the directive with an announcement (*I'm gonna turn it off again*).

At the beginning of this excerpt, Romeo made a request for Andrea to turn on the television. In response, Andrea displayed her stance toward Romeo's request. He demonstrates understanding of Andrea's stance for the rest of the interaction in his ability to repeat exactly what she said (*You're not gonna turn it back on*) and his replacement of his directive toward her with an announcement. Thus, Romeo displays an awareness of Andrea's stance but persists even though the possible effect on his social image may be negative. In addition, he is unable to make a decision about whether he wants to watch television. He appears to be driven by his immediate desire to watch the television or not, and does not think, in the long term, of what he really wants to do. This is highlighted by his remark reporting knowledge of the agreement he had made earlier starting with *but ... now*, which indicates a shift in his desire; he wants the television to be turned on again. Romeo's behavior may also demonstrate a deficit in the appraisals related to coping potential as he is not conscious that he is socially failing. He stubbornly insists on his way, regardless of how Andrea might perceive him. This sequence may also reflect a deficit in Romeo's appraisal for what is pleasant or not, because in spite of Andrea's displayed annoyance and her attempts to withdraw from playing a part in his social failing (i.e. holding the newspaper to create a social barrier), Romeo unapologetically persists in his behavior and does not display an attempt to restrain himself. Perhaps the value of having a pleasant interactive experience is affected as well. Thus, it may be a combination of appraisal deficits in this interaction that accounts for Romeo's extraordinary behavior.

Stimulus appraisal and language pragmatics

The examples above may indicate how FTD affects one's social cognition as a result of an inability to appraise a social situation appropriately. In each of the examples, we can also see that the FTD patients' interlocutors are making known their disapproval of their behaviors through their gestures and pragmatics of their talk. The next turns of interlocutors following the responses of FTD patients are assessments often marked with exasperation and derision. Therefore, one can argue that perhaps FTD patients may also have difficulties assessing the pragmatics of their interlocutors. If this is so, then we would suspect that FTD patients in talk-in-interaction should also exhibit a loss in pragmatic sensitivity as result of their inability to appraise social situations appropriately and act accordingly.

Schumann (1999) has argued that the stimulus appraisal system may be relevant to 'language pragmatics, which involves decisions about what to say and how to say it in relation to an individual's own intentions and dispositions and his/her perceptions of the intentions and dispositions of others' (283) and maintain social relations with others (Fiske, 1991). As Schumann states:

> In normal social situations we make judgments about our inter-locutors' intentions, emotions, beliefs, and behaviors. We appraise these judgments according to their novelty (i.e. conformity or dis-crepancy with what is expected), pleasantness, and how they might challenge our ability to cope with this situation. In addition, we assess judgments about our interlocutor's state of mind and behav-ior according to whether they foster our goals and according to whether they are enhancing our self and social image. On the basis of these appraisals, we decide (consciously or unconsciously) to be polite or rude, aggressive or calm, direct or indirect, loud or quiet, clever or vague, truthful or untruthful, dominant or submis-sive, and we choose our phonology, prosody, grammar and lexicon accordingly.
>
> (Schumann, 1999: 294; 2010: 245)

He thus suggested that if the discourse of patients with frontal damage and FTD patients is analyzed, social interactions are likely to contain fre-quent pragmatic anomalies (Schumann, 1999: 304; see also Schumann, 2010). Indeed, Schumann initially found some support for his speculations from early researchers who studied the language pragmatics of prefrontal patients (Brickner, 1936). For example, one patient's 'inability to appraise a social situation on the dimension of self and social image resulted in offen-sive sexual braggadocio' (Schumann, 1999: 304). In addition, analyses of FTD patients, in talk-in-interaction, display pragmatic impairments, which may be due to a loss in ability to appraise social situations, leading to inappropriate behavior and pragmatics.

In this first example, the FTD patient is Kelly. She is in a hotel room with 'Maria', the director of the nursing home she stays at, and the two graduate researchers whom she has just met – Andrea and Lisa. This instance occurs prior to going out to dinner with Andrea and Lisa, thus she has known them for less than an hour. Kelly is sitting on a bed, while Andrea is sitting on the bed across from her. The other graduate researcher (Lisa) and Maria are sitting in chairs nearby. Here, Kelly has been telling them about her experiences of studying abroad in Germany. Then she shares two memories: one memory is the time she got lyme disease and the second is about how she got an abortion.

After Kelly tells her story of how she contracted lyme disease, she begins another narrative in such a way that projects multi-unit turns of talks. She also prefaces the story with the assessment as one that was *kinda weird* and then is on her way to explaining that she ended up getting an *abortion*, but cuts off before ending the turn to correct the course of events: She got

Extract 10 The other memory that was kinda weird
Kelly 13 March, 2007A

```
01 KEL    Well the other memory that was kinda weird is:::: I was
02        dating this guy(.8) and I ended up getting a- (.) pregnant
03        and I aborted.
04 AND    mhm
05 KEL    ↑Well I didn't know the stupid asshole was married (.) I
06        think what happened he (.2) worked in Frankfurt but then he
07        lived in [K(??) so he'd go home on the the weekend to be
08 AND             [((slowly nodding))
09 KEL    with his wi:fe.   ](.) And then I was his girlfriend in
10 AND    ((slowly nodding))]
11 KEL    Frankfurt(.5) and I didn't know the stupid idiot was
12        married.
13 AND    (.8) ((nodding))
14 KEL    >And I don't think I should ha:ve (.) been at any risk of
15        getting pregnant but I think I was in the hospital with lyme
16        disease I  think it screwed up the monthly hormone cycle.
17 AND    ↑huh [((nodding))                                          ]
18 KEL    [So.][Its just that my period was a couple days late and so
19        I aborted.
20 LIS    [°hm]
21 AND    Right.((nodding))
22 KEL    ↑I don't have too many guilt feelings for it because at that
23        point I was [still in the middle of my doctoral degree.]=
24 AND                [((nodding))]
25 AND    =Mhm.
26 KEL    And if I'd have the kid because that idiot was married I
27        would have to raise it by myself [so,]
28 AND                                     [((nodding))]
29 AND    =°True
30        (.6)
31 KEL    That's how I made that decision.=Oh here he comes.
32 AND    Who's he?
33 KEL    My husband.
```

pregnant and then aborted. When Kelly has concluded her turn, of the three other participants who have withheld their talk, only Andrea provides a continuer (*mhm*). Andrea's continuer demonstrates that she is listening to Kelly, and sustains Kelly's talk (Schegloff, 1982). In line 5, Kelly begins to qualify why she had an abortion, beginning with the man's character, describing him as a *stupid asshole* that was already *married*. She then tells them how she thinks he was able to succeed with his ploy (lines 5–8). In line 9, she reiterates that she did not know that he was married, perceiving herself as a victim not only of the man, but also of her circumstances – that contracting lyme disease *screwed* up her hormonal cycle, which increased her risk of getting pregnant (lines 10–12).

Other than the initial continuer provided by Andrea, before Kelly launched her extended sequence of turns, no other continuers or markers that sustain a teller's talk are provided by her interlocutors. In fact, throughout her telling from lines 5–12, there are pauses at the end of her turns in which her recipients could have encouraged Kelly to keep talking about her topic (lines, 5, 8 and 9). Mid-telling nods were visible from Andrea (lines 8, 10, 13, 17, 24, 28) which Kelly seems to have treated as adequate uptake during her telling (Stivers, 2008). However, they do not provide other continuers or expressions often produced by recipients to show their engagement, alignment and, in a sense, continue the interaction, such as 'really?', 'oh?' , 'my goodness', and questions such as 'he did?' (Heritage, 1984). As she concludes her explanation, the lack of her recipients' uptake at the end of any of the turn construction units she completes, emphasizes a problem in her talk. Particularly in line 8, after she has reiterated that she didn't know that the *stupid idiot was married,* her interlocutors do not provide a downgraded, a same evaluation, or an upgraded assessment of the man that would display a preferred agreement (Pomerantz, 1984). Instead, as Kelly concludes, Andrea provides a minimal response that simply acknowledges receipt of Kelly's story, while Lisa provides a weak response. Neither take a stance to align with Kelly. Thus, in line 14, after Kelly provides an account of how she knew she was pregnant, Andrea's assessment again acknowledges receipt of information and a confirmation of Kelly's explanation, but still does not take a stance. When Kelly further discusses why she made her decision in line 18 (she was in the middle of the doctoral degree and would have had to raise the kid by herself), Andrea again provides receipt and acceptance of the logic behind Kelly's decision, but still does not take a strong stance. Kelly's explanation shows that there is room for her past action to be considered wrong (*I have no guilt feelings for it*) and therefore may affect her interlocutors' perception of her. Thus, she attempted to qualify her decisions. Furthermore, though Andrea provided mid telling nods, not all nods are affiliative or show alignment. At possible story final, marked by the repetition of the relevant event (line 19), Andrea who has been producing nods, upgrades her response to a vocal response (line 21), but then downgrades to nodding (line 28), non-elaborated continuers (line 25), and quiet commentary (line 29), instead of fuller vocal affiliative responses, which are often found in final response position (Stivers, 2008). Nor did any of the other recipients initiate any further talk related to her telling when relevant (Jefferson, 1978).

In this interaction, Kelly tells this narrative to researchers she has just met. The frequent pauses during her telling, with or without minimal responses from her interlocutors, indicates that the content of her talk is problematic (Jefferson, 1978; Schegloff, 2007), which she acknowledges in line 18 and results in her explanation. The absence of her recipients' talk is dramatic. Thus, what she chose to say, and to whom she chose to say it to, was inappropriate. In this situation, because of the personal nature of the content of her talk, her inappropriate telling may be due to a problem in her appraisal of how what she said would affect her social image to the researchers she had just met.

In this next excerpt, which we have already seen in Chapter 6, Romeo's behavior may have been due to a deficit in appraising his goals and needs. Recall that Juliet has been talking about how she has been coping with her back pains and other difficulties in her life. She is visibly and audibly distraught as evidenced by her facial expressions and crying voice. As she

Extract 11 More Coffee
Romeo 12 December 2006 (*=crying)

```
01   JLT   I don't know how to run my life.
02         (2.0)
03   JLT   tch .h * sometimes I'm so overwhelmed I don't even know
04         (1.0) what I should do ne:xt. *
```

```
05   ROM   (8.0) ((clears throat))
```

```
06   ROM   °more coffee°
07         (4.2)
```

ends her turn in line 4, her gaze is directed toward Romeo, who is already looking at her, and thus identifies him as the next speaker. Romeo, however, turns away, gets up, and announces that he is going to get *more coffee*, which is in stark contrast to the graduate researcher who demonstrates participation and concern.

Although Romeo is selected as next speaker, which solicits his participation, Romeo's appraisal of his most immediate need is for *more coffee*, rather than to fulfill his social obligations, resulting in a pragmatic failure.

In this next example, we see how damage to the frontal areas may lead to deficits along the coping potential dimension and also how it may affect one's pragmatics. Kelly is supposed to take her medication once on Tuesday. For this nearly 37 minute segment, Kelly is in the hotel room with Andrea, Lisa, and Maria. Her husband Bron is bringing the luggage. A few turns prior, Kelly has asked, *Is today Tuesday?* to which she was given the answer. In fact, by this sequence, she has already asked and been given the answer to the same question twice. Now, Bron has returned to the room with some of the luggage, but will still need to get more. However, he is staying in the hotel room for a while.

In line 1, Kelly calls out to Bron for his attention. However, he has spoken at the same time with his announcement that he *has already brought something*, though his task is still incomplete (line 2). As soon as his turn is done, Kelly once again calls out to Bron while looking at what is presumably a paper with some guidelines for when to take her medication (line 4). Bron then responds to her summons (line 5), which acknowledges that he will be the recipient of her next turn. She then asks *Is today Tuesday?* Her question makes a response or answer relevant from Bron (Sacks *et al.*, 1974), but there is a .4 pause. Instead, Bron requests that he be allowed to take off his jacket. Having not received a response, Kelly pursues the second pair part and repeats her question, which has now made an answer from Bron 'accountably due' (Heritage, 1984). Bron, however, ignores her question and never provides the second pair part due and comments on the weather (line 10). Andrea, who is not the addressee, but a coparticipant, acknowledges the obligation for a response to Kelly's question and provides the answer (line 11). Kelly then immediately states that she has already taken her bedtime medication (line 12), which she had also reiterated just minutes before. However, Kelly has not yet taken her medication. Having heard Bron's assessment of the weather, Andrea aligns with him with the same evaluation (Pomerantz, 1984) (line 13). In the second turn unit, she asks Bron if he needs any help with the luggage, which he declines twice (lines 16 and 18), and then leaves the room once again. After Bron leaves, Andrea and Maria (the director) are discussing something relevant to Kelly when she once again asks *Is today Tuesday?* (line 25).

Extract 12A Is today Tuesday?
Kelly 13 March, 2007A


```
01 KEL    [Bron]
02 BRN    [So  ]I already brought something but I sti:ll need to go
03        over there.
04 KEL    Hey Bron? ((Looking at prescription paper?))
05 BRN    Yes.
06 KEL    Is today Tuesday?
07        (.4)
08 BRN    But if you allow me I would like to take off my jacket.
09 KEL    Bron, is today Tuesday?
10 BRN    It's [ve:::ry hot.
11 AND         [It is Tuesday.
12 KEL    Oh I've already taken my bedtime medication.
13 AND    It is very hot. Do you need help downstairs bringing stuff
14        up?
15 MAR    [Oh I'll
16 BRN    [Oh no no no no I already have it
17 AND    Are you sure?
18 BRN    And it's not very far.
```


Extract 12B Is today Tuesday?
Kelly 13 March, 2007A


```
19 AND    Uh::::::::::::: Yeah, she has all three of them [so::
20 MAR                                                   [oh:::
21 AND    So enjoy fi(hhh)guring that out h h.
22 MAR    Which one?
23 AND    We can just- we can just stick it on the door and see
24        which one doesn't work.
                  ---------------
                         |
          22:56 — 23:04 omitted
          (Indistinct talk)
                         |
                  ---------------
25 KEL    Is today Tuesday?
26 LIS    Yes.
27 KEL    Oh God I have taken my bedtime medication already.
28        (1.0)
29 KEL    That's crazy.
30 LIS    h Yeah it's only four forty-five↑
31 KEL    Well, it says here at eight forty-five on it. Today is
32        Tuesday?←
33 LIS    Yes.
34 KEL    Yeah, says I do it at eight forty five.
35        (.2)
36 LIS    huh↑.
37 KEL    Well that's [crazy.
38 LIS                [Three hours early. hhh
39 KEL    How did I screw that one [up?
40 LIS                             [hhh
41 KEL    Today's Tuesday?
42 LIS    It is Tuesday.
```

This time, Kelly's question, *Is today Tuesday?*, is answered by Lisa. Kelly then responds with the same formulaic response, that she has already taken her medication. She then adds an assessment (line 29: *that's crazy*). Lisa confirms Kelly's assessment by providing a reason *why* it is crazy (line 30: *it's only 4:45*) and that she is supposed to take her medication at 8:45 (line 31). In doing so, she has brought the discrepancy between reality and Kelly's claim that she has already taken her medication to Kelly's attention. Kelly then looks at the paper and states that she should take her medicine at 8:45 on Tuesday. Thus, she again requests a confirmation that *Today is Tuesday?* (lines 31–32), which Lisa emphatically provides. Kelly is then confused by the discrepancy as she again looks at what is written on the paper. She wonders why she has already taken her medication when she is supposed to take it at 8:45. Lisa, however, does not to try to help clarify Kelly's mistake to her, but rather after Kelly makes another assessment of what is happening (*well that's crazy*), and just states that she if she has taken the medication already then she has done so a few hours early. Kelly then asks a rhetorical question (*how did I screw that one up?),* and then again asks, *Today's Tuesday?* followed by Lisa's confirmation. Though Kelly is still confused, Lisa assures Kelly that she's *good for today* (line 44).

In this sequence, Kelly's constant request for the day of the week is responded to in different ways. Bron, her husband, ignores her despite the fact that she pursues a second pair part. Andrea and Lisa, on the other hand, both reply. Though her husband ignores her, she does not shows signs of annoyance for being ignored or view Bron's behavior as a signal that her question is not appropriate. Andrea and Lisa, however, at multiple times, treat her question as suitable. Though her repetition of the question to Bron may have been legitimate, as her question demands a response, her reiterations of the same question to Andrea and Lisa are not. Her pragmatic failure is even more noticeable given that within the 37 minute long interaction, Kelly asks the question 22 times. At one point, Kelly holds Bron's arm and asks the question; in response, Bron visibly brushes off her hand, and she still persists in asking the question. Kelly's behavior seems to demonstrate an ignorance of the social cues given by others, and despite having the sense that something is not quite right, she persists. Her dementia may have affected her ability to appraise the social cues as negative, resulting in a mis-assessment of her coping potential. In addition, it appears that she is unaware of how the social cues contribute to her negative social image. In fact, her self-image remains seemingly unaffected. Her feelings are not hurt, despite being ignored by Bron. In addition, she is not concerned with how she may appear to her interlocutors as one who has taken her medication much earlier than recommended.

Extract 13 Saying Grace
(*=crying voice)

```
01   JLT   Prayer. ((Romeo puts spoon down and leans back))
02         (3.0)
03   J/R   In the name of the Father, and of the Son, and the Holy
04         Spirit, Amen. ((Romeo moves forward and starts to eat his
05         cereal while continuing to say the blessing)). Bless us oh
06         Lord with these thy gifts we are about to receive from thy
07         bounty through Christ our Lord Amen. ((Romeo continues to
08         eat)).
09   JLT   *We give thanks for this day and ask oh Lord help me with
10         (2.0) what to do:. (.8 )Give him everything. Amen.
11   ROM   Amen.
```

In extract 13, we see Romeo being driven by his immediate wants rather than following the proper courses of action before eating.

As Romeo and Juliet sit to eat breakfast, he picks up his spoon and is about to start eating his cereal. However, Juliet reminds him of the proper course of events – saying grace before eating (line 1). Romeo acknowledges this and puts the spoon down and leans back. Together they begin to say their meal prayer. As soon as they come to the end of the turn construction unit signaled with an 'Amen', Romeo starts to eat his cereal while continuing to say the blessing with Juliet (lines 4–8). When they have come to another signal of the end of the prayer, Juliet continues to pray. Her voice, however, has an audibly crying tone as she asks the Lord for *help* on what to do, and pleads for Romeo as well. During this emotional moment, Romeo has continued to eat. When she concludes her prayer, Romeo echoes her 'Amen.'

Though Romeo is able to successfully say 'grace', when and how he is supposed to say grace is precluded by his wanting to eat. Even if he starts to say 'grace' appropriately, at the first sign of its completion (line 4: *Amen*), Romeo immediately starts to eat. Although he still is able to go through the prayer, he does so in an inappropriate manner. It is perhaps because the appraisal of his immediate goals/need to eat is more important than acting as a conscientious member of society.

Other recent analyses of patients with frontotemporal dementia (FTD), typically demonstrate a loss in pragmatic sensitivity (Mates *et al.*, 2010). Smith (2010) reported observing an FTD patient in a store call a stranger 'a little munchkin', and then proceed to speak to him and touch him. The same patient apparently also approaches strangers in the street and engages them in conversation. Fiske (2010) also reports an FTD patient who flew to his brother's to visit his dying father. Upon arrival, however, the patient 'flopped down and turned the TV on without asking about their father or going to see him' (210). In another interaction, when an ethnographer, who had not visited the FTD patient (Romeo) in months, knocked on the door of Romeo's home, he simply 'opened the door, paused, said "Hi" – and then walked away to watch TV' (Fiske, 2010: 207). The ethnographer noted, 'He asked no questions of me. He followed up no questions with extensions' (Gervais, August 9, 2007: field notes). In Chapter 8, I illustrated a situation when Romeo was selected as next speaker by his emotionally distraught wife through a gaze, but did not respond, and actually stood up and walked away, resulting in a noticeable pragmatic failure. I also described an instance in which Romeo's wife was making an emotionally charged complaint while driving, and in the middle of her talk he interrupts and requests the ethnographer to play something on the tape player. Another ethnographer had also noticed that interaction with Romeo was 'odd' due to his 'lack of initiation', 'lack of extending talk' (Mates, November 20, 2006: field notes), and 'relatively unsatisfactory and short answers' (Mates, August 22, 2007: field notes). Romeo's discourse is particularly striking as his wife described him as chatty and engaged prior to FTD. Mikesell (2010) also shows that though a patient may reply to a question, they do so in a way that fails to 'respond to the conversational demands for a more elaborated personal reply' (206). As Fiske (2010) notes: 'In short, the [FTD] patients do not hold up their end of the conversations, leaving their interlocutors to do all the conversation "work"' (208). Though research also demonstrates that frontotemporal dementia patients have preserved many of their pragmatic abilities (Joaquin, 2010a, in prep; Mikesell, 2010), research has also shown that one characterization of FTD is a loss in pragmatic sensitivity. They have a diminished sensitivity on what to say and what not to say, when to say something, how to say something, and to whom.

Furthermore, because of the central role of this appraisal system in modulating interactive behavior, we can also speculate that if any part of this system is damaged one's interactional tendencies may also be affected and compromised. In these cases, patients will no longer find it rewarding to maintain social relationships. Recall that the appraisal regions are also involved in the integration of reward (a positive feeling generated by affiliative stimuli) with context leading to the formation of affiliative memories (see Chapter 4) which motivate and determine future courses of action and lead to the maintenance of interaction. This may be why in some cases, damage to the amygdala and/or the prefrontal areas may lead to a lack of communication, which may be interpreted as an inability or lack of desire to communicate. This is perhaps most striking in FTD patients who display mutism in later stages. Thus, FTD patients may have deficits in the ability to appraise their actions and their talk-in-interaction as pleasurable. In other words, they might lose the pleasure of affiliating with another. Fiske (2010) also suggests that FTD affects social emotions, including affiliative emotions and consummatory emotions, or those emotions that motivate people in seeking to form relationships, and those that are rewards for forming and sustaining relationships.

In addition, the examples, illustrations, and anecdotes in this and the preceding chapter have shown that FTD seemingly affects a patient's desire to initiate interaction, the ability to perceive and understand emotions, and the ability to understand dialogic practices and communicative cues, which I have argued to be behavioral manifestations of the interactional instinct. Thus, damage to these regions in the brain seems to affect our ability to do what is needed to form and maintain social relationships, which we have acquired through our extensive period of socialization.

10 Challenges to the Theory and Conclusion

In this book, I have suggested that languages are acquired as a result of: 1. children's motivation to attune to, seek out, and attend to others; 2. their abilities for frequency and pattern detection; 3. opportunity provided by society for socialization and exposure to a shared language; and 4. a biology that subserves children's interactional proclivities and caregivers' socialization practices. Such a perspective gives a sociocultural view of how languages are acquired. Central to this proposal is an innate motivation in children to entrain to caregivers. In this chapter, I discuss potential challenges to the perspective, including autism and the sociality of other animals.

Understanding the interactional instinct through autism

Autism spectrum disorders (ASD)[1] affect approximately 1 in 110 children in the US ('Autism Spectrum Disorders,' 2010).[2] It is defined by the onset of three core disturbances before the age of three: atypical social behavior, disrupted verbal and non-verbal communication, and unusual patterns of highly restricted interests and repetitive behaviors. Specifically, individuals with ASD display abnormal reciprocal social interactions including lack of eye contact, joint attention, and empathy. They also display perseverative behaviors and other behaviors such as hand-flapping, and toe-walking. In addition, children with ASD also have language deficits. In fact, current estimates show that up to 50% of individuals with autism will never develop useful speech (Pickett *et al.*, 2009). Other deficits include lack of reward from social contact, and dysfunction in the ability to form social attachments (Baird *et al.*, 2003). Additional symptoms of autism involve deficits in imitative behaviors and in the ability to read emotions in others through facial and vocal cues. Thus, the manifestations of autism have implications for what we have called the interactional instinct. Given the claim that the interactional instinct is a powerful developmental precursor to language acquisition, if the instinct is impaired, how then do some autistic children acquire language? In this section, I address the implications of autism for the interactional instinct and suggest that an understanding of autism may provide insight into the powerful underlying emotional motivation that drives enculturation and thus, language acquisition.

Oxytocin and vasopressin in autistics

Although the exact causes of autism are still unknown (Tager-Flusberg and Joseph, 2003; Geschwind and Levitt, 2007), researchers are taking important steps toward understanding some of the biological processes connected with the ASD. As mentioned earlier in Chapter 4, the neuropeptides (oxytocin and vasopressin) appear to be connected to the rewarding nature of social interactions and have been implicated in social attachment and social recognition. Because of their role in social cognition, researchers have examined the effects of such neuropeptides on ASD symptoms. In one recent study (Andari *et al.*, 2010), researchers investigated the effects of oxytocin in 13 children with Asperger's Syndrome. In the first part of the study, the social behavior of patients while interacting with three other people during a ball tossing game was observed. One player always returned the ball to the patient, another did not return the ball, and the third returned the ball to the patient and to other players. Each time the patient received the ball he/she also won money. Under a placebo, the patients returned the ball indiscriminately to his/her partners. However, patients treated with oxytocin were able to discriminate between the different players and tossed the ball to the cooperative player. Thus, patients exhibited 'stronger interactions with the most socially cooperative partner and had enhanced feeling of trust and preference' (4389). In the second part of the study, patients were then asked to look at photographs of faces. Under a placebo, patients typically looked at the mouth or away from the stimuli. However, patients treated with oxytocin, 'selectively increased patients' gazing time on the socially informative region of the face, namely the eyes' (4389).

In another study (Guastella *et al.*, 2010), adolescents with ASD were administered a single dose of oxytocin via a nasal spray, and then a placebo a week after. After each administration, participants were asked to complete a facial expression recognition task that measures emotional recognition. The results showed that participants improved when they received the oxytocin spray.

The role of oxytocin in autism has also been explored by comparing the level of oxytocin in the blood of 30 typically developing children and 29 autistic children. The study showed that autistic children had significantly less oxytocin in their blood (Modahl *et al.*, 1998). Furthermore, the study showed that oxytocin levels increased with age in the normal children but not in the autistic children. Other studies created knock-out mice that lacked oxytocin (OTKO) (Ferguson, 2001, 2000). The mice in these studies behaved normally, except that they could not recognize other mice even after repeated social exposure. They also could not recognize their mother's scent, even though their sense of smell was normal. However, when a single dose of oxytocin was injected into the brain prior to interaction, the mice were cured. Other studies have shown that injecting a synthetic form of oxytocin (pitocin) into the blood-stream of adults with autism rapidly and significantly reduces repetitive behaviors (Hollander *et al.*, 2003). At the Seaver and New York Autism Center of Excellence, Hollander and colleagues have also looked at the effects of oxytocin on the ability of autistics to read affective cues in speech (i.e. anger, sadness, and happiness) (Hollander and Bartz, 2006). The study found that participants injected with pitocin demonstrated an improvement in their ability to retain and assign affective significance to speech even after two weeks passed, whereas the controls who were given placebo injections, did not show the same ability.

Vasopressin, another social behavior modulator, is reported to stimulate social communication in birds, frogs, and hamsters (Young, 1999), as well as to increase affiliative and paternal behaviors in voles (Young *et al.*, 1999). Studies of vasopressin in mice with a mutation in a vasopressin gene (V1aR) reveal that they lack the ability to recognize familiar conspecifics despite repeated exposures (Bielsky *et al.*, 2004). In humans, one experiment examined the effects of vasopressin when intranasally administered to adult autistics (Thompson *et al.*, 2004). The experiment reported that vasopressin enhanced responses toward emotionally expressive facial expressions. Though research explaining the possibility of defective oxytocin and vasopressin systems in autistics is still inconclusive, from these studies it seems plausible to suggest that impairments in these systems may impair the interactional instinct.

Mirror neurons in autistics

Research also suggests that a dysfunction in the mirror neuron system may have a role in impeding observation and imitation. Recall from Chapter 7 that the observation of an action made by a human blocks the mu rhythm of observers (Cochin *et al.*, 1998). In one study, mu wave suppression was examined in ten high functioning individuals with autism and ten controls while watching a video of a moving hand or the movement of their own hand (Oberman *et al.*, 2005). Control subjects showed significant mu suppression when observing both their own hand movements and the movements of others. However, the autistics showed significant mu suppression to self-performed hand movements, but not to observed hand movements. The researchers concluded that their study was evidence for a dysfunctional mirror neuron system in high-functioning autistics. Other studies have implicated a dysfunctional mirror neuron system for an autistic's inability to perceive emotions. In one study (Dapretto *et al.*, 2006), 10 high functioning autistics and 10 typically developing children underwent fMRI while imitating and observing 80 photos of emotional expressions such as anger, fear, happiness, or sadness. Both groups showed activations in the fusiform gyrus and the amygdala, which are areas associated with face processing. Thus, both groups seem to have been attending to the face stimuli. But the study also revealed that the autistics have virtually no activity in the pars opercularis of the inferior frontal gyrus, a central part of the mirror neuron system. Furthermore, the high functioning autistics showed reduced activity in the insula and limbic structures – areas associated with emotion understanding (Carr *et al.*, 2003), providing a possible explanation for why autistics generally show an inability to perceive emotions. In another study, cortical thickness in 14 high functioning ASD adults and a group of controls was examined (Hadjikhani *et al.*, 2005). The results showed that several areas central to the mirror neuron system, including the pars opercularis, IPL (inferior parietal lobule), and STS (superior temporal sulcus), were significantly thinner in autistics. The study also showed that severity of cortical thinning in the areas of the mirror neuron system correlated with the severity of ASD symptoms.

There is also some evidence that an impaired mirror neuron system may be related to the imitative deficits that also characterize autistics. Using fMRI and an experimental design to determine the neural substrate for imitation, Williams *et al.* (2006) compared activity in the mirror neuron network in 16 males with ASD to a control group. They found that activity in areas associated with mirror neurons was less extensive in autistics. In addition, McIntosh *et al.* (2006), through electromyography (EMG) readings, found that autistics appear to have an inability to 'automatically' mimic emotional faces, though the same subjects also demonstrated an ability to voluntarily imitate emotional expressions. They suggest that perhaps the deficit is due to a dysfunctional mirror neuron system. Therefore, as the instinct to attune to others is biologically subserved, dysfunctions in these systems may constrain the behavioral manifestations of the instinct including imitation and emotional perception and expression.

Language learning and use in autistics

Clearly, some autistics develop language. If the interactional instinct is obstructed by dysfunctions in its biological systems, and therefore impedes the social interaction that is necessary to acquire language, then how and why do some autistics acquire language? First, abilities that may contribute to language learning of some autistics may manifest differently in typically developing individuals. Gernsbacher *et al.* (2008a, b) argue that autistics have deficits in motor skills that may account for a lower frequency of behaviors that are considered to be overt manifestations of joint attention. In fact, they argue that 'autistics do initiate joint attention, perhaps even as frequently as their nonautistic peers, but they do so in unconventional ways' (Gernsbacher *et al.* 2008a: 42). In addition, they note that autistics also exhibit more covert attention and can analyze and retain what they see within a shorter span of time than typically developing individuals (Casey *et al.*, 1993; Greenaway and Plaisted, 2005). Some autistics may have heightened abilities to learn language via overhearing.

Second, the language and social competence of autistics is often based on clinical diagnostic descriptors and not on their performance in real social contexts. Looking at language use in genuine social contexts reveals that individuals with ASD demonstrate some interactional proclivities and competencies. In 2000, the DSM IV-TR Diagnostic Criteria for autistic disorder included that autistics display a 'marked impairment in the ability to initiate or sustain a conversation with others' ('DSM-IV-TR Diagnostic Criteria,' 2000: 75). Certainly, research has shown that autistics have deficits in communicative competence; however, using theoretical frameworks of interactional sociology, ethnomethodology, and conversation analysis, high functioning autistics are found to be quite skillful (Dobbinson *et al.*, 1998; Ochs *et al.*, 2004). For example, the system of turn-taking in conversation is a complex activity that involves participants' mutual monitoring to recognize when a turn change is relevant. Competent conversational partners are expected to evaluate whether a 'turn constructional unit' could be coming to possible completion, when the current speaker is projecting to continue with yet another turn constructional unit (TCU), or when another speaker's turn could begin (Sacks *et al.*, 1974). Monitoring the speaker's TCU allows for the interlocutor to take the next turn without hesitation. Ethnographic studies have shown that the understanding of this basic interpersonal organization does in fact appear to be 'within the grasp of persons with autistic spectrum disorders' and they 'displayed few difficulties taking their turns at talk at expected transition relevant places' (Ochs *et al.*, 2004: 160). In fact, autistics were found to be so skilled in projecting the end of their interlocutor's turn that they latched at the end of one turn and even overlapped during the beat prior to the end of an interlocutor's turn with a preferred second pair part.

Using conversation analysis, Stribling *et al.* (2007) examined an autistic girl, Helen, and her use of repetition, which is a general characteristic of the language of persons with ASD. Though repetition is often viewed as meaningless and inappropriate, examining its use within its sequential contexts suggests that repetition constitutes an adaptation to interacting with a limited lexicon. In particular, two forms of repeats frequently occurred – *Prior turn repeats* and *Within-turn repeats*. Prior turn repeats were often deployed when the interlocutor specifically addressed Helen, making a response from her relevant. Her repetition was used to demonstrate that she had heard and was orienting to that prior turn. With respect to the use of Within-turn repeats, or repeats of the first item within Helen's own prior talk, the repeats were bound to non-vocal activities, such as handing an object to a co-participant; the repetitions ceased when the object reached its recipient. Thus, using conversation analysis, ASD patients may be more interactionally competent language users and co-participants than often assumed.

Pollock *et al.* (2008) have also studied 11 severely autistic children in naturally occurring interactions at home and school. Their data showed that even severely autistic children were capable of interacting skillfully with others, given that there was relevant shared knowledge between the autistic child and their interlocutors. They were able to initiate requests despite profound difficulties with speech and language. Studies have also shown that ASD patients recognize communicative breakdowns and as a result employ repair strategies such as clarification requests. Furthermore, in a study in which episodes of communicative breakdowns with individuals with ASD and normals were engineered by researchers, results showed that although the participants with ASD were more likely to respond with an inappropriate response, they were also similar to normals in the use of repair strategies (Volden, 2004).

The emphasis on the deficits of ASD patients may also be averting attention from other displays of communicative competence. For example, in one study (Stone *et al.*, 1997) designed to elicit requesting and commenting behavior from 14 autistics and children with developmental delays and/or language impairments (DD/LI), autistics were more likely to issue requests and comment on interesting situations (i.e. a slinky dropping from the ceiling, the accidental spilling of a cup of juice, etc.) less than controls. Autistic children were also less likely to point, show objects, or use eye gaze to communicate. However, autistics were more likely to directly manipulate the researcher's hand. In addition, autistic children also used less complex combinations of behaviors to communicate. Though this study emphasized the deficits in comparison to other children with developmental delays, the study also shows that autistics have interactional competencies.

How might we interpret such research on autistics? More generally, the research shows that autism is in extremely heterogeneous affliction; it has many etiologies and its core features are variable. For example, mental retardation is a core feature, and yet current data suggests that less than 50% of all individuals with autism have significant cognitive impairments (Chakrabarti and Fombonne, 2005; Geschwind and Levitt, 2007). Social impairments also vary – 'some individuals with ASD display an aloof style of social interaction, whereas others seek personal interactions, albeit in a socially odd manner' (Geschwind and Levitt, 2007: 103). There are also major differences in developmental courses – some children manifest signs from early infancy while others show signs in the second or third year of life. With regard to language, some autistics acquire language and others do not. Typically, if a child does not develop useful speech by the age of 5, it is highly improbable that they will. However, there are studies that do report a small minority of children with ASD that develop speech after the age of 5. Some children even begin to communicate at the age of 10 or older (Pickett *et al.*, 2009). Language skills are one of the most strikingly variable characteristics of children and adults with autism. By later preschool and early school age, some children with autism are highly fluent with a large vocabulary and complex grammar, while others have no real meaningful production of words and minimal language comprehension. Moreover, many fall in between (Thurm *et al.*, 2007). The reality is 'little is known about the specific relationship between etiologies, mechanisms, and the resulting phenotypes', such that some researchers have suggested that it might be constructive to think of ASD as 'the autisms' (Geschwind and Levitt, 2007).

Thus, because of this heterogeneity, the relevance of the syndrome to the interactional instinct can only be worked out on a case-by-case basis. In order to use autism as either support or counterevidence for the interactional instinct, one would have to know the etiology of the disease (i.e. age of onset and the child's linguistic ability prior to onset). Additionally, one would want to know the child's attachment profile (i.e. his/her performance on tests of attachment (e.g. The Strange Situation), his/her ability to hypothesize about the intentions and dispositions of others (e.g. Theory of Minds tests), his/her current ability to communicate, and as research increasingly explores autism as a neurodevelopmental syndrome, one has to understand the developmental processes of each individual, such as neurogenesis, neuronal migration, axon pathfinding, synaptogenesis, and so on (Geschwind and Levitt, 2007; Lee *et al.*, 2009).

Manifestations of the interactional instinct in nonhuman primates

From the preceding chapters on infant behavior, I have argued that human beings are born to seek out social engagement. However, sociality is obviously not distinct to human beings. Studies comparing the behaviors of adult non-human primates with humans have shown similarities in face-to-face inter-action behavior. Adult chimpanzees have been observed to take turns in communication (de Waal, 1989), to communicate with gestures (Gardner and Gardner, 1989), to use natural and artificial sign systems, and to follow the gaze and other interactional behaviors of conspecifics (Savage-Rumbaugh *et al.*, 1978; Tomasello *et al.*, 1998). The social behaviors of adult nonhuman primates make it seem even more logical to assume that they may have simi-lar neonate behavior, and perhaps an interactional instinct that manifests itself similarly.

It seems that nonhuman primates parallel human development in signifi-cant ways. In fact, Bard (1998) reports that at least newborn chimpanzees exhibit the same kind of 'helplessness' and dependency on the mother as human newborns. Both are unable to support their own weight by clinging (Bard, 1995; Plooij, 1984); and both are unable to survive without active cradling and nurturing (Bard, 1994; van de Rijt-Plooij and Plooij, 1987). Like human neonates, neonatal chimpanzees also have a capacity for sustained attention to visual and auditory stimuli and have been found to respond sig-nificantly more to social stimuli than nonsocial stimuli throughout their neo-natal period (Bard, 1992).

With regard to their communicative abilities, infant nonhuman primates exhibit a repertoire of communicative tools within the first days of life. Neonate chimpanzees have been reported to show emotional expressions in appropriate interactional contexts. Infant chimpanzees smile, fuss, show distress, and cry. They also greet, make a scream face without vocalization, vocalize effort grunts, pout, show anger, tongue click, and laugh when tick-led and when playing games (Bard, 1998, 2003). In addition, infant gorillas seem to initiate interaction; they have been observed to encourage an other-wise non-engaged mother to share food, play, or follow them (Maestripieri *et al.*, 2002). Neonate chimpanzees also imitate facial gestures of tongue protrusion, mouth opening, and lip pursing as early as 1-week-old (Myowa, 1996; Myowa-Yamakoshi *et al.*, 2004). In addition, as I have mentioned, cot-ton-top tamarin monkeys seem to have pattern finding skills as well as mirror neurons (Ramus *et al.*, 2000; Rizzolatti and Craighero, 2004; Bard, 2007). Indeed, research indicates that human beings may not be alone in their abil-ity for cultural learning (Kawamura, 1959). There are, however, findings that seem to suggest that early human dyadic interaction is qualitatively different from early nonhuman dyadic interaction. First, human beings are dependent on caregivers for a much longer period of time than nonhuman primates. Also, some communicative interactions, such as play dialogue with adults, which is found in human 3-month-olds, have not been reported in nonhuman primates. In interaction, other social animals imitate far less than humans. Furthermore, nonhuman primate mothers seem to interact with their infants qualitatively differently than humans. For example, though neonatal chimpanzees have been found to engage in mutual eye gaze with their mothers, the mothers appear to encourage quick glances by the infant instead of prolonging mutual gaze transactions (van de Rijt-Plooij and Plooij, 1987; Bard, 1994). Western lowland gorilla mothers also seem to show little encouragement to their infants (Maestripieri *et al.*, 2002). Furthermore, though neonatal chimpanzees show an interest in imitating others just as human infants do, by 12 weeks after birth, infant chimpanzees seem to lose interest in doing so. This was the same course found in subsequent studies with chimpanzees (Bard, 2007). Similarly, Ferrari *et al.* (2006) demonstrated the same ability to imitate in neonate rhesus monkeys. However, the urge to imitate faded by day seven. Rhesus monkeys are also reported to mutually gaze and lipsmack, which resembles human mother-infant interactions, but such interactions significantly decrease after the first month of life (Ferrari *et al.*, 2009). Thus, primates may demonstrate early attempts for the interactional activity, but no longer seem interested after a few weeks, while the interest develops and intensifies in human children (Jones, 2007; Hrdy, 2009).

However, because of the lack of studies to date of infant nonhuman primates in comparison to the numerous studies of humans, the uniqueness of neonatal behaviors in both human and nonhuman species has yet to be established. Such striking similarities in early infant primate behavior and abilities could be viewed as a challenge to the notions of unique human propensities and the interactional instinct as a significant developmental precursor that guarantees the acquisition of language for all typically developing children – an adaptation that sets human beings apart from other species.

Tomasello (1999) has argued that it is the human's ability to understand other humans as intentional beings like themselves that ultimately separates humans from nonhuman primates. He also suggests that human infants are not just social like other primates, but emphasizes that they are 'ultra-social' (59). Unlike chimpanzees and other apes, humans are naturally eager to collaborate with others, to engage others, even strangers, and to read and share the feelings and concerns of others. Such proclivities ultimately set us apart from nonhuman primates.

Greenfield (2006) suggests another perspective based on the theoretical and evolutionary connections between ontogeny and phylogeny:

> First, earlier stages of development are more universal within a species than are later stages of development. Second, earlier stages of development are more similar among phylogenetically-related species than are later stages in development. In other words, as

> phylogenetic divergence progresses, the evolutionarily later devel-
> opments are more likely to occur later than earlier in ontogenetic
> sequence. In that way phylogenetic changes interfere less with
> subsequent ontogenetic developments that may have depended on
> something that has disappeared through evolutionary modification.
> Note that this formulation is contrary to the evolutionary myth that
> adult chimpanzees resemble human children. The notion is simply
> that human and chimpanzee babies will be more alike than human
> and chimpanzee adults ... Third, characteristics among groups that
> are phylogenetically-related indicates that characteristic was likely
> a part of the common ancestor of those species.
>
> (Greenfield, 2006: 504)

Thus, because they are phylogenetically-related, humans and chimpanzees may, at the earlier stages, display similar characteristics that exhibit an innate drive for interaction and pattern finding abilities. This drive is part of the foundation of both species. The studies of chimpanzee imitation and observation, key components to primate cultural learning (Greenfield *et al.*, 2000) and the interactional instinct, suggest that these processes go back to the origins of humans and chimpanzees as well. However, as humans and primates diverged, the accumulation of ontogenetic changes within humans eventually led to a disparity in abilities that support language. This is supported by Greenfield (1991), who argued that early in the ontogeny of humans the neural mechanisms for language (including Broca's area) are not so distinct from the mechanisms underlying tool use and object combination, but with maturation and increased complexity of language and object combination abilities, each eventually generates its own specialized circuitry.

Therefore, to the challenge raised by cross-species comparisons of the behavioral manifestations and underlying mechanisms, I make two points. First, the interactional instinct is phylogenetically and ontogenetically basic in both humans and nonhuman primates. Thus, it is not surprising that characteristics that show readiness for interaction are seen in both humans and nonhuman primates. Second, the innate readiness and drive for interaction is only argued to be necessary, but not completely sufficient for the development and transmission of language. Perhaps the ways in which humans are 'ultra-social' compared to nonhuman primates may provide the clues to the points of divergence between species. The position taken here is that all social animals have an interactional instinct commensurate with their socialization needs, but because humans have such prolonged infancy, childhood, juvenility, and adolescence, their socialization demands are extended. For this reason, the interactional instinct may be much stronger and more elaborated than in other animals, even closely related primates (Lee *et al.*, 2009).

Conclusion

In this book, I have discussed the different cultural practices and ideologies related to how a child is taught and learns the normative ways of being in his/her culture. Chapter 2 proposed these practices to be eavesdropping, observation, participation, imitation, and language socialization. Though a culture may seem to have an exclusive belief in one ideology, research often shows that the practices are not mutually exclusive. Children in Western societies, known for explicit teaching, must also learn a great deal implicitly. Likewise, traditional societies in which the burden of acquiring their culture is often placed on the child, caregivers often reward, punish, and at times prompt children toward normative behavior. With respect to Vygotsky's sociocultural theory, I have attempted to explore, given these varying contexts, how language is acquired via the cultural practices involved in socialization and enculturation, and the biology that subserves these processes. What emerges is a picture of an elegant dance between biology and culture.

At the core of the argument proposed in this book, which is proposed by Lee *et al.* (2009), and further developed in Chapter 3, is the claim that children are born with an interactional instinct which drives them to seek interaction with conspecifics. This instinct is supported by a typically developing infant's endowed abilities that facilitate interaction with conspecifics. Children are born with sufficiently developed sensory systems that allow them to see, hear, smell, and touch social stimuli. They have a repertoire of facial expressions and gestures, and they have the ability to attend and attune to social stimuli in the environment. These abilities provide a newborn with communicative equipment and behaviors that are powerful enough to elicit and engage in interactions with caregivers. Therefore, very young infants appear to have an underlying motivation to engage in interactional activity, show agency in the initiation of interactional activity, communicate pleasure and distress when desired interaction occurs or fails, have a bias for interaction with conspecifics, understand the interactional import of communicative and social cues, and more generally are attuned to adults' responses and actions. Such behaviors, I suggest, are manifestations of the interactional instinct, which provides the motivation to attend to, seek out, imitate, and engage in interaction with conspecifics.

In Chapters 4 and 5, I discussed what might support the interactional instinct. I discussed the role of endogenous opiates and neuropeptides (e.g. oxytocin, vasopressin, and dopamine), which make interaction with caregivers inherently rewarding and entrain a child's attentional mechanisms on caregivers and serves as a hardwired motivational mechanism. Neuropeptides are also a part of a system that appraises and marks interactions and the contexts in which they occur as pleasurable or not. Thus, as the child grows, the rewarding aspect of the attachment bond becomes part of the child's memory, which leads to the approach and development of affiliative bonds with caregivers and ensures socialization and language acquisition. A similar biology guides the behaviors of caregivers, who, through motherese and infant directed speech, serve to facilitate and increase affiliation and attachment between the infant and caregiver. Furthermore, such behaviors assist in the acquisition of cultural information – including language and everyday actions.

In addition to simplified speech from caregivers, infants have brains that assess statistical properties of input from the environment. In Chapter 6, I examined how infants are able to extract the grammar of the language which itself has been molded by cultural evolution to fit their brains. The research on discriminating abilities, frequency effects, and priming suggests that aspects of language are not inaccessible to children and that very early in life we have abilities suitable for learning language in a variety of ways and sociocultural contexts. Chapter 7 explored how mirror neurons may be part of the system underlying these skills. The prefrontal cortex, which subserves the processes of socialization, enculturation, and education, guides the acquisition of pragmatics for the appropriate social use of language, and this brain region remains available for adaptation to social variation well into adulthood. What the interactional instinct provides is the motivation to engage in interaction, attend to the language, and learn how it is used in the course of routine everyday interactions. The picture that emerges indicates that biology is nature and culture is nurture, but there is no nurture without nature, and it is nurture that provides for the phylogenetic development of our biological nature. The ontogenesis of language behavior (i.e. its acquisition) cannot occur without its evolved biology or without its evolved cultural practices for socialization.

Notes

1.   Autism spectrum disorders (ASD) include autism (autistic disorder), Asperger's Syndrome, and Pervasive Developmental Disorder not otherwise specified (PPD-NOS or Atypical Autism).
2.   Though researchers often explicitly distinguish between different types of autism, other researchers do not and may simply refer to the participants as autistic. I have noted when such distinctions are made.

Appendix A: Transcription conventions

Adapted from Sacks *et al.* (1974)

[ ]	Square brackets between lines or bracketing two lines of talk indicate the beginning ([) and end (]) of overlapping talk.
(.4)	Numbers in parentheses represent silence measured to the nearest tenth of a second.
(.)	A dot enclosed in parentheses indicates a short, untimed silence (sometimes called a micropause), generally less than two- or three-tenths of a second.
End of line= =Start of line	Latching symbols. When attached to the end of one line and the beginning of another, they indicate that the later talk was 'latched onto' the earlier talk with no hesitation, perhaps without even waiting the normal conversational rhythm or 'beat.'
> <	The combination of more than and less than symbols indicates that the talk between them is compressed or rushed.
< >	The combination of the less than and more than symbols indicate that a stretch of talk is markedly slowed or drawn out.
<	The less than symbol by itself indicates that the immediately following talk is 'jump-started' i.e. sounds like it starts with a rush.
<u>Wait</u> a minute	Underlining shows vocal stress of emphasis.
STOP	Uppercase letters represents noticeable loudness.
°wait	Indicates words are spoken softly.
Oh: no:::	Colons indicate an elongated syllable; the more colons, the more the syllable or sound is stretched.
Wait a mi-	A hyphen shows a sudden cutoff of speech.
This is a (guess)	Parentheses around words indicate transcriber doubt about what those words are, and in the case of softly spoken or overlapped talk.
This is a ( )	Empty parentheses indicate that some talk was not audible or interpretable at all.

((coughing))	Double parentheses and italicization enclose transcriber comments.
.	Indicates a drop in pitch.
_:	If the letter(s) preceding the colon is underlined, then there is an inflected falling intonation contour (you can hear the pitch turn downward)
:_	If a colon itself is underlined, then there is an inflected rising intonation contour. You can hear the pitch turn upward.
?	Indicates a rising pitch (not necessarily a question).
,	Indicates a flat pitch or a slight rising-then-falling pitch.
!	Indicates 'lively' or animated speech.
	Indicates a sudden sharp increase in pitch.
.hh	The h preceded by a period indicates an audible inbreath.
hh St(h)upid	The h without a leading period represents an audible exhaling, sometimes associated with laughter.

References

Abravanel, E. and DeYong, N. (1991). Does object modeling elicit imitative-like gestures from young infants? *Journal of Experimental Child Psychology*, 52(1), 22–40.

Ackerly, S. and Benton, A. L. (1948). Report of a case of bilateral frontal lobe defect. *Association for Research in Nervous and Mental Disease*, 27, 479–504.

Adamson, L. and Frick, J. (2003). The still-face: A history of shared experimental paradigm. *Infancy*, 4(4), 451–473.

Adleman, N., Menon, V., Blasey, C., White, C., Warsofsky, I., Glover, G., and Reiss, A. L. (2002). A developmental fMRI study of the Stroop Color-Word task. *NeuroImage*, 16, 61–75.

Adolphs, R. (2002). Trust in the brain. *Nature Neuroscience*, 5, 192–193.

Adolphs, R. (2003). Cognitive neuroscience of human social behavior. *Nature Reviews Neuroscience*, 4, 165–178.

Adolphs, R., Tranel, D., Damasio, H. and Damasio, A. (1994). Impaired recognition of emotion in facial expressions following bilateral damage to the human amygdala. *Nature*, 372, 669–672.

Aggleton, J. (ed.) (1999). *The Amygdala: Neurobiological Aspects of Emotion, Memory, and Mental Dysfunction*. New York: Wiley-Liss.

Aharon, I., Etcoff, N., Ariety, D., Chabris, C., O'Connor, E. and Breiter, H. (2001). Beautiful faces have variable reward value: fMRI and behavioral evidence. *Neuron*, 32, 537–551.

Ahn, H. J. (2005). Child care teachers' strategies in children's socialization of emotion. *Early Childhood Development and Care*, 175(1), 49–61.

Akhtar, N. (2005). The robustness of learning through overhearing. *Developmental Science*, 8, 199–209.

Akhtar, N. and Gernsbacher, M. A. (2007). Joint attention and vocabulary development: a critical look. *Language & Linguistics Compass*, 1, 195–207.

Akhtar, N. and Montague, L. (1999). Early lexical acquisition: the role of cross-situational learning. *First Language*, 19, 347–358.

Akhtar, N. and Tomasello, M. (2000). The social nature of words and word learning. In R. Golinkoff (ed.), *Becoming a Word Learner*, 115–135. Oxford: Oxford University Press.

Akhtar, N., Jipson, J. and Callanan, M. (2001). Learning words through overhearing. *Child Development*, 72(2), 416–430.

Aldridge, M., Stillman, R. D. and Bower, T. G. R. (2001). Newborn categorization of vowel-like sounds. *Developmental Science*, 4, 220–232.

Als, H., and Brazelton, T. B. (1981). Assessment of the behavioral organization of a preterm and full-term infant. *Journal of the American Academy of Child Psychiatry*, 20, 239–263.

Als, H., Tronick, E. and Brazelton, T. B. (1980). Affective reciprocity and the development of autonomy: The study of a blind infant. *Journal of the American Academy of Child Psychiatry*, 19, 22–40.

American Psychiatric Association (2000). *Diagnostic and Statistical Manual of Mental Disorders* (Revised 4th edn). Washington, DC: American Psychiatric Assoc.

Andari, E., Duhamel, J., Zalla, T., Herbrecht, E., Leboyer, M. and Sirigu, A. (2010). Promoting social behavior with oxytocin in high-functioning autism spectrum disorders. *Proceedings of the National Academy of Sciences*, 107(9), 4389–4394.

Anderson, S., Barrash, J., Bechara, A. and Tranel, D. (2006). Impairments of emotion and real-world complex behavior following childhood – or adult onset damage to ventromedial prefrontal cortex. *Journal of International Neuropsychological Society*, 12, 224–235.

Anderson, S., Bechara, A., Damasio, H., Tranel, D. and Damasio, A. (1999). Impairments of social and moral behavior related to early damage in human prefrontal cortex. *Nature Neuroscience*, 2(11), 1032–1037.

Anderson, B., Vietze, P. and Dokecki, P. (1978). Interpersonal distance and vocal behavior in the mother-infant dyad. *Infant Behavior and Development*, 1, 381–391.

Annett, L., McGregor, A. and Robbins, T. (1989). The effects of ibotenic acid lesions of the nucleus accumbens on spatial learning and extinction in the rat. *Behavioral Brain Research*, 31, 231–242.

Apicella, P., Ljungberg, T., Scarnati, E. and Schultz, W. (1991). Responses to reward in monkey dorsal and ventral striatum. *Experimental Brain Research*, 85, 491–511.

Arbuckle, T. and Pushkar-Gold, D. (1993). Aging, inhibition, and verbosity. *Journal of Gerontology*, 48, 225–232.

Aronfreed, J. (1969). The problem of imitation. In L. P. Lipsitt, and H. W. Reese (eds), *Advances in Child Development and Behavior (vol. 4)*. New York: Academic Press.

Attneave, F. (1953). Psychological probability as function of experienced frequency. *Journal of Experimental Psychology*, 46(2), 81–86.

Autism Spectrum Disorders (2010). Retrieved June 12, 2010, from http://www.cdc.gov/ncbddd/autism/addm.html

Backen Jones, L., Rothbart, M. and Posner, M. (2003). Development of executive attention in preschool children. *Developmental Science*, 6(5), 498–504.

Baird, A., Dewar, B., Critchley, H., Dolan, R., Shallice, T. and Cipolotti, L. (2006). Social and emotional functions in three patients with medial frontal lobe damage including the anterior cingulate cortex. *Cognitive Neuropsychiatry*, 11(4), 369–388.

Baird, G., Cass, H., and Slonims, V., (2003). Diagnosis of autism. *BMJ* 327, 488–493.

Bakeman, R. and Adamson, L. (1984). Coordinating attention to people and objects in mother-infant and peer-infant interactions. *Child Development*, 55, 1278–1289.

Bar, M., Kasam, K. S., Ghuman, A. S., Boshyan, J., Schmid, A.M., Dale, A. M., Hamalainen, M. S., Marinkovic, K., Schacter, D. L., Rosen, B. R. and Halgren, E. (2006). Top-down facilitation of visual recognition. *Proceedings in the National Academy of Sciences*, 103(2), 449–454.

Bard, K. (1994). Evolutionary roots of intuitive parenting: maternal competence in chimpanzees. *Early Development and Parenting*, 3, 19–28.

Bard, K. (1995). Parenting in primates. In M. Bornstein (ed.), *Handbook of Parenting* (vol. 2), 27–58. Mahwah, NJ: Erlbaum.

Bard, K. (1998). Social-experiential contributions to imitation and emotion in chimpanzees. In S. Braten (ed.), *Intersubjective Communication and Emotion in Early Ontogeny*, 208–227. Cambridge: Cambridge University Press.

Bard, K. (2003). Development of emotional expression in chimpanzees (Pan troglodytes). *Annual New York Academy of Sciences*, 1000, 88–90.

Bard, K. (2007). Neonatal imitation in chimpanzees (Pan troglodytes) tested with two paradigms. *Animal Cognition*, 10, 233–242.

Bard, K., Platzman, K., Lester, B. and Suomi, S. (1992). Orientation to social and nonsocial stimuli in neonatal chimpanzees in humans. *Infant Behavior and Development*, 15, 43–56.

Barlow, H. and Mollon, JD. (eds) (1982). *The Senses*. Cambridge: Cambridge University Press.

Bates, E. (1979). *The Emergence of Symbols: Cognition and Communication in Infancy*. New York: Academic Press.

Bateson, M. C. (1979). The epigenesis of conversational interaction: A personal account of research development. In M. Bullowas (ed.), *Before Speech: The Beginning of Human Communication* , 63–77. London: Cambridge University Press.

Bechara, A., Damasio, A. R., Damasio, H. and Anderson, S. W. (1994). Insensitivity to future consequences following damage to human prefrontal cortex. *Cognition*, 50, 7–15.

Bechara, A., Damasio, H., Tranel, D. and Anderson, S. W. (1998). Dissociation of working memory from decision makng within the human prefrontal cortex. *Journal of Neuroscience*, 18, 428–437.

Bechara, A., Damasio, H., Tranel, D. and Damasio, A. (1997). Deciding advantageously before knowing the advantageous strategy. *Science*, 275, 1293–1295.

Beebe, B., Stern, D. and Jaffe, J. (1979). The kinesic rhythm of mother-infant interactions. In S. F. Aron W. Siegman (eds), *Of Speech and Time*, 23–34. Hillsdale, NJ: Lawrence Erlbaum.

Belin, P. and Zatorre, R. J. (2003). Adaptation to a speaker's voice in right anterior temporal lobe. *Neuroreport*, 14, 2105–2109.

Benton, A. and Tranel, D. (2000). Historical notes on reorganization of function and neuroplasticity. In H. Levin and J. Grafman (eds), *Cerebral Organization of Function After Brain Damage*, 3–23. New York: Oxford University Press.

Berducci, D. (2010). *From infant reacting to understanding: Infant/caregiver interaction, turn-taking and sequencing*. Paper presented at the International Conference on Conversation Analysis.

Bhimji, F. (2002). '*Dile Famile': Socializing language skills with directives in three families in South Central Los Angeles*. Unpublished Dissertation, University of California Los Angeles, Los Angeles.

Bielsky, I., Hu, S. B., Szegba, K. L., Westphal, H. and Young, L. (2004). Profound impairment is social recognition and reduction inanxiety-like behavior in vasopressin V1a receptor knockout mice. *Neuropsychopharmacology*, 29, 483–493.

Bijeljac-Babic, R., Bertocini, J. and Mehler, J. (1991). How do four-day-old infants categorize multisyllabic utterances? *Developmental Psychology*, 29, 711–721.

Bissiere, S., Humeau, Y. and Luthi, A. (2003). Dopamine gates LTP induction in lateral amydala by suppressing feedforward inhibition. *Nature Neuroscience*, 103, 15–23.

Blair, J. R. and Cipolotti, L. (2000). Impaired social response reversal: A case of 'acquired sociopathy'. *Brain*, 123, 1122–1141.

Blakemore, S. and Choudhury, S. (2006). Development of the adolescent brain: Implications for executive function and social cognition. *Journal of Child Psychology and Psychiatry*, 47(3/4), 296–312.

Blass, E. and Shah, A. (1994). Pain-reducing properties of sucrose in human newborns. *Chemical Senses*, 20(1), 29–35.

Blass, E., Ganchrow, J. R. and Steiner, J. E. (1984). Classical conditioning in newborn humans 2-48 hours of age. *Infant Behavior and Development*, 7, 223–235.

Bock, J. K. (1986). Syntactic persistence in language production. *Cognitive Psychology*, 18, 355–387.

Bock, K. and Griffin, Z. (2000). The persistence of structural priming: Transient activation or implicit learning? *Journal of Experimental Psychology*, 129, 1771–1792.

Bolin, I. (2006). *Growing Up in a Culture of Respect: Child Rearing in Highland Peru*. Austin, TX: University of Texas Press.

Bonneh, Y., Belmonte, M., Pei, F., Iversen, P., Kenet, T., Akshoomoff, N. A., Adini, Y., Simon, H., Moore, C., Houde, C. and Merzenich, M. (2008). Cross-modal extinction in a boy with severely autistic behaviour and high verbal intelligence. *Cognitive Neuropsychology*, 25(5), 635–652.

Bosacki, S. and Astington, J. W. (1999). Theory of Mind in preadolescence: Relations between social understanding and social competence. *Social Development*, 8(2), 237–255.

Boukydis, C. F. Z. (1979). *Adult response to infant cries.*Unpublished manuscript, Unpublished PhD dissertation, Pennsylvania State University, University Park.

Bower, B. (2004). Teen brains on trial. *Science News*, 165(19), 291.

Bower, T. G. (1977). *A Primer of Infant Development*. San Francsico, CA: Freeman.

Bowlby, J. (1969). *Attachment and Loss* (vol. 1). New York: Basic Books.

Boyland, J. (ed.). (2001). *Hypercorrect Pronoun Case in English? Cognitive Processes that Account for Pronoun Usage*. Amsterdam: Benjamins.

Brand, R. and Shallcross, W. L. (2008). Infants prefer motionese to adult-directed action. *Developmental Science*, 11, 853–861.

Brand, R., Baldwin, D. and Ashburn, L. (2002). Evidence for 'motionese': Modifications in mothers' infant-directed action. *Developmental Science*, 5(1), 72–83.

Branigan, H., Pickering, M. and Cleland, A. (2000). Syntactic co-ordination in dialogue. *Cognition*, 75, B13–25.

Brazelton, T. B. (1981). Precursors for the development of emotions in early infancy. In R. Plutchik, H. Kellerman (eds), *Emotion, Theory, Research and Experience* (vol. 2), 35–55. New York: Academic Press.

Brazelton, T. B. and Cramer, B. (1990). *The Earliest Relationship: Parents, Infants, and the Drama of Early Attachment*. Reading, MA: Addison-Wesley Publishing Company, Inc.

Brazelton, T. B., Koslowski, B. and Main, M. (1974). The origins of reciprocity: the early mother-infant interaction. In M. Lewis and L. Rosenblum (eds), *The Effect of the Infant on its Caregiver.*, 49–76. New York: Wiley.

Brickner, R. (1936). *The Intellectual Functions of the Frontal Lobes: Study Based upon Observation of a Man after a Partial Bilateral Frontal Loboctomy*. New York: Macmillan.

Brothers, L. (1997). *Friday's Footprints: How Society Shapes the Human Mind*. New York: Oxford University Press.

Brown, A., Jones, T. C. and Mitchell, D. B. (1996). Single and multiple repetition priming in implicit memory. *Memory*, 4, 159–173.

Brugger, A., Lariviere, L. A., Mumme, D. L. and Bushnell, E. (2007) Doing the right thing: Infants' selection of actions to imitate from observed event sequences. *Child Development*, 78(3), 806–824.

Bruner, J. (1983). *Child's Talk: Learning to Use Language*. New York: W. W. Norton & Company.

Bryant, G. and Barrett, H. C. (2007). Recognizing intentions in infant-directed speech: Evidence for universals. *Psychological Science*, 18(8), 746–751.

Buccino, G., Binkofski, F., Fink, G. R., Fadiga, L., Fogassi, L., Gallese, V., Seitz, R. J., Zilles, K., Rizzolatti, G. and Freund, H. J. (2001). Action observation activates premotor and parietal areas in a somatotopic manner: an fMRI study. *European Journal of Neuroscience*, 13, 400–404.

Buccino, G., Vogt, S., Ritzl, A., Fink, G. R., Zilles, K., Freund, H. J. and Rizzolatti, G. (2004). Neural circuits underlying imitation of hand actions: an event related fMRI study. *Neuron*, 42, 323–334.

Burdelski, M. (2010). Socializing politeness routines: Action, other-orientation, and embodiment in a Japanese preschool. *Journal of Pragmatics*, 42, 1606–1621.

Bybee, J. and Hopper, P. (eds) (2001). *Frequency and the Emergence of Linguistic Structure*. Amsterdam: Benjamins.

Caine, S. and Koob, G. (1993). Modulation of cocaine self-administration in the rat through D-3 dopamine receptors. *Science*, 260, 1814–1816.

Cairns, G. and Butterfield, E. C. (1975). Assessing infants' auditory functioning. In B. Z. Friedlander (ed.), *Exceptional Infant* (vol. 2), 84–108. New York: Brunner/Mazel.

Caron, A., Caron, R., Roberts, J. and Brooks, R. (1997). Infant sensitivity to deviations in dynamic facial-vocal displays: The role of eye regard. *Developmental Psychology*, 33, 802–813.

Carpenter, G. C. (1973). Differential response to mother and stranger within the first month of life. *Bulletin of British Psychological Society* 26, 138.

Carpenter, G. C., Tecce, J. J., Stechler, G. and Freidmann, S. (1970). Differential visual behavior to human and humanoid faces in early infancy. *Merrill-Palmer Quarterly*, 16, 91–108.

Carr, L., Iacoboni, M., Dubeau, M., Mazziota, J. and Lenzi, G. (2003). Neural mechanisms of empathy in humans: A relay from neural systems for imitation to limbic areas. *Proceedings in the National Academy of Sciences of the United States of America*, 100(9), 5497–5502.

Carter, C. S. and Altemus, M. (2006). Integrative functions of lactational hormones and social behavior and stress management. *Annals of the New York Academy of Sciences*, 807(1), 164–174.

Carter, C. S. and Keverne, E. B. (2002). The neurobiology of social affiliation and pair bonding. In D. Pfaff (ed.), *Hormones, Brain and Behavior*, 299–337. San Diego, CA: Academic Press.

Carter, C. S., DeVries, A. C. and Getz, L. L. (1995). Physiological substrates of mammalian monogamy: The prairie vole model. *Neuroscience Biobehavioral Reviews*, 19, 303–314.

Casey, B. J., Gordon, C. T., Mannheim, G. B., and Rumsey, J. M. (1993). Dysfunctional attention in autistic savants. *Journal of Clinical Experimental Neuropsychology*, 15, 933–946.

Casey, B. J., Tottenham, N., Liston, C. and Durston, S. (2005). Imaging the developing brain: What have we learned about cognitive development? *Trends in Cognitive Science*, 9(3), 104–110.

Casey, B. J., Trainor, R., Orendi, J., Schubert, A., Nystrom, L., Giedd, J., Castellanos, F., Haxby, J., Noll, D., Cohen, J., Forman, S., Dahl, R. and Rapoport, J. (1997). A developmental functional MRI study of prefrontal activation during performance of a Go-No-Go task. *Journal of Cognitive Neuroscience*, 9(6), 835–847.

Chakrabarti, S. and Fombonne, E. (2005). Pervasive developmental disorders in preschool children: Confirmation of high prevalence. *American Journal of Psychiatry*, 162, 1133–1141.

Champagne, F., Chretian, P., Stevenson, C. W., Zhang, T. Y., Gratton, A. and Meaney, M. J. (2004). Variations in nucleus accumbens dopamine associated with individual differences in maternal behavior in the rat. *Journal of Neuroscience*, 24, 4113–4123.

Chang, C.-Y. (2006). *The Neurobiology of Frequency Effects*. Los Angeles, CA: UCLA.

Charlesworth, W. and Kreutzer, M. A. (1973). Facial expressions of infants and children. In P. Ekman (ed.), *Darwin and Facial Expressions*, 91–168. New York: Academic Press.

Chartrand, T. and Bargh, J. A. (1999). The chameleon effect: The perception-behavior link and social interaction. *Journal of Personality and Social Psychology*, 76, 893–910.

Chomsky, N. (1959). A review of B. F. Skinners 'Verbal Behavior'. *Language*, 35, 26–58.

Choudhury, S., Blakemore, S. and Charman, T. (2006). Social cognitive development during adolescence. *SCAN*, 1, 165–174.

Christiansen, M., Allen, J. and Seidenberg, M. S (1998). Learning to segment speech using multiple cues: A connectionist model. *Language and Cognitive Processes*, 13, 221–268.

Christophe, A., Gout, A., Peperkamp, S. and Morgan, J. (2003). Discovering words in the continuous speech stream: The role of prosody. *Journal of Phonetics*, 31, 585–598.

Christophe, A., Mehler, J. and Sebastian-Galles, Nuria (2001). Perception of prosodic boundary correlates by newborn infants. *Infancy*, 2(3), 385–394.

Church, B. and Fisher, C. (1998). Long-term auditory word priming in preschoolers: Implicit memory support for language acquisition. *Journal of Memory and Language*, 39, 523–542.

Cochin, S., Barthelemy, C., Roux, C. and Martineau, J. (1998). Perception of motion and qEEG activity in human adults. *Electrocenphalography in Clinical Neurophysiology*, 107, 287–445.

Cochin, S., Barthelemy, C., Roux, S. and Martineau, J. (1999). Observation and execution of movement: Similarities demonstrated by qualified electroencephalography. *European Journal of Neuroscience*, 11, 1839–1842.

Cohn, J. and Tronick, E. (1983). Three-month-old infants' reaction to simulated maternal depression. *Child Development*, 54, 185–193.

Cohn, N., Dustman, R. and Bradford, D. C. (1984). Age related decrements in Stroop color test performance. *Journal of Clinical Psychology*, 40, 1244–1250.

Comalli, P. E., Wapner, S. and Werner, H. (1962). Interference effects of Stroop-color test performance. *Journal of Genetic Psychology*, 100, 47–53.

Condon, W. S. (1977). A primary phase in the organization of infant responding. In H. R. Schaffer (ed.), *Studies on Mother-infant Interaction*, 153–176. London: Academic Press Inc.

Condon, W. S. (1980). Cultural microrhythms. In M. Davis (ed.), *Interaction Rhythm. Proceedings of the First Annual Research Conference of the Institute for Nonverbal Communication Research, Teachers College, Columbia University, 1979.* New York: Human Science Press.

Condon, W. S., and Sander, L.W. (1974a). Neonate movement is synchronized with adult speech: Interactional participation and language acquisition. *Science*, 183, 99–101.

Condon, W. S. and Sander, L.W. (1974b). Synchrony demonstrated between movements of the neonate and adult speech. *Child Development* 45, 456–462.

Conklin, H., Luciana, M., Hooper, C. and Yarger, R. (2007). Working memory performance in typically developing children and adolescents: Behavioral evidence of protracted frontal lobe development. *Developmental Neuropsychology*, 31(1), 103–128.

Cook, H. (2000). *The acquisition of social meaning: The case of the Japanese honorific masu form.* Paper presented at the Annual Conference of the Japanese Society for Language Sciences, Kyoto, Japan.

Coontz, S. (1992). *The Way We Never Were: American Families and the Nostalgia Trap.* New York: Basic Books.

Cooper, R. and Aslin, R. (1990). Preference for infant-directed speech in the first month after birth. *Child Development*, 61, 1584–1595.

Cooper, R., Abraham, J., Berman, S. and Staska, M. (1997). The development of infant's preference for motherese. *Infant Behavior and Development*, 20, 477–488.

Corkum, V. and Moore, C. (1995). Development of joint visual attention in infants. In C. Moore and P. J. Dunham (eds), *Joint Attention: Its Origins and Role in Development*. Hillsdale, NJ: Erlbaum.

Corter, C. and Fleming, A. S. (1995). Psychobiology of maternal beahvior in human beings. In M. Bornstein (ed.), *Handbook of Parenting: Biology and Ecology of Parenting*, 87–116. Marwah, NJ: Lawrence Erlbaum.

Crago, M. (1988). *Cultural context in the communicative interaction of young Inuit children.* Unpublished Doctoral Dissertation, McGill University.

Crago, M. (1992). Communicative interaction and second language acquisition: An Inuit example. *TESOL Quarterly*, 26(3), 487–505.

Crone, E. and van de Molen, M. (2007). Development of decision making in school-aged children and adolescents: Evidence from heart rate and skin conductance analysis. *Child Development*, 78(4), 1288–1301.

Crone, E., Venel, I. and van der Molen, M. (2003). Decision-making in disinhibited adolescents and adults: Insensitivity to future consequences or driven by immediate reward. *Personality and Individual Differences*, 34, 1–17.

Crown, C. L., Feldstein, S., Jasnow, M., Beebe, B. and Jaffe, J. (2002). The cross-modal coordination of interpersonal timing: Six-week-olds infants' gaze with adults' vocal behavior. *Journal of Psycholinguistic Research*, 31(1), 1–23.

Csibra, G. (2010). Recognizing communicative intentions in infancy. *Mind & Language*, 25(2), 141–168.

Csibra, G. and Gergely, G. (2006). Social learning and social cognition: The case for pedagogy. In Y. Munakata and Johnson, M. H. (eds), *Attention and Performance*

XXI: Processes of Change in Brain and Cognitive Development, 249–274. Oxford: Oxford University Press.

Csibra, G. and Gergely, G. (2009). Natural pedagogy. *Trends in Cognitive Sciences*, 13, 148–153.

Cummings, J. (1993). Frontal-subcortical circuits and human behavior. *Neurology*, 50(8), 873–880.

Damasio, A. (1994). *Descartes Error: Emotion, Reason, and the Human Brain*. New York: Putnam.

Damasio, A. (1995). Toward a neurobiology of emotion and feeling: Operational concepts and hypotheses. *The Neuroscientist*, 1, 19–25.

Damasio, A., Tranel, D. and Damasio, H. (1990). Individuals with sociopathic behavior caused by frontal damage fail to respond autonomically to social stimuli. *Behavioural Brain Research*, 41, 81–94.

Dapretto, M., Davies, M., Pfeifer, J., Scott, A., Sigman, M., Bookheimer, S. and Iacoboni, M. (2006). Understanding emotions in others: mirror neuron dysfunction in children with autism spectrum disorders. *National Review of Neurosciences*, 9(1), 28–30.

Darwin, C. (1965). *The Expression of Emotions in Man and Animals*. Chicago, IL: The University of Chicago Press.

Davis, M. (1999). The role of the amygdala in conditioned fear. In J. Aggleton (ed.), *The Amygdala: Neurological aspects of emotion, memory, and mental dysfunction*, 255–306. New York: Wiley-Liss.

Davis, M., Walker, D. and Lee, Y. (1997). Roles of the amygdala and bed nucleus of the stria terminalis differentially involved in fear versus anxiety measured with the acoustic startle reflex. *Annals of the New York Academy of Sciences*, 877, 281–291.

De Leon, L. (2008). The emergent participant: Interactive patterns in the socialization of Tzotzil (Mayan Infants). *Journal of Linguistic Anthropology*, 8(2), 131–161.

De Vries, G. and Villalba, C. (1997). Brain sexual dimorphism and sex differences in parental and other behaviors. In C. S. Carter, Lederhendler, I. I., and Kirkpatrick, B. (eds), *Annals of the New York Academy of Sciences: Vol. 807, The Integrative Neurobiology of Affiliation*, 273–286. New York: Academy of Sciences.

de Waal, F. (1989). *Peacemaking Among Chimpanzees*. Cambridge, MA: Harvard University Press.

deCasper, A. and Spence, M. J. (1986). Newborns prefer a familiar story over an unfamiliar one. *Infant Behavior and Development*, 9, 133–150.

DeHaene, S. (1997). *The Number Sense: How the Mind Creates Mathematics*. Oxford: Oxford University Press.

Dehaene-Lambertz, G., Dehaene, S., Anton, J. L., Campagne, A., Ciuciu, P., Dehaene, G., Denghien, I., Jobert, A., LeBihan, D., Sigman, M., Pallier, C. and Poline, J. B. (2006). Functional segregation of cortical language areas by sentence repetition. *Human Brain Mapping*, 27, 360–371.

Dehaene-Lambertz, G. and Gliga, T. (2004). Common neural basis for phoneme processing in infants and adults. *Journal of Cognitive Neuroscience*, 16, 1375–1387.

Dempster, F. (1992). The rise and fall of the inhibitory mechanism: Toward a unified theory of cognitive development and aging. *Developmental Review*, 12, 45–75.

Depue, R. and Collins, P. (1999). Neurobiology of the structure of personality: Dopamine, facilitation of incentive motivation, and extraversion. *Behavioral and Brain Sciences*, 22: 491–569.

Depue, R. and Morrone-Strupinsky, J. V. (2005). A neurobehavioral model of affiliative bonding: Implications for conceptualizing a human trait of affiliation. *Brain and Behavioral Sciences*, 28(3), 313–350.

Di Chiara, G. and North, R. A. (1992). Neurobiology of opiate abuse. *Trends in the Physiological Sciences*, *13*, 185–193.

Dixon, S. D., Yogman, M. W., Tronick, E., Als, H., Adamson, L. and Brazelton, T. B. (1981). Early infant social interaction of parents and strangers. *Journal of the American Academy of Child Psychiatry*, 20, 32–52.

Dobbinson, S., Perkins, M. R. and Boucher, J. (1998). Structural patterns in conversation with a woman who has autism. *Journal of Communication Disorders*, 31, 113–134.

Duncan, J. and Owen, A. M. (2000). Common regions of the human frontal lobe recruited by diverse cognitive demands. *Trends in Neurosciences*, 23, 475–483.

Dunn, J. and Richards, M. P. (1977). Observations on the developing relationship between mother and baby in the neonatal period. In H. Schaffer (ed.), *Studies in Mother-infant Interaction*, 427–455. New York: Academic Press.

Eckerman, C., Oehler, J., Medvin, M. and Hannan, T. (1994). Premature newborns as social partners before term age. *Infant Behavior and Development*, 17, 55–70.

Edwards-Lee, T., Miller, B. L., Benson, D. F., Cumming, J. L., Russell, G. L., Boone, K. and Mena, I. (1997). The temporal variant of frontotemporal dementia. *Brain*, 120, 1027–1040.

Eibl-Eibesfeldt, I. (1973). The expressive behaviour of the deaf-and-blind born. In M. Cranach and Vine, I. (ed.), *Social Communication and Movement*, 163–194. London: Academic Press.

Eimas, P. (1975). Auditory and phonetic coding of the cues for speech: Discrimination of the [r-l] distinction by young infants. *Perception and Psychophysics*, 18, 341–347.

Eimas, P. and Miller, J. L. (1980). Discrimination of information for manner of articulation by young infants. *Infant Behavior and Development*, 3, 367–375.

Eimas, P., Siqueland, E. R., Jusczyk, P. and Vigorito, J. (1971). Speech perception in infants. *Science*, 171, 303–306.

Eisenberg, R. (1975). *Auditory Competence in Early Life: The Roots of Communicative Behavior*. Baltimore, MD: University Park Press.

Ellis, N. (2002). Frequency effects in language processing and acquisition: A review with implications for theories of implicit and explicit language acquisition. *Studies in Second Language Acquisition*, 24, 143–188.

Ellis, R. and Ellingson, R. (1972). Responses to electrical stimulation of the median nerve in the human newborn. *Developmental Psychobiology*, 6(3), 235–244.

Emery, N. and Amaral, D. G (2000). The role of the amygdala in primate social cognition. In B. Lane and Nadel, L. (eds), *Cognitive Neuroscience of Emotion*, 156–191. Oxford: Oxford University Press.

Erting, C. and Prezioso, C., O'Grady-Hynes, M. (1990). The interactional context of deaf mother-infant communication. In V. Volterra and Erting, C. J. (eds), *From Gesture to Language in Hearing and Deaf Children*, 97–106. New York: Springer.

Eslinger, P. and Biddle, K. (2000). Adolescent neuropsycholical development after early right prefrontal cortex damage. *Developmental Neuropsychology*, 18(3), 297–329.

Eslinger, P., Biddle, K. and Grattan, L. M. (1997). Cognitive and social development in children with prefrontal cortex lesions. In N. Krasnegor, Lyon, G. R. and Goldman-Rakic, P. S. (eds), *Develoment of the Prefrontal Cortex: Evolution, Neurobiology, and Behavior*, 215–335. Baltimore, MD: Paul H. Brookes Publishing.

Everitt, B. and Robbins, T. (1992). Amygdala-ventral striatal interactions and reward-related processes. In J. Aggleton (ed.), *The Amygdala: Neurobiological Aspects of Emotion, Memory and Mental Dysfunction*, 401–483. New York: Wiley-Liss.

Fabre-Nys, C., Ohkura, A. and Kendrick, K. M. (1997). Male faces and odours evoke differential patterns of neurochemical release in the mediobasal hypothalamus of the ewe during oestrus: An insight into sexual motivation? *European Journal of Neuroscience*, 9, 1666–1677.

Fadiga, L., Fogassi, L., Pavesi, G. and Rizzolatti, G. (1995). Motor facilitation during action observation: A magnetic simulation study. *Journal of Neurophysiology*, 73, 2608–2611.

Fadiga, L. C. L., Buccino, G. and Rizzolatti, G. (2002). Speech listening specifically modulates the excitability of tongue muscles: A TMS study. *European Journal of Neuroscience*, 15, 399–402.

Falk, D. (2009). *Finding our Tongues*. New York: Basic Books.

Fantz, R. L. (1963). Pattern vision in newborn infants. *Science*, 140, 296–297.

Farroni, T., Csibra, G., Simion, F. and Johnson, M. (2002). Eye contact detection in humans from birth. *Proceedings in the National Academy of Sciences*, 99, 9602–9605.

Farroni, T., Massaccesi, S., Pividori, D. and Johnson, M. (2004). Gaze following in newborns. *Infancy*, 5(1), 39–60.

Feldman, R., Weller, A., Zagoory-Sharon, O. and Levine, A. (2007). Evidence for a neuroendocrinological foundation of human affiliation: Plasma oxytocin levels across pregnancy and the postpartum predict mother-infant bonding. *Psychological Science*, 18, 965–970.

Ferguson, C. (1978). *Talking to Children: A Search for Universals*. Stanford, CA: Stanford University Press.

Ferguson, J., Aldag, M., Insel, T. and Young, L. (2001). Oxytocin in the medial amygdala is essential for social recognition in the mouse. *The Journal of Neuroscience*, 21(20), 8278–8285.

Ferguson, J., Young, L. J., Hearn, E. F., Matzuk, M. M., Insel, T. R. and Winslow, J. T. (2000). Social amnesia in mice lacking the oxytocin gene. *Nature Genetics*, 25, 284–288.

Fernald, A., Taeschner, T., Dunn, J., Papousek, M., de Boysson-Bardies, B. and Fukui, I. (1989). A cross-language study of prosodic modifications in mothers' and fathers' speech to preverbal infants. *Journal of Child Language*, 16, 477–501.

Ferrari, P., Paukner, A., Ionica, C. and Suomi, S. J. (2009). Reciprocal face-to-fae communication between rhesus macaque mothers and their newborn infants. *Current Biology*, 19, 1768–1772.

Ferrari, P., Visalberghi, E., Paukner, A., Fogassi, L., Ruggiero, A. and Suomi, J. (2006). Neonatal imitation in rhesus monkeys. *PLos Biology*, 4(9), e302.

Ferris, C., Kulkarni, P., Sullovan Jr, J. M., Harder, J., Mesenger, T. and Febo, M. (2005). Pup suckling is more rewarding than cocaine: Evidence from functional magnetic resonance imaging and three-dimensional computational analysis. *The Journal of Neuroscience*, 25(1), 149–156.

Fibiger, H. and Philiips, A. (1987). Role of catecholamine transmitters in brain reward systems: Implications for the neurobiology of affect. In J. Engel and Oreland, L. (eds), *Brain Reward Systems and Abuse*, 61–74. New York: Raven Press.

Field, T. (1984). Early interactions between infants and their postpartum depressed mothers. *Infant Behavior and Development*, 7, 517–522.

Field, T. (1985). Neonatal perception of people: Maturational and individual differences. In T. Field and Fox, N. (eds), *Social Perception in Infants*, 31–52. Norwood, NJ: Ablex.

Field, T., Woodson, R., Cohen, D., Greenberg, R., Garcia, R. and Collins, K. (1983). Discrimination and imitation of facial expressions by term and preterm neonates. *Infant Behavior and Development*, 6, 485–490.

Field, T., Woodson, R., Greenberg, R. and Cohen, D. (1982). Discrimination and imitation of facial expressions by neonates. *Science*, 218, 179–181.

Filipi, A. (2007). A toddler's treatment of mm and mm hm in talk with a parent. *Australian Review of Applied Linguistics*, 30(3), 33.31–33.17.

Firth, R. (1970). Education in Tikopia. In J. Middleton (ed.), *From Child to Adult: Studies in the Anthropology of Education*, 75–90. New York: The Natural History Press.

Fisher, C., Church, B. and Chambers, K. (2004). Learning to identify spoken words. In D. Hall and Waxman, S. R. (eds), *Weaving a Lexicon*, 3–40. Cambridge, MA: MIT Press.

Fisher, C., Church, B. and Hunt, C. (in prep). Auditory word priming in 18-month-old infants.

Fisher, C., Hunt, C., Chambers, K. and Church, B. (2001). Abstraction and specificity in preschoolers' representations of novel spoken words. *Journal of Memory and Language*, 45(4), 665–687.

Fiske, A. (1991). *Structures of Social Life: The Four Elementary Forms of Human Relations*. New York: Free Press.

Fiske, A. (2004). Four modes of constituting relationships: Consubstantial assimilation; space, magnitude, time, and force; concrete procedures; abstract symbolism. In N. Haslam (ed.), *Relational Models Theory: A Contemporary Overview*, 61–146. Mahwah, NJ: Lawrence Erlbaum

Fiske, A. (2010). Dispassionate heuristic rationality fails to sustain social relationships. In A. Mates, Mikesell, L. and Smith, M. (eds), *Language, Interaction and Frontotemporal Dementia*. London: Equinox.

Fiske, A. (unpublished manuscript). Learning a culture the way informants do: Observing, imitating, and participating. University of California, Los Angeles.

Fiske, A. and Haslam, N. (1997). Prerequisites for satifactory relationships. In L. Meyer, Grenot-Scheyer, M., Harry, B., Park, H.-S. and Schwartz, I. (eds), *Making Friends: The Influences of Culture and Development*, 385–392. Baltimore, MD: Ph. Brooks.

Fiske, A. and Schubert, L. (2012). How to relate to people: The extra-terrestial's guide to Homo sapiens. In O. Gillath, Adams, G. and Kunkel, A. D. (eds), *New Directions in Relationship Research: Integrating Across Disciplines and Theoretical Approach*: Washington, DC: American Psychological Association.

Fleming, A., Corter, C., Stallings, J. and Steiner, M. (2002). Testosterone and prolactin are associated with emotional responses to infant cries in new fathers. *Hormones and Behavior*, 42, 399–413.

Fleming, A., O'Day, D. H. and Kraemer, G. W. (1999). Neurobiology of mother-infant interactions: Experience and central nervous system plasticity across development and generations. *Neuroscience and Biobehavioral Reviews*, 23, 673–685.

Fleming, A., Ruble, D., Krieger, H. and Wong, P.Y. (1997). Hormonal and experiential correlates of maternal responsiveness during pregnancy and the puerperium in human mothers. *Hormones and Behavior*, 31, 145–158.

Fleming, A., Steiner, M. and Anderson, V. (1987). Hormonal and attitudinal correlates of maternal behavior during the early postpartum period. *Journal of Reproductive and Infant Psychology*, 5, 193–205.

Floor, P. and Akhtar, N. (2006). Can 18-month-old infants learn words by listening in on conversation? *Infancy*, 9(3), 327–339.

Fogassi, L., Ferrari, P. F., Gesierich, B., Rozzi, S., Chersi, F. and Rizzolatti, G. (2005). Parietal lobe: From action understanding to intention understanding. *Science*, 308, 662–667.

Fontaine, R. (1984). Imitative skills between birth and six months. *Infant Behavior and Development*, 7, 323–333.

Fox Adams, G. (forthcoming). Infant attachment and language exposure across cultures. In A. D. L. Joaquin and J. H. Schumann (eds), *Exploring the Interactional Instinct*. Oxford: Oxford University Press.

Fraiberg, S. (1974). Blind infants and their mothers: An examination of the sign system. In M. Lewis and Rosenblum, L. (eds), *The Effects of the Infant on its Caregiver*, 215–232. New York: Wiley.

Franceschini, R., Venturini, P. L., Cataldi, A., Barreca, T., Ragni, N. and Rolandi, E. (1989). Plasma beta-endorphin concentrations during suckling in lactating women. *BJOG: An International Journal of Obstetrics and Gynaecology*, 96(6), 711–713.

Frazier, L., Tapt, L., Roeper, T. and Clifton, C. (1984). Parallel structure: A source of facilitation in sentence comprehension. *Memory and Cognition*, 12, 421–430.

Freedle, R. and Lewis, M. (1977). Prelinguistic conversation. In M. Lewis and Rosenblaum, L. (ed.), *Interaction, Conversation and the Development of Language* (Vol. 5), 157–185. New York: John Wiley and Sons.

Friederici, A. and Wessels, J. M. I. (1993). Phonotactic knowledge of word boundaries and its use in infant speech-perception. *Perception and Psychophysics*, 54, 287–295.

Frith, C. and Frith, U (1999). Interacting minds – A biological basis. *Science*, 286, 1692–1695.

Fuster, J. (1989). *The Prefrontal Cortex*. New York: Raven Press.

Gaffan, D. (1992). Amygdala and the memory of reward. In J. Aggleton (ed.), *The Amygdala: Neurobiological Aspects of Emotion, Memory and Mental Dysfunction*, 471–483. New York: Wiley-Liss.

Gallese, V. (2006). Intentional attunement: A neurophysiological perspective on social cognition and its disruption in autism. *Cognitive Brain Research*, 1079(1), 15–24.

Gardner, B. and Gardner, R. A. (1989). Prelinguistic development of children and chimpanzees. *Human Evolution*, 4, 433–460.

Gaskins, S. and Lucy, J. A. (1987). *The role of children in the production of adult culture: A Yucatec case.* Paper presented at the American Ethnological Society.

Geidd, J., Blumenthal, J., Jeffries, N., Castellanos, F. X., Liu, H., Zijdenbos, A., Paus, T., Evans, A. and Rapoport, J. (1999). Brain development during childhood and adolescence: A longitudinal MRI study. *Nature Neuroscience*, 2(10), 861–863.

Gerardi-Caulton, G. (2000). Sensitivity to spatial conflict and the development of self-regulation in children 24-36 months of age. *Developmental Science*, 3(4), 397–404.

Gergely, G. and Csibra, G. (2005). The social construction of the cultural mind: Imitative learning as a mechanism of human pedagogy. *Interaction Studies*, 6, 463–481.

Gernsbacher, M. A., Stevenson, J., Khandakar, S., and Goldsmith, H. H. (2008a). Why does joint attention look atypical in autism? *Child Development Perspectives*, 2(1), 38–45.

Gernsbacher, M. A., Stevenson, J., Khandakar, S., Goldsmith, H. H. (2008b). Autistics' atypical joint attention: Policy implications and empirical nuance. *Child Development Perspectives*, 2(1), 49–52.

Geschwind, D. and Levitt, P. (2007). Autism spectrum disorders: Developmental disconnection syndromes. *Current Opinion in Neurobiology*, 17, 103–111.

Gianino, A. and Tronick, E. (1988). The mutual regulation model: The infant's self and interactive regulation coping and defense. In T. Field, McCabe, P. and Schneiderman, N. (eds), *Stress and Coping.* Hillsdale, NJ: Erlbaum.

Gliga, T. and Csibra, G. (2009). One-year-old infants appreciate the referential nature of deictic gestures and words. *Psychological Science*, 20(3), 347–353.

Goddard, M., Durkin, K. and Rutter, DR. (1985). The semantic focus of maternal speech: A comment on Ninio and Bruner. *Journal of Child Language*, 12, 209–213.

Gogtay, N., Giedd, J., Lusk, L., Hayashi, K., Greenstein, D., Vaituzis, A., Nugent, T., Herman, D., Clasen, L., Toga, A., Rapoport, J. and Thompson, P. (2004). Dynamic mapping of human cortical development during childhood through early adulthood. *Proceedings in the National Academy of Sciences*, 101(21), 8174–8179.

Goldinger, S. (1996). Echoes of echoes? An episodic theory of lexical access. *Psychological Review*, 105, 251–279.

Goldman-Rakic, P. S. (1992). Working memory and the mind. *Scientific American*, 267, 111–117.

Gomez, G. and Gerken, L. (1999). Artificial grammar learning by 1-year-olds leads to specific and abstract knowledge. *Cognition*, 70, 109–135.

Goodsitt, J., Morgan, J. L. and Kuhl, P. K. (1993). Perceptual strategies in prelingual speech segmentation. *Journal of Child Language*, 20, 229–252.

Goodwin, C. (1979). The interaction construction of a sentence on natural conversation. In G.Psathas (ed.), *Everyday Language: Studies in Ethnomethodology*, 97–121. New York: Irvington Publishers.

Goodwin, C. (1980). Restarts, pauses, and the achievement of a state of mutual gaze at turn-beginning. *Sociological Inquiry*, 503(3–4), 272–302.

Goodwin, C. (1981). *Conversational Organization: Interaction Between Speakers and Hearers.* New York: Academic.

Goodwin, C. (2003). *Conversation and Brain Damage*. Oxford: Oxford University Press.

Goodwin, C. and Goodwin, M. H. (2004). Participation. In A. Duranti (ed.), *A Companion to Linguistic Anthropology*, 222–244. Malden: Blackwell.

Goodwin, M. (1983). Searching for a word as an interactive activity. In J. Deely and Lenhart, M. (eds), *Semiotics*, 129–138. New York: Plenum.

Goodwin, M. H. (1990). *He-Said-She-Said: Talk as Social Organization Among Black Children*. Bloomington and Indianapolis, IN: Indiana University Press.

Gopnik, A. (2009). *The Philosophical Baby: What Children's Minds Tell us About Truth, Love, and the Meaning of Life*. New York: Farrar, Straus and Giroux.

Goren, C., Sarty, M. and Wu, P. (1975). Visual following and pattern discrimination of face-like stimuli by newborn infants. *Pediatrics*, 56, 544–549.

Gottlieb, A. (2004). *The Afterlife is Where we Come From: The Culture of Infancy in West Africa*. Chicago, IL: Chicago University Press.

Grattan, L. and Eslinger, P. (1991). Frontal lobe damage in children and adults: A comparative review. *Developmental Neuropsychology*, 7, 283–326.

Gray, P. (2003). Marriage, parenting, and testosterone variation among Kenyan Swahili men. *American Journal of Physical Anthropology*, 122, 279–286.

Greenaway, R. and Plaisted, K. (2005). Top-down attentional modulation in autistic spectrum disorders is stimulus-specific. *Psychological Science*, 15, 987–994.

Greenfield, P. (1991). Language, tools and brain: The ontogeny and phylogeny of hierarchically organized sequential behavior. *Behavioral and Brain Sciences*, 14(4), 531–551.

Greenfield, P. (2006). Implications of mirror neurons for the ontology and phylogeny of cultural processes: The examples of tools and language. In M. Arbib (ed.), *Action to Language via the Mirror Neuron System*, 501–533. Cambridge: Cambridge University Press.

Greenfield, P., Matnard, A., Boehm, C. and Yut-Schmidtling, E. (2000). Cultural apprenticeship and cultural change: Tool learning and imitation in chimpanzee and humans. In S. Parker, Langer, J. and McKinney, M. L. (eds), *The Evolution of Behavioral Ontogeny*, 237–277. Santa Fe, NM: SAR Press.

Greenfield, P., Pfeifer, J., Fiske, A. P., Thomsen, L., Lovelace, V., Blazelko, A., Lik, H. C. and Dapretto, M. (unpublished manuscript). The development of children's understanding of social relations: communal sharing and authority ranking.

Gregory, C., Lough, S., Stone, V., Erzinclioglu, S., Martin, L., Baron-Cohen, S. and Hodges, J. R. (2002). Theory of mind in patients with frontal variant frontotemporal dementia and Alzheimer's disease: Theoretical and practical implications. *Brain*, 125, 752–764.

Groenewegen, H., Mulder, A. B., Beijer, A. V. J., Wright, C. I., Lopez da Silva, F. and Pennartz, C. M. A. (1999). Hippocampal and amydaloid interactions in the nucleus accumbens. *Psychobiology*, 27(2), 149–164.

Grossman, M. (2003) What is frontotemporal dementia: A clinical perspective. In L. Rudin and Rudin, G. (eds), *What if it's not Alzheimer's*, 41–54. Amherst, NY: Prometheus Books.

Guastella, A., Einfeld, S., Gray, K., Rinehart, N., Tonge, B., Lambert, T. and Hickie, I. (2010). Intranasal oxytocin improves emotion recognition for youth with autism spectrum discorders. *Biological Psychiatry*, 67(7), 692–694.

Guastella, A., Mitchell, P. and Matthews, F. (2008). Oxytocin enhances the encoding of positive social memories in humans. *Biological Psychiatry*, 64(3), 256–258.

Gutierrez, K. (2002). Studying cultural practices in urban learning communities. *Human Development*, 45(4), 312–321.

Hadjikhani, N., Joseph, R., Snyder, J. and Tager-Flusberg, H. (2005). Anatomical differences in the mirror neuron system and social cognition network in autism. *Cerebral Cortex* 16(1), 1276–1282.

Hains, S. and Muir, D. W. (1996). Infant sensitivity to adult eye direction information. *Child Development*, 67, 1940–1951.

Hallan, N. (2001). Paths to prepositions? A corpus-based study of the acquisition of a lexico-grammatical category. In J. Bybee and Hopper, P. (eds), *Frequency and the Emergence of Linguistic Structures*, 91–122. Amsterdam: Benjamins.

Hamilton, A. and Grafton, S. T (2008). Action outcomes are represented in human inferior frontoparietal cortex. *Cerebral Cortex*, 18, 1160–1168.

Han, N. (2004). *Language socialization of Korean-American preschoolers: Becoming a member of a community beyond the family.* Unpublished Dissertation, University of California, Los Angeles, Los Angeles.

Hardacre, B. (2009). *Psychological and Biological Basis of Engagement in SLA.* Los Angeles, CA: University of California, Los Angeles.

Harlow, H., Dodsworth, R. and Harlow, M. (1965). Total isolation in monkeys. *Proceedings in the National Academy of Sciences*, 54, 90–97.

Hasher, L. and Chromiak, W. (1977). The processing of frequency information: An automatic mechanism? *Journal of Verbal Learning and Verbal Behavior*, 16, 173–184.

Haskett, G. J. and Lenfestey, W. (1974). Reading-related behavior in an open classroon: Effects of novelty and modeling on preschoolers. *Journal of Applied Behavioral Analysis*, 7, 233–241.

Hasson, U., Nusbaum, H. and Small, S. (2006). Repetition suppression for spoken sentences and the effect of task demands. *Journal of Cognitive Neuroscience*, 18(12), 2013–2029.

Haug, H., Knebel, G., Mecke, E., Orun, C. and Sass, N.-L. (1981). The aging of cortical cytoarchitectonics in the light of stereological investigation. *Progress in Clinical and Biological Research* 59B, 193–197.

Haxby, J., Ungerledier, L. G., Clark, V. P., Schouten, J. L., Hoffman, E. A. and Martin, A. (1999). The effect of face inversion on activity in human neural systems for face and object perception. *Neuron*, 22(1), 189–199.

He, A. (2000). The grammatical and interactional organization of teacher's directives: Implications for socialization of Chinese American children. *Linguistics and Education*, 11(2), 119–140.

Heath, S. (1983). *Ways with Words: Language, Life, and Work in Communities and Classrooms*. Cambridge: Cambridge University Press.

Heatherton, T., Wyland, C. L., Macrae, C. N., Demos, K. E., Denny, B. T. and Kelley, W. M. (2006). Medial prefrontal activity differentiates self from close others. *Social Cognitive and Affective Neuroscience*, 1, 18–25.

Heimann, M. (1989). Neonatal imitation, gaze aversion, and mother-infant interaction. *Infant Behavior and Development*, 12, 495–505.

Heimann, M. (2002). Notes on individual difference and the assumed elusiveness of neonatal imitation. In A. Meltzoff, Prinz, W. (eds), *The Imitative Mind:*

Development, Evolution, and Brain Bases, 74–84. Cambridge: Cambridge University Press.

Henry, J., von Hippel, W. and Baynes, K. (2009). Social inappropriateness, executive control, and aging. *Psychology and Aging*, 24(1), 239–244.

Henson, R. (2003). Neuroimaging studies of piming. *Progress in Neurobiology*, 70, 53–81.

Heritage, J. (1984). *Garfinkel and Ethnomethodology.* Cambridge: Polity Press.

Hess, E. (1975). The role of pupil size in communication. *Scientific American*, 233, 110–119.

Hewlett, B. (1991). *Intimate Fathers: The Nature and Context of Aka Pygmy Paternal Infant Care.* Ann Arbor, MI: University of Michigan Press.

Hewlett, B., Lamb, M., Shannon, D., Leyendecker, B. and Scholmerich, A. (1998). Culture and early infancy among central African foragers and farmers. *Developmental Psychology*, 34(4), 653–661.

Hickok, G. (2009). Eight problems for the Mirror Neuron Theory of action understanding. *Journal of Cognitive Neuroscience*, 21(7), 1229–1243.

Hickok, G. and Poeppel, D. (2007). The cortical organization of speech processing. *Nature Reviews Neuroscience*, 8, 393–402.

Hilliard, S., Domjan, M., Nguyen, M. and Cusato, B. (1998). Dissociation of conditioned appetitive and consummatory sexual behavior: Satiation and extinction tests. *Animal Learning and Behavior*, 26(1), 20–33.

Hogbin, H. (1970). A New Guinea childhood: From weaning till the eighth year in Wogeo. In J. Middleton (ed.), *From Child to Adult: Studies in the Anthropology of Education*, 134–162. New York: The Natural History Press.

Hohne, E. and Jusczyk, P (1994). Two-month-old infants' sensitivity to allophonic differences. *Perception and Psychophysics*, 56, 613–623.

Hollander, E., and Bartz, J. (2006). *New research suggests oxytocin's potential for treatment of two core autism symptom domains.* Paper presented at the ACNP Annual Meeting Outlines Effects of Key Symptoms, Hollywood , FL.

Hollander, E., Novotny, S., Hanratty, M., Yaffe, R., DeCaria, C. M., Aronowitz, B. R. and Mosovich, S. (2003). Oxytocin infusion reduces repetitive behaviors in adults with autistic and Asperger's disorders. *Neuropsychopharmacology*, 28, 193–198.

Holman, S. and Goy, RW (1995). Experiential and hormonal correlates of care-giving in rhesus macaques. In C. Pryce, Martin, R. D. and Skue, D. (eds), *Motherhood in Human and Nonhuman Primates. Biosocial Determinants*, 87–93. Basel: Karger Publishers.

Hooper, C., Luciana, M., Conklin, H. and Yarger, R. (2004). Adolescents' performance on the Iowa gambling task: Implications for the development of decision making and ventromedial prefrontal cortex. *Developmental Psychology*, 40(6), 1148–1158.

Hornak, J., Rolls, E. T. and Wade, D. (1996). Face and voice expression identification in patients with emotional and behavioral changes following ventral lobe damage. *Neuropsychologia*, 34(4), 247–261.

Howard, A. (1970). *Learning to be Rotuman.* New York: Teachers College Press.

Howard, K. (2004). Socializing respect at school in Northern Thailand. *Working Papers in Educational Linguistics*, 20(1), 1–30.

Howard, K. (2009). 'When meeting Khun teacher, each time we should pay respect': Standardizing respect in a Northern Thai classroom. *Linguistics and Education*, 20, 254–272.

Howard, K. (2010). Social relationships and shifting languages in Northen Thailand. *Journal of Sociolinguistics*, 14(3), 313–340.

Hrdy, S. (2009). *Mothers and Others*. Cambridge, MA: Harvard University Press.

Hunt, C., Fisher, C. and Church, BA. (1998). *Long term auditory non-word priming in 2.5-year-old children*. Paper presented at the 11th Biennial International Conference on Infant Studies.

Huttenlocher, J., Vasilyeva, M., Cymerman, E. and Levine, S. (2002). Language input and child syntax. *Cognitive Psychology*, 45, 337–374.

Huttenlocher, J., Vasilyeva, M. and Shimpi, P. (2004). Syntactic priming in young children. *Journal of Memory and Language*, 50, 182–195.

Huttenlocher, P. (1979). Synaptic density in human frontal cortex-developmental changes and effects of aging. *Brain Research*, 163, 195–205.

Huttenlocher, P. and Dabholkar, A. (1997). Regional differences in synaptogenesis in human cerebral cortex. *Journal of Comparative Neurology*, 387, 167–178.

Iacoboni, M., Koski, L., Brass, M., Bekkering, H., Woods, R., Dubeau, M., Mazziota, J. and Rizzolatti, G. (2001). Reafferent copies of imitated actions in the right superior temporal cortex. *Proceedings in the National Academy of Sciences*, 98(24), 13995–13999.

Iacoboni, M., Molnar-Szakacs, I., Gallese, V., Buccino, G., Mazziotta, J.C. and Rizzolatti, G. (2005). Grasping the intentions of others with one's own mirror neuron system. *PLoS Biology*, 3(3), e79.

Iacoboni, M., Woods, R., Brass, M., Bekkering, H., Mazziota, J. and Rizzolatti, G. (1999). Cortical mechanisms of human imitation. *Science*, 286, 2526–2528.

Ingold, T. (1993). Tool-use, sociality and intelligence. In K. R. Gibson, and Ingold, T. (eds), *Tools, Language and Cognition in Human Evolution*, 429–445. Cambridge: Cambridge University Press.

Insel, T. (2003). Is social attachment an addictive disorder? *Physiology & Behavior*, 79, 351–357.

Insel, T. and Harbaugh, C. R (1989). Lesions of the hypothalamic paraventricular nucleus disrupt the initiation of maternal behavior. *Physiology & Behavior*, 45, 1033–1041.

Iversen, P. (2006). *Strange Son*. New York: Riverhead Books.

Iversen, P. (2007). Strange Son. *The Autism Perspective*, 3, 8–13.

Izard, C. (1978). Emotions and motivations: An evolutionary-developmental perspective. In H. Howe (ed.), *Nebraska Symposium of Motivation* (vol. 26), 163–199. Lincoln, NE: University of Nebraska Press.

Jaffe, J., Beebe, B., Feldstein, S., Crown, C. and Jasnow, M. (2001). *Rhythms of Dialogue in Infancy: Coordinated Timing in Development* (vol. 66). Boston, MA: Blackwell Publishers.

Jamner, L. and Leigh, H. (1999). Repressive/defensive coping, endogenous opioids and health: How a life so perfect can make you sick. *Psychiatry Research*, 85, 17–31.

Jefferson, G. (1973). A case of precision timing in ordinary conversation: Overlapped tag-positioned address terms in closing sequences. *Semiotica*, 9, 47–96.

Jefferson, G. (1974). Error correction as an interactional resource. *Language in Society*, 2, 181–199.

Jefferson, G. (1978). Sequential aspects of storytelling in conversation. In J. Schenkein (ed.), *Studies in the Organization of Conversational Interaction*, 219–248. New York, Academic Press.

Jefferson, G. (1983). Notes on some orderliness of overlap onset. *Tilburg Papers in Language and Literacy, 28.*

Jefferson, G. (1985). An exercise in the transcription and analysis of laughter. In T. A. van Dijk (ed.), *Handbook of Discourse Analysis* (vol. 3). London: Academic Press.

Joaquin, A. (2005). *How we dialogic interaction: Some biological and ontogentic precursors to Resonance.*Unpublished manuscript, University of California, Los Angeles.

Joaquin, A. (2008). *Socializing the Prefrontal Cortex.* Paper presented at the American Association of Applied Linguistics, Washington, DC.

Joaquin, A. (2010a). Language, sociality, and the prefrontal cortex: Comparing child-adult and frontotemporal dementia-caregiver interactions. *Discourse Studies,* 12(4), 443–464.

Joaquin, A. (2010b). The prefrontal cortex: Through education, socialization, and regression. In A. Mates, Mikesell, L., Smith, M. (eds), *Language, Interaction, and Frontotemporal Dementia: Reverse Engineering the Social Mind,* 161–190. London: Equinox Publishing.

Joaquin, A. (in prep). Repair in caregiver-frontotemporal dementia interactions.

Johnson, E. and Jusczyk, P. (2001). Word segmentation by 8-month-olds: When speech cues count more than statistics. *Journal of Memory and Language,* 44, 548–567.

Johnson, M., Dziurawiec, S., Ellis, H. and Morton, J. (1991). Newborn's preferential tracking of face-like stimuli and its subsequent decline. *Cognition* 40, 1–19.

Jones, S. (1996). Imitation or exploration? Young infants' matching of adults' oral gestures. *Child Development,* 67, 1952–1969.

Jones, S. (2007). Imitation in infancy: The development of mimicry. *Psychological Science,* 18(7), 593–599.

Jordan, B. (1989). Cosmopolitan obstetrics: Some insights from the training of traditional midwives. *Social Science Medicine,* 28(9), 925–944.

Jusczyk, P. and Hohne, E. (1997). Infants' memory for spoken words. *Science,* 277, 1984–1986.

Jusczyk, P., Luce, P. A. and Charles-Luce, J. (1994). Infants' sensitivity to phonotactic patterns in the native language. *Journal of Memory and Language,* 33, 630–645.

Karmiloff, K. and Karmiloff-Smith, A. (2001). *Pathways to Language: From Fetus to Adolescent.* Cambridge, MA: Harvard University Press.

Kawamura, S. (1959). The process of sub-culture propagation among Japanese macaques. *Primates,* 2, 43–60.

Kelley, W., Macrae, C. N, Wyland, C., Caglar, S., Inati, S. and Heatherton, T. F. (2002). Finding the self: An event related fMRI study. *Journal of Cognitive Neuroscience,* 14, 785–794.

Kendon, A. (1970). Movement coordination in social interaction: Some examples described. *Acta Psychologica,* 32, 100–125.

Kendon, A. (1985). Some uses of gesture. In D. Tannen and Saville-Troike, M. (eds), *Perspectives on Silence,* 215–234. Norwood, NJ: Ablex Publishing.

Kendrick, K. (2000). Oxytocin, motherhood and bonding. *Experimental Physiology,* 85S, 111–124S.

Kenyatta, J. (1953). *Facing Mount Kenya: The Tribal Life of the Gikuyu.* London: Secker & Warburg.

Keverne, E. B. (2005). Neurobiological and molecular approaches to attachment and bonding. In C. S. Carter, Ahnert, L., Grossman, K. E., Hrdy, S. B., Lamb, M. E., Porge, W. and Sachser, N. (eds), *Attachment and Bonding: A New Synthesis*, 101–118. Cambridge, MA: The MIT Press in cooperation with Dahlem University Press.

Kilner, J., Neal, A., Weiskopf, N., Friston, K. and Frith, C. (2009). Evidence of mirror neurons in human inferior frontal gyrus. *The Journal of Neuroscience*, 29(32), 10153–10159.

Klopfer, P. (1971). Mother love: What turns it on? *American Scientist*, 59, 404–407.

Koepke, J., Hamm, M., Legerstee, M. and Russell, M. (1983). Neonatal imitation: Two failures to replicate. *Infant Behavior and Development*, 6, 97–102.

Koterba, E. A. and Iverson, J. M. (2009). Investigating motionese: The effect of infant directed action on infants' attention and object exploration. *Infant Behavior and Development*, 32, 437–444.

Krawczyk, D. (2002). Contributions of the prefrontal cortex to the neural basis of human decision making. *Neuroscience and Biobehavioral Reviews*, 26, 631–664.

Kringelbach, M. (2005). The human orbitofrontal cortex: Linking reward to the hedonic experience. *Nature Reviews*, 6, 691–702.

Kringelbach, M., Lehtonen, A., Squire, S., Harvey, A., Craske, M., Holliday, I., Green, A., Aziz, T., Hansen, P., Cornelissen, P. and Stein, A. (2008). A specific and rapid neural signature for parental instinct. *PLoS Biology*, 3(2), 1–7.

Kugiumutzakis, G. (1998). Neonatal imitation in the intersubjective companion space. In S. Braten (ed.), *Intersubjective Communication and Emotion in Early Ontogeny*, 63–88. Cambridge: Cambridge University Press.

Kugiumutzakis, G. (1999). Genesis and development of early infant mimesis to facial and vocal models. In J. Nadel and G. Butterworth (eds), *Imitation in Infancy*, 36–59. Cambridge: Cambridge University Press.

Kuhl, P. (2000). A new view of language acquisition. *Proceedings in the National Academy of Sciences*, 97(22), 11850–11857.

Kuhl, P., Andruski, J., Chistovich, I., Chistovich, L., Kozhevnikova, E., Ryskina, V., Stolyarova, E., Sundberg, U. and Lacerda, F. (1997). Cross-language analysis of phonetic units in language addressed to infants. *Science*, 277, 684–686.

Kuhl, P. A. (2004). Early language acquisition: Cracking the speech code. *Nature* 5, 831–843.

Lancy, D. (1996). *Playing on the Motherground*. New York: The Guilford Press.

Lancy, D. (2008). *The Anthropology of Childhood*. Cambridge: Cambridge University Press.

Lave, J. and Wenger, E. (1992). *Situated Learning: Legitimate Peripheral Participation*. Cambridge: Cambridge University Press.

Leckman, J., Carter, C. S., Hennessy, M. B., Hrdy, S. B., Keverne, E. B., Klann-Delius, G., Schradin, C., Todt, D. and von Holst, D. (2005). Group report: Biobehavioral processes in attachment and bonding. In C. S. Carter, Ahnert, L., Grossman, K. E., Hrdy, S. B., Lamb, M. E., Porges, W. and Sachser, N. (eds), *Attachment and Bonding: A New Synthesis*, 301–348. Cambridge, MA: The MIT Press.

Lee, N. and Schumann, J. H. (2005). *The Interactional Instinct: The Evolution and Acquisition of Language*.Unpublished manuscript, Los Angeles.

Lee, N., Mikesell, L., Joaquin, A. D. L., Mates, A. and Schumann, J. (2009). *The Interactional Instinct: The Evolution and Acquisition of Language*. Oxford: Oxford University Press.

Legerstee, M. (1991). The role of person and object in eliciting early imitation. *Journal of Experimental Child Psychology*, 51, 424–433.

Legerstee, M. P. A., Malcuit, G. and Feider, H. (1987). The development of infants' responses to people and a doll: Implications for research in communication. *Infant Behavior and Development*, 10, 81–95.

Lelwica, M. and Haviland, J. M. (1983). *Response or imitation: Ten-week-old infants; reactions to three emotion expressions*. Paper presented at the The biennial meeting of the Society for Research in Child Development.,

Leon-Carrion, J., Garcia-Orza, J. and Perez-Santamaria, F. J. (2004). Development of the inhibitory component of the executive functions in children and adolescents. *International Journal of Neuroscience*, 114(10), 1291–1311.

Lester, B., Hoffman, J. and Brazelton, B. (1985). The rhythmic structure of mother-infant interaction in term and preterm infants. *Child Development*, 56(1), 15–27.

LeVine, R. (1973). *Culture, Behavior, and Personality*. Chicago, IL: Aldine.

Levine, R., Dixon, S., Levine, S., Richman, A., Leiderman, P. H., Keefer, C., Brazelton, T. B. (1994). *Child Care and Culture: Lessons from Africa*. New York: Cambridge University Press.

Lewis, M. and Ellis, H. D (1999). Repeated repetition priming in face recognition. *The Quarterly Journal of Experimental Psychology*, 52A, 927–955.

Lewis, M. and Freedle, R. O. (1973). Mother-infant dyad: The cradle of meaning. In L. K. P. Pilner and T. Alloway (eds), *Communication and Affect: Language and Thought*, 127–155. New York: Academic Press.

Li, S., Cullen, W. K., Anwyl, R. and Rowan, M. J. (2003). Dopamine-dependent facilitation of LTP induction in hippocampal CA1 by exposure to spatial novelty. *Nature Neuroscience*, 6, 526–531.

Liberman, A. M. and Mattingly, I. G. (1985). The motor theory of speech perception revised. *Cognition*, 21, 1–36.

Liu, Y. and Wang, Z. Y. (2003). Nucleus accumbens oxytocin and dopamine interact to regulate pair bond formation in female prairie voles. *Neuroscience*, 121(3), 537–545.

Liu, H., Kuhl, P. and Tsao, F. (2003). An association between mother's speech clarity and infants' speech discrimination skills. *Developmental Science*, 6(3), F1–F10.

Loberbaum, J., Newman, J. D., Horwitz, A. R. Dubno, J. R., Lydiard, R. B., Hamner, M. B., Bohning, D. E. and George, M. S. (2002). A potential role for thalamocingulate circuitry in human maternal behavior. *Biological Psychiatry*, 51, 431–445.

LoBue, V., Nishida, T., Chiong, C., DeLoache, J. S. and Haidt, J. (2009). When getting something good is bad: Even three-year-olds react to inequality. *Social Development*, 20(1), 154–170.

Locke, J. L. (1986). The linguistic significance of babbling. In B. Lindblom, Zetterstrom, R. (eds), *Precursors of Early Speech*, 143–162. Stockholm: M. Stockton Press.

Lockman, J. (2001). *Infant-directed action: Maternal and sibling input*. Paper presented at the Symposium conducted at the meeting of the Society for Research in Child Develoment, Minneapolis, MN.

Lorenz, K. (1971). *Studies in Animal and Human Behavior (vol. 2)*. London: Methuen Publishers.

Lotto, A., Hickok, G. and Holt, L. (2009). Reflections on mirror neurons and speech perceptions. *Trends in Cognitive Sciences*, 13(3), 110–114.

Lowi, R. (2007). *Building understanding through language and interaction: Joint attention, social modals and directives in adult-directed speech to children in two preschools.* Unpublished Dissertation, University of California Los Angeles, Los Angeles.

Luciana, M. and Nelson, C. (1998). The functional emergence of prefrontally-guided working memory systems in four- to eight-year-old children. *Neuropsychologia*, 36(3), 273–293.

Luciana, M. and Nelson, C. (2002). Assessment of neuropsychological function through the use of the Cambridge Neuropsychological Testing Automated Battery: Performance in 4- to 12- year old child. *Developmental Neuropsychology*, 22(3), 595–624.

Luria, A. (1976). *Cognitive Development: Its Cultural and Social Foundations.* Cambridge, MA: Harvard University Press.

Lyons, J. (1967). *Introduction to Theoretical Linguistics*. Cambridge: Cambridge University Press.

MacFarlane, A. (1975). Olfaction in the development of social preferences in the human neonate. In R. Porter, O'Connor, M. (eds), *Parent-Infant Interaction*, 103–117. Amsterdam: Elsevier.

Maestripieri, D., Ross, S. and Megna, N. (2002). Mother-infant interactions in Western lowland gorillas (Gorilla gorilla gorilla): Spatial relationships, communication, and opportunities for social learning. *Journal of Comparative Psychology*, 116(3), 219–227.

Mah, L., Arnold, M. and Grafman, J. (2004). Impairment of social perception associated with lesions of the prefrontal cortex. *American Journal of Psychiatry*, 161, 1247–1255.

Mah, L., Arnold, M. and Grafman, J. (2005). Deficits in social knowledge following damage to the ventromedial prefrontal cortex. *Journal of Neuropsychiatry*, 17(1), 66–74.

Makin, J. and Porter, R. (1989). Attractiveness of lactating females' breast odors to neonates. *Child Development*, 60(4), 803–810.

Malatesta, C. and Izard, C. E. (1984). The ontogenesis of human social signals: From biological imperative to symbol utilization. In N. Fox and Davidson, R. J. (eds), *The Psychobiology of Affective Development*, 161–206. Hillsdale, NJ: Erlbaum.

Manes, F., Sahakian, B., Clark, L., Rogers, R., Antoun, N., Aitken, M. and Robbins, T. (2002). Decision-making processes following damage to the prefrontal damage. *Brain*, 125(3), 624–639.

Maratos, O. (1973). *The Origin and Development of Imitation in Early Infancy.* Geneva University, Geneva.

Marcus, G., Vijaya, S., Bandi Rao, S. and Vishton, P. M. (1999). Rule learning by seven-month-old-infants. *Science*, 283, 77–80.

Maretzki, T. and Maretzki, H. (1966). *Taira: An Okinawan village. Six Cultures Series*. New York: John Wiley and Sons.

Marlowe, W. (1992). The impact of a right prefrontal lesion on the developing brain. *Brain and Cognition*, 20, 205–213.

Masataka, N. (1992). Motherese in a signed language. *Infant Behavior and Development*, 15, 453–460.

Mates, A., Mikesell, L. and Smith, M. (eds) (2010). *Language, Interaction, and Frontotemporal Dementia: Reverse Engineering the Social Mind.* London: Equinox.

Matthiesen, A., Ransjo-Arvidson, A. B., Nissen, E. and Uvnas-Moberg, K. (2001). Postpartum maternal oxytocin release by newborns: Effects of infant hand massage and sucking. *Birth*, 28(1), 13–19.

Mattson, B., Williams, S., Rosenlatt, J. S. and Morrell, J. I. (2001). Comparison of two positive reinforcing stimuli: Pups and cocaine throughout the postpartum period. *Behavioral Neuroscience* 115, 683–694.

Maurer, D. (1985). Infants' perception of facedness. In T. Field and Fox, N. (ed.), *Social Perception in Infancy*, 73–100. Norwood, NJ: Ablex.

Maurer, D. and Barrera, M. (1981). Infants' perception of natural and distorted arrangements of a schematic face. *Child Development*, 52, 196–202.

McCarthy, G., Puce, A., Gore, J. C. and Allison, T. (1997). Face-specific processing in the human fusiform gyrus. *Journal of Cognitive Neuroscience*, 9, 605–610.

McDougall, W. (1908). *An Introduction to Social Psychology*. London: Methuen.

McGivern, R., Anderson, J., Byrd, D., Mutter, K. L. and Reilly, J. (2002). Cognitive efficiency on a match to sample task decrease at the onset of puberty in children. *Brain and Cognition*, 50(1), 73–89.

McIntosh, D., Reichmann-Decker, A., Winkielman, P. and Wilbarger, J. (2006). When the social mirror breaks: Deficits in automatic, but not voluntary, mimicry of emotional facial expressions in autism. *Developmental Science*, 9(3), 295–302.

McKenzie, B. and Over, R. (1983). Young infants fail to imitate facial and manual gestures. *Infant Behavior and Development*, 6, 85–95.

McPhee, C. (1955). Children and music in Bali. In M. Mead and Wolfenstein, M. (eds), *Childhood in Contemporary Cultures*, 70–98. Chicago, IL: Chicago University Press.

Mehler, J. and Christophe, A. (1995). Maturation and learning of language in the first year of life. In M. S. Gazzaniga (ed.), *The Cognitive Neurosciences: A Handbook for the Field*, 943–954. Cambridge, MA: MIT Press.

Mehler, J., Jusczyk, P., Lambertz, G., Halsted, N., Bertoncini, J. and Amiel-Tison, C. (1988). A precursor of language acquisition in young infants. *Cognition*, 29, 143–178.

Meister, I., Wilson, S., Deblieck, C. and Wu, A. (2007). The essential role of premotor cortex in speech perception. *Current Biology*, 17, 1692–1696.

Meltzoff, A. (1988). Infant imitation after a 1-week delay: Long-term memory for novel acts and multiple stimuli. *Developmental Psychology*, 24(4), 470–476.

Meltzoff, A. (1998). Infant intersubjectivity: Broadening the dialogue to include imitation, identity and intention. In S. Braten (ed.), *Intersubjective Communication and Emotion in Early Ontogeny*, 47–62. Cambridge: Cambridge University Press.

Meltzoff, A. and Decety, J. (2003). What imitation tells us about social cognition: A rapprochement between developmental psychology and cognitive neuroscience. *Biological Sciences*, 358(1431), 491–500.

Meltzoff, A. and Moore, M. K. (1977). Imitation of facial and manual gestures by human neonates. *Science*, 198(4312), 75–78.

Meltzoff, A. and Moore, M. K. (1983). Newborn infants imitate adult facial gestures. *Child Development*, 54, 702–709.

Meltzoff, A. and Moore, M. K. (1989). Imitation in newborn infants: Exploring the range of gestures imitated and the underlying mechanisms. *Developmental Psychology* 25, 954–962.

Meltzoff, A. and Moore, M. K. (1992). Early imitation within a functional framework: The importance of person identity, movement, and development. *Infant Behavior and Development*, 15, 479–505.

Meltzoff, A. and Moore, M. K. (1994). Imitation, memory, and the representation of persons. *Infant Behavior and Development*, 17, 83–99.

Meltzoff, A. and Moore, M. K. (1997). Explaining facial imitation: A theoretical model. *Early Development and Parenting*, 6, 179–192.

Mikesell, L. (2010). Examining perservative behaviors of a frontotemporal dementia patient and caregiver responses: The benefits of observing ordinary interactions and reflections on caregiver stress. In A. Mates, Mikesell, L. and Smith, M. (eds), *Language, Interaction and Frontotemporal Dementia*. London: Equinox.

Miller, B., Seeley, P., Mychack, P., Rosen, H., Mena, I. and Boone, K. (2001). Neuroanatomy of the self: Evidence from patients with frontotemporal dementia. *Neurology*, 57(5), 817–821.

Mirenowicz, J. and Schultz, W. (1996). Preferential activation of midbrain dopamine neurons by appetitive rather than aversive stimuli. *Nature*, 379, 449–451.

Modahl, C., Green, L., Fein, D., Morris, M., Waterhouse, L., Feinstein, C. and Levin, H. (1998). Plasma oxytocin levels in autistic children. *Biological Psychiatry*, 43(4), 270–277.

Moon, C., Cooper, R. P. and Fifer, W. P. (1993). Two-day-olds prefer their native language. *Infant Behavior and Development*, 16, 495–500.

Morgan, J. (1996). A rhythmic bias in preverbal speech segmentation. *Journal of Memory and Language*, 35, 666–688.

Morgan, J. and Saffran, J. (1995). Emerging integration of sequential and suprasegmental information in preverbal speech segmentation. *Child Development*, 66, 911–936.

Morse, P. (1972). The discrimination of speech and nonspeech stimuli in early speech. *Experimental Child Psychology*, 13, 477–492.

Mulligan, N., Duke, M. and Cooper, A. (2007). The effects of divided attention on auditory priming. *Memory & Cognition*, 35(6), 1245–1254.

Murray, L. and Trevarthen, C. (1985). Emotional regulations of interactions between two-month-olds and their mothers. In Field, T and Fox, N. (eds), *Social Perception in Infants*, 177–198. Norwood, NJ: Ablex.

Myowa, M. (1996). Imitation of facial gestures by an infant chimpanzee. *Primates*, 37, 207–213.

Myowa-Yamakoshi, M., Tomonaga, M., Tanaka, M. and Matsuzawa, T. (2004). Imitation in neonatal chimpanzees (Pan troglodytes). *Developmental Science*, 7(4), 437–442.

Nadel, J., Guerini, C., Peze, A. and Rivet, C. (1999). The evolving nature of imitation as a format for communication. In J. Nadel and Butterworth, G. (eds), *Imitation in Infancy*, 209–234. Cambridge: Cambridge University Press.

Nadel, J., Prepin, K. and Okanda, M. (2005). Experiencing contingency and agency: First step toward self-undersatnding in making a mind? *Interaction Studies*, 6(3), 447–462.

Nagy, E. (2006). From imitation to conversation: The first dialogues with human neonates. *Infant and child development*, 15, 223–232.

Nagy, E. and Molnar, P. (1994). Homo imitans or homo provocans. *International Journal of Psychophysiology*, 18(2), 128.

Nagy, E. and Molnar, P. (2004). Homo imitans or homo provocans? Human imprinting model of neonatal imitation. *Infant Behavior and Development*, 27, 54–63.

Nakamura, K. (1996). The use of polite language by Japanese preschool children. In D. Slobin, Gerhardt, J., Kyratzis, A. and Guo, J. (eds), *Social Context and Language: Essays in Honor of Susan Ervin-Tripp*, 235–250. Hillsdale, NJ: Lawrence Erlbaum.

Nakamura, K. (2000). *Polite language usage in Japanese mother-infant interactions: A look at language socialization.* Paper presented at the Annual International Conference of the Japanese Society of Language Sciences, Kyoto, Japan.

Nazzi, T., Bertoncini, J. and Mehler, J. (1998). Language discrimination by newborns: Toward an understanding of the role of rhythm. *Journal of Perception and Performance*, 24(3), 756–766.

Newport, E., Gleitman, H. and Gleitman, L. (1977). Mother, I'd rather do it myself: Some effects and non-effects of maternal speech style. In C. Snow and Ferguson, C. (eds), *Talking to Children*, 109–150. New York: Cambridge.

Nishitani, N., Avikainen, S. and Hari, R. (2004). Abnormal imitation-related cortical activation sequences in Asperger's Syndrome. *American Neurological Association*, 55, 558–562.

Nishitani, N.and Hari, R. (2000). *Temporal dynamics of cortical representation for action.* Paper presented at the Proceedings of National Academy of Sciences.

Nissen, E., Gustavsson, P., Widstrom, A. M. and Uvnas-Moberg, K. (1998). Oxytocin, prolactin, and cortisol levels in response to nursing in women after Sectio Caesarea and vaginal delivery-relationship with changes in personality patterns post partum. *Journal of Psychosomatic Obstetics and Gynaecology*, 19, 49–58.

Nonaka, A. (2004). The forgotten endangered languages: Lessons on the importance of remembering from Thailand's Ban Khor Sign Language. *Language in Society*, 33, 737–767.

Noppeney, U. and Price, C. J. (2004). An fMRI study of syntactic adaptation. *Journal of Cognitive Neuroscience*, 16(4), 702–713.

Numan, M. (1974). Medial preoptic area and maternal behavior in the female rat. *Journal of Comparative Physiology and Psychology*, 87, 746–759.

Numan, M. (1994). A neural circuitry analysis of maternal behavior in the rat. *Acta Paediatrica Supplement*, 397, 19–28.

Numan, M., Corodimas, K. P., Numan, M. J., Factor, E. M. and Piers, W. D. (1988). Axon-paring lesions of the preoptic region and substantia innominata disrupt maternal behavior in rats. *Behavioral Neuroscience*, 102, 381–396.

O'Donnell, P. (1999). Ensemble coding in the nucleus accumbens. *Psychobiology*, 27(2), 187–197.

O'Donnell, P. (2003). Dopamine gating of forebrain neural ensembles. *European Journal of Neuroscience*, 17, 429–435.

Oberman, L., Hubbard, E., McCleery, J., Altschuler, E., Ramachandran, V. and Pineda, J. (2005). EEG evidence for mirror neuron dysfunction in autism spectrum disorders. *Cognitive Brain Research*, 24, 190–198.

Ochs, E. and Kremer-Sadlik, T. (2007). Introduction: Morality as family practice. *Discourse and Society*, 18(1), 5–10.

Ochs, E. and Schieffelin, B. (1994). Language acquisition and socialization: Three developmental stories and their implications. In B. Blount (ed.), *Language, Culture, and Society*, 470–512. Prospect Heights, NY: Waveland Press, Inc.

Ochs, E. and Schieffelin, B. (2001). Language acquisition and socialization: Developmental stories and their implications. In A. Duranti (ed.), *Linguistic Anthropology: A Reader*, 263–301. Malden: Blackwell Publishers.

Ochs, E. and Schieffelin, B. (1984). Language socialization: Three developmental stories. In R. A. Shweder and R. A. Levine (eds), *Culture Theory: Essays on Mind, Self, and Emotion*, 276–320. Cambridge: Cambridge University Press.

Ochs, E., Kremer-Sadlik, T., Gainer Sirota, K. and Solomon, O. (2004). Autism and the social world: An anthropological perspective. *Discourse Studies*, 6(2), 147–183.

Olazabal, D. and Young, LJ (2006). Oxytocin receptors in the nucleus accumbens facilitate 'spontaneous' maternal behavior in adult female prairie voles. *Neuroscience*, 141, 559–568.

Orfanidou, E., Marslen-Wilson, W. D. and Davis, M. (2006). Neural response suppression predicts repetition priming of spoken words and pseudowords. *Journal of Cognitive Neuroscience*, 18(8), 1237–1252.

Oshima-Takane, Y. (1988). Children learn from speech not addressed to them: The case of personal pronouns. *Journal of Child Language*, 15, 95–108.

Oshima-Takane, Y. (1999). The learning of first- and second person pronouns in English. In R. Jackendoff, Bloom, P. and Wynn, K. (eds), *Language, Logic, and Concept: Essays in Memory of John MacNamara*, 373–409. Cambridge, MA: MIT Press.

Oshima-Takane, Y., Goodz, E. and Derevensky, J. L. (1996). Birth-order effects on early language development: Do secondborn children learn from overheard speech? *Child Development*, 67, 621–634.

Over, H. and Carpenter, M. (2009). Eighteen-month old infants show increased helping following priming with affiliation. *Psychological Science*, 20(10), 1189–1193.

Papousek, H. and Papousek, M. (1987). Intuitive parenting: A didactic counterpart to the infant's precocity in integrative capacities. In J. Osofsky (ed.), *Handbook of Infant Development* (vol. 2), 669–720. New York: Wiley.

Paugh, A. (2005). Learning about work at dinnertime: Language socialization in dual-earner American families. *Discourse and Society*, 16(1), 55–78.

Pawlby, S. (1977). Imitative interaction. In H. R. Schaffer (ed.), *Studies in Mother-infant Interaction*, 203–226. London: Academic Press Inc.

Peak, L. (1986). Training learning skills and attitudes in Japanese early educational settings. In W. Fowler (ed.), *Early Experience and the Development of Competence*, 111–123. San Francisco, CA: Jossey-Bass.

Pedersen, C. (1997). Oxytocin control of maternal behavior: Regulation by sex steroids and offspring stimuli. In C. S. Carter, Ledehendler, I. I. and Kirkpatrick, B. (eds), *The Integrative Neurobiology of Affiliation. Annals of the New Academy of Sciences.* (vol. 807), 126–145. New York: Wiley.

Pedersen, C. and Boccia, M. (2002). Oxytocin links mothering received, mothering bestowed and adult stress responses. *Stress*, 5(4), 259–267.

Pedersen, C., Caldwell, C. D., Drago, F., Noonan, L. R., Petersen, G., Hood, L. E. and Prange, A. J. (1988). Oxytocin activates the postpartum onset of rat maternal behavior in the ventral tegmental area and the medial preoptic areas. *Behavioral Neuroscience*, 108, 1163–1171.

Pederson, C., Vadlamunci, S. V., Boccia, M. L. and Amico. J. A. (2006). Maternal behavior deficits in nulliparous oxytocin knockout mice. *Genes, Brain, and Behavior*, 5(3), 274–281.

Phillips, A. and Fibiger, H. (1978). The role of dopamine in maintaining intracranial self-stimulation in the ventral tegmentum, nucleus accumbens and medial prefrontal cortex. *Reviews of Canadian Psychology*, 32, 58–66.

Pickett, E., Pullara, O., O'Grady, J. and Gordon, B. (2009). Speech acquisition in older nonverbal individuals with autism. *Cognitive Behavioral Neurology*, 22(1), 1–21.

Plooij, F. (1984). The behavioral development of free living chimpanzee babies and infants *Monographs of Infancy* (vol. 3). Norwood, NJ: Ablex.

Pollock, C., Auburn, T., Clibbens, J. and Phillips, C. (2008). *Interactions of children with severe autism*. Paper presented at the International Meeting for Autism Research.

Pomerantz, A. (1984). Agreeing and disagreeing with assessments: Some features of preferred/dispreferred turn shapes. In J. Atkinson and Heritage, J. (ed.), *Structures of Social Action: Studies in Conversational Analysis*, 57–101. Cambridge: Cambridge University Press.

Popik, P. and Van Ree, J. M. (1992). Long-term facilitation of social recognition in rats by vasopressin related peptides: A structure-activity study. *Life Sciences*, 50(8), 567–572.

Porges, S. (2001). The polyvagal theory: Phylogenetic substrates of a social nervous system. *International Journal of Psychophysiology*, 42(2), 123–146.

Porges, S. (2003). Social engagement and attachment: A phylogenetic perspective. *Annals of the New York Academy of Sciences*, 1008, 31–47.

Porges, S. (2005). The role of social engagement in attachment and bonding. In C. S. Carter, Ahnert, L., Grossman, K. E., Hrdy, S. B., Lamb, M. E., Porge, S. W. and Sachser, N. (eds), *Attachment and Bonding: A New Synthesis*, 33–54. Cambridge, MA: The MIT Press.

Potter, J.,and Wetherell, M. (1987). Foundations of discourse analysis. In J. Potter and Wetherell, M (eds), *Discourse and Social Psychology: Beyond Attitudes and Behavior*, 9–31. London: Sage Publications.

Powell, K. and Voeller, K. (2004). Prefrontal executive function syndromes in children. *Journal of Child Neurology*, 19, 785–797.

Price, B., Daffner, K., Stowe, R. and Mesulam, M. (1990). The comportmental learning disabilities of early frontal lobe damage. *Brain*, 113, 1383–1393.

Przednowek, M. (2009). *Uncovering the Scope of Infant-directed Action: Are Mother-infant Interactions Unique?* Hamilton, Ontario: McMaster University.

Pye, C. (1986a). An ethnography of Mayan speech to children. *Working papers in Child Language*, 1, 30–58.

Pye, C. (1986b). Quiche Mayan speech to children. *Journal of Child Language*, 13, 85–100.

Quinn, N. (2005). Universals of child rearing. *Anthropological Theory*, 5(4), 477–516.

Rakison, D. and Oakes, L. M. (eds). (2003). *Early Category and Concept Development: Making Sense of Blooming, Buzzing Confusion*. Oxford: Oxford University Press.

Ramus, F. (2001). *Perception of linguistic rhythms by newborn infants.* Unpublished manuscript, Paris.

Ramus, F. (2002). Language discrimination by newborns. *Annual Review of Language Acquisition*, 2, 85–115.

Ramus, F., Hauser, M., Miller, C., Morris, D. and Mehler, J. (2000). Language discrimination by human newborns and by cotton-top tamarin monkeys. *Science*, 288, 349–351.

Raz, N. (2000). Aging of the brain and its impact on cognitive performance: Integration of structural and functional findings. In F. Craik and Salthouse, T. (eds), *The Handbook of Aging and Cognition*, 1–90. Mahwah, NJ: Lawrence Erlbaum.

Raz, N., Lindenberger, U., Rodrigue, K. M., Kennedy, K., Head, D., Williamson, A., Dahle, C., Gerstorf, D. and Acker, J. (2005). Regional brain changes in aging healthy adults: General trends, individual differences and modifiers. *Cerebral Cortex*, 15(11), 1676–1689.

Redington, M. and Chater, N. (1998). Connectionist and statistical approaches to language acquisition: A distributional perspective. *Language and Cognitive Processes*, 13, 129–192.

Reissland, N. (1988). Neonatal imitation in the first hour of life: Observations in rural Nepal. *Developmental Psychology*, 24(4), 464–469.

Reissland, N., Francis, B., Mason, J. and Lincoln, K. (2011). Do facial expressions develop before birth? *PLoS One*, 8(8), 1–7.

Reynolds, J. (2008). Socializing Puros Pericos (Little Parrots): The negotiation of respect and responsibility in Antonero Mayan sibling and peer networks. *Journal of Linguistic Anthropology*, 18(1), 82–107.

Rijt-Plooij, H. van de and Plooij, F. X (1987). Growing independence, conflict, and learning in mother-infant relations in free-ranging chimpanzees. *Behavior*, 101, 191–221.

Rizzolatti, G. (2005). The mirror neuron system and imitation. In S. Hurley and Chater, N. (eds), *Mechanisms of Imitation and Imitation in Animals* (Vol. 1), 55–76. Cambridge, MA: MIT Press.

Rizzolatti, G. and Craighero, L. (2004). The mirror neuron system. *Annual Review of Neuroscience* 27, 167–192.

Rizzolatti, G., Fabbri-Destro, M. and Cattaneo, L. (2009). Mirror neurons and their clinical relevance. *Nature* 5(1), 24–34.

Rogoff, B. (2003). *The Cultural Nature of Human Development.* Oxford: Oxford University Press.

Rogoff, B., Moore, L., Najafi, B., Dexter, A., Correa-Chávez, M. and Solís, J. (2007). Children's development of cultural repertoires through participation in everyday routines and practices. In J. Gruseca and Hastings, P. (eds), *Handbook of Socialization: Theory and Research*, 490–515. New York: Guilford Press.

Rogoff, B., Paradise, R., Mejia Arauz, R., Correa-Chavez, M. and Angelillo (2003). Firsthand learning through intent participation. *Annual Review of Psychology*, 54, 175–203.

Rolls, E. (1998). The orbitofrontal cortex. In A. Roberts, Robbins, T. W. and Weiskrantz, L. (eds), *The Prefrontal Cortex*, 67–86. Oxford: Oxford University Press.

Rosen, H., Perry, R., Murphy, J., Kramer, J., Mychack, P., Schuff, N., Weiner, M., Levenson, R. and Miller, B. (2002). Emotion comprehension in the temporal variant of frontotemporal dementia. *Brain*, 125, 2286–2295.

Rowe, A., Bullock, P. R., Polkey, C. E. and Morris, R. G. (2001). 'Theory of mind' impairments and the relationship to executive functioning following frontal lobes excisions. *Brain*, 124, 600–616.

Russell, W. (1959). *Brain, Memory, Learning*. London: Oxford University Press.

Sacks, H. (1984). Notes on methodology. In J. Atkinson and Heritage, J. (ed.), *Structures of Social Action: Studies in Conversation Analysis*, 21–27. Cambridge: Cambridge University Press.

Sacks, H., Schegloff, E. and Jefferson, G. (1974). A simplest systematics for the organization of turn-taking for conversation. *Language*, 50(4), 696–736.

Saffran, J. (2001). Words in a sea of sounds: The output of infant statistical learning. *Cognition*, 81, 149–169.

Saffran, J., Aslin, R. and Newport, E. (1996). Statistical learning by 8-month old infants. *Science*, 274(5294), 1926–1928.

Saffran, J. and Thiessen, E. (2003). Pattern induction by infant language learners. *Developmental Psychology*, 39(3), 484–494.

Santi, A., Servos, P., Vatikiotis-Bateson, E., Kuratate, T. and Munhall, K. (2003). Perceiving biological motion: Dissociating visible speech from walking. *Journal of Cognitive Neuroscience*, 15(6), 800–809.

Savage-Rumbaugh, E., Rumbaugh, D. M. and Boysen, S. T. (1978). Symbolic communication between two chimpanzees (Pan troglodytes). *Science*, 201, 641–644.

Saver, J. and Damasio, A. (1991). Preserved access and processing of social knowledge in a patient with acquired sociopathy due to ventromedial frontal damage. *Neuropsychologia*, 29(12), 1241–1249.

Scarpa, A. and Raine, A. (2004). The psychophysiology of child misconduct. *Pediatric Annals*, 33(5), 296–304.

Schegloff, E. (1982). Discourse as an interactional achievement: Some uses of 'uh huh' and other things that come between sentences. In D. Tannen (ed.), *Analyzing Discourse: Text and Talk*, 71–93. Washington DC: Georgetown University Press.

Schegloff, E., Jefferson, G. and Sacks, H. (1977). The preference for self-correction in the organization of repair in conversation. *Language*, 53, 361–382.

Schegloff, E. A. (1968). Sequencing in conversational openings. *American Anthropologist*, 70(6), 1075–1095.

Schegloff, E. A. (2000). Overlapping talk and the organization of turn taking for conversation. *Language in Society* 29, 1–63.

Schegloff, E. A. (2003). Conversation analysis and communication disorders. In C. Goodwin (ed.), *Conversation and Brain Damage*, 21–55. Oxford: Oxford University Press.

Schegloff, E. A. (2007). *Sequence Organization in Interaction: A Primer in Conversation Analysis* (vol. 1). Cambridge: Cambridge University Press.

Scheibel, M. and Scheibel, A. B. (1975). Dendrite bundles, central programs, and the olfactory bulb. *Brain Research*, 95, 407–424.

Scherer, K. (1984). Emotion as a multi-component process: A model and some cross-cultural data. In P. Shaver (ed.), *Review of Personality and Social Psychology: Emotions, Relationships and Health* (vol. 5), 57–63. Beverly Hills, CA: Sage.

Schieffelin, B. (1991). *The Give and Take of Everyday Life: Language Socialization of Kaluli Children*. Tucson, AZ: Fenestra Books.

Schieffelin, B. and Ochs, E. (1986). Language socialization. *Annual Review in Anthropology*, 115, 163–191.

Schultz, W. (1986). Responses of midbrain dopamine neurons to trigger stimuli in the monkey. *Journal of Neurophysiology*, 56, 1439–1461.

Schultz, W. (2007). Behavioral dopamine signals. *Trends in Neurosciences*, 30(5), 203–210.

Schultz, W., Apicella, P., Scarnati, E. and Ljungberg, T. (1992). Neuronal activity in monkey ventral striatum related to the expectation of reward. *Journal of Neuroscience*, 12, 4595–4599.

Schultz, W., Dayan, P. and Montague, P. R. (1997). A neural substrate of prediction and reward. *Science*, 275, 1593–1599.

Schultz, W., Romo, R., Ljungberg, T., Mirenowicz, J., Hollerman, J. and Dickinson, A. (1995). Reward related signals carried by dopamine neurons. In J. Houk, David, J. J., Beiser, D. (ed.), *Models of Information Processing in the Basal Ganglia*, 233–248. Cambridge, MA: MIT Press.

Schumann, J., Wood, L. A., Lee, N., Jones, N. E. and Crowell, S. E. (2004). *The Neurobiology of Learning: Perspectives from Second Language Acquisition* Mahwah, NJ: Lawrence Erlbaum.

Schumann, J. H. (1997). *The Neurobiology of Affect in Language*. Los Angeles, CA: Blackwell Publishers.

Schumann, J. H. (1999). A neurobiological basis for decision making in language pragmatics. *Pragmatics & Cognition*, 7(2), 283–311.

Schumann, J. H. (2010). Brain, language, society: Where FTD has led us. In A. Mates, Mikesell, L. and Smith, M. (eds), *Language, Interaction, and Frontotemporal Dementia: Reverse Engineering the Social Mind.* London: Equinox Publishing.

Scollon, R. and Scollon, S. (1981). *Narrative, Literacy, and Face in Interethnic Communication.* Norwood, NJ: Ablex

Selden, N., Everitt, B. J., Jarrard, L. E. and Robbins, T. W. (1991). Complementary roles for the amygdala and hippocampus in aversive conditioning to explicit and contextual cues. *Neuroscience*, 42(2), 335–350.

Senju, A. and Csibra, G. (2008). Gaze following in human infants depends on communicative signals. *Current Biology*, 18, 668–671.

Seymour, S. (1999). *Women, Family, and Child Care in India: A World in Transition.* New York: Cambridge University Press.

Shapiro, B. (1969). The subjective estimate of relative word frequency. *Journal of Verbal Learning and Verbal Behavior*, 8, 248–251.

Skolnick, D. and Fernald, A. (2003). *Incidental word learning by two-year-olds,* Poster presented at the Biennial meeting of the Society for Research in Child Development. Tampa, FL.

Smith, M. (2010). Exploring the moral basis of social action in frontotemporal dementia. In A. Mates, Mikesell, L. and Smith, M. (eds), *Language, Interaction and Frontotemporal Dementia*. London: Equinox.

Southgate, V., Johnson, M. H., Osborne, T. and Csibra, G. (2009). Predictive motor activation during action observation in human infants. *Biology Letter*, 5, 769–772.

Sowell, E., Thompson, P., Holems, C., Jernigan T. and Toga, A. (1999). In vivo evidence for post-adolescent brain maturation in frontal and striatal regions. *Nature Neuroscience* 2(10), 859–861.

Spitz, R. A. (1949). The role of ecological factors in emotional development in infancy. *Child Development*, 20(3), 145–155.

Steiner, J. (1979). Human facial expressions in response to taste and smell stimulation. In H. Reese and Lipsitt, L. P. (eds), *Advances in Child Development and Behavior* (vol. 13), 257–295. New York: Academic Press.

Stern, D. (2002). *The First Relationship*. Cambridge, MA: Harvard University Press.

Stevenson, M., Ver Hoeve, J., Roach, M. and Leavitt, L. (1986). The beginning of conversation: Early patterns of mother-infant vocal responsiveness. *Infant Behavior and Development*, 9, 423–440.

Stivers, T. (2008). Stance, alignment, and affiliation during storytelling: When nodding is a token of affiliation. *Research on Language and Social Interaction*, 41(3), 31–57.

Stone, V., Baron-Cohen, S. and Knight, K. (1998). Frontal lobe contributions to theory of mind. *Journal of Cognitive Neuroscience*, 10, 640–656.

Stone, W., Ousley, O., Yoder, P., Hogan, K. and Hepburn, S. (1997). Nonverbal communication in two- and three-year-old children with autism. *Journal of Autism and Developmental Disorders*, 27(6), 677–696.

Storey, A., Walsh, C. J., Quinton, R. L. and Wynne-Edwards, K. E. (2000). Hormonal correlates of paternal responsiveness in new and expectant fathers. *Evolution and Human Behavior*, 21, 79–95.

Strathearn, L., Li, J., Fonagy, P. and Montague, P. R. (2008). What's in a smile? Maternal brain responses to infant facial cues. *Pediatrics*, 122, 40–51.

Stribling, P., Rae, J. and Dickerson, P. (2007). Two forms of spoken repetition in a girl with autism. *International Journal of Language and Communication Disorders*, 42(4), 427–444.

Strutt, G., Andersom, D. R. and Well, A. D. (1975). A developmental study of the effects of irrelevant information on speeded classification. *Journal of Experimental Child Psychology*, 20, 127–135.

Sundara, M., Namasivayam, A. K. and Chen, R. (2001). Observation-execution matching system for speech: A magnetic stimulation study. *NeuroReport*, 12, 1341–1344.

Sutherland, R. and McDonald, R. (1990). Hippocampus, amygdala, and memory deficits in rats. *Behavioral and Brain Research*, 37, 57–79.

Swain, J., Lorberbaum, J., Kose, S. and Strathearn, L. (2007). Brain basis of early parent-infant interactions: Psychology, physiology, and in vivo functional neuroimaging studies. *Journal of Child Psychology and Psychiatry*, 48(3/4), 262–287.

Tager-Flusberg, H. and Joseph, R. (2003). Identifying neurocognitive phenotypes in autism. *Philosophical Transactions of the Royal Society of London Biological Sciences*, 358, 303–314.

Tanaka, Y. and Arayama, T. (1969). Fetal responses to acoustic stimuli. *Practica Oto-Rhino-Larygologica*, 31, 269–273.

Terry, R., De Teresa, R. and Hansen, L. A. (1987). Neocortical cell counts in normal adult aging. *Annals of Neurology*, 21, 530–539.

Thompson, R., Gupta, S., Miller, K., Mills, S. and Orr, S. (2004). The effects of vasopressin on human facial responses related to social communication. *Psychoneuroendocrinology*, 29, 35–48.

Thomsen, L., Frankenhuis, W. E., Ingold-Smith, M. and Carey, S. (2011). Big and mighty: Preverbal infants mentally represent social dominance. *Science*, 331, 477–480.

Thurm, A., Lord, C., Lee, L. and Newschaffer, C. (2007). Predictors of language acquisition in preschool children with autism spectrum disorders. *Journal of Austism and Developmental Disorders*, 37, 1721–1734.

Tinbergen, N. (1951). *The Study of Instinct*. Oxford: Clarendon Press of Oxford University Press.

Tobin, J., Wu, D. and Davidson, D. (1989). *Preschool in Three Cultures: Japan, China, and the United States*. New Haven, CT: Yale University Press.

Tomasello, M. (1999). *The Cultural Origins of Human Cognition*. Cambridge, MA: Harvard University Press.

Tomasello, M. (2003). *Constructing a Language: A Usage based Theory of Language Acqusition*. Cambridge, MA: Harvard University Press.

Tomasello, M. (2008). *Origins of Human Communication*. Cambridge, MA: MIT Press.

Tomasello, M., Call, J. and Hare, B. (1998). Five primate species follow the visual gaze of conspecifics. *Animal Behavior*, 55(4), 1063–1069.

Tomasello, M. and Farrar, M. (1986). Joint attention and early language. *Child Development*, 57, 1454–1463.

Tomasello, M., Kruger, A. C. and Ratner, H. H. (1993). Culture learning. *Behavioral and Brain Sciences*, 16, 495–552.

Torralva, T., Kipps, C. M., Hodges, J. R., Clark, L., Bekinsctein, T., Roca, M., Calcagno, M. L. and Manes, F. (2007). The relationship between the affective decision making and theory of mind in the frontal variant of fronto-temporal dementia. *Neuropsychologia*, 45(2), 342–349.

Torrisi, S. (2010). Social regulation in frontotemporal dementia: A case study. In A. Mates, Mikesell, L. and Smith, M. (eds), *Language, Interaction and Frontotemporal Dementia*, 23–47. London: Equinox.

Tranel, D. and Eslinger, P. J. (2000). Effects of early onset brain injury on the development of cognition and behavior: Introduction to the special issue. *Developmental Neuropsychology*, 18(3), 273–280.

Trehub, S. (1973). Infants' sensitivity to vowel and tonal contrasts. *Developmental Psychology*, 9, 91–96.

Trehub, S., Trainor, L. J. and Unyk, A. M. (1993). Music and speech processing in the first year of life. *Advances in Child Development and Behaviour*, 24, 1–35.

Trevarthen, C. (1974). Conversations with a two-month-old. *New Scientist*, 62, 230–235.

Trevarthen, C. (1977). Descriptive analyses of infant communicative behavior. In H. R. Schaffer (ed.), *Studies in Mother-infant Interaction*, 227–270. London: Academic Press Inc.

Trevarthen, C. (1979). Communication and cooperation in early infancy: A description of primary intersubjectivity. In M. M. Bulowa (ed.), *Before Speech: The Beginning of Interpersonal Communication*, 321–347. New York: Cambridge University Press.

Trevarthen, C. (2005). Stepping away from the mirror: Pride and shame in adventures of companionship. In C. Carter, Ahnert, L., Grossman, K. E., Hrdy, S. B., Lamb, M. E., Porges, W. and Sachser, N. (eds), *Attachment and Bonding: A New Synthesis*, 55–84. Cambridge, MA: The MIT Press.

Tronick, E. (1989). Emotions and emotional communication in infants. *American Psychologist*, 44(2), 112–119.

Tronick, E., Als, H. and Adamson, L. (1979). Structure of early face-to-face communicative interactions. In M. Bullowa (ed.), *Before Speech*, 349–370. Cambridge: Cambridge University Press.

Tronick, E., Als, H., Adamson, L., Wise, S. and Brazelton, TB (1978). The infant's response to entrapment between contradictory messages in face-to-face interaction. *Journal of Child Psychiatry*, 17, 1–13.

Uemura, E. and Hartman, H. A. (1978). RNA content and volume of nerve cell bodies in human brain. I. Prefrontal cortex in aging normal and demented patients. *Journal of Neuropathology and Experimental Neurology*, 37, 487–496.

Ullstadius, E. (1998). Neonatal imitation in a mother-infant setting. *Early Development and Parenting*, 7, 1–8.

Umilta, M. A., Kohler, E., Gallese, V., Fogassi, L., Fadiga, L., Keysers, C. and Rizzolatti, G. (2001). 'I know what you are doing': A neurophysiological study. *Neuron*, 32, 91–101.

Underwood, B. (1971). Recognition of memory. In H. Kendler and Spence, J. T. (ed.), *Essays in Neobehaviorism*, 313–335. New York: Appleton-Century-Crofts.

Uvnäs-Moberg, K. (1998). Oxytocin may mediate the benefits of positive social interactions and emotions. *Psychoneuroendicronology*, 23(8), 819–835.

Uvnäs-Moberg, K. and Petersson, M. (2005). Oxytocin, a mediator of anti-stress, well-being, social interaction, growth and healing. *Z Psychosom Med Psychother*, 51(1), 57–80.

Uvnäs-Moberg, K., Widstrom, A. M., Nissen, E. and Bjorvell, H., (1990). Personality traits in women 4 days post partum and their correlation with plasma levels of oxytocin and prolactin. *Psychosomatic Obstetics and Gynaecology*, 11, 261–273.

Van Rees, S. and de Leeuw, R. (1987). *Born Too Early: The Kangaroo Method with Premature Babies*. Leveroy, The Netherlands.

Vanderwolf, C. (1962). Medial thalamic functions in voluntary behavior. *Canadian Journal of Psychology*, 16, 318–330.

Vinter, A. (1986). The role of movement in eliciting early imitations. *Child Development*, 57, 66–71.

Volden, J. (2004). Conversational repair in speakers with autism spectrum disorder. *International Journal of Language and Communication Disorders*, 39(2), 171–189.

von Hippel, W. (2007). Aging, executive function, and social control. *Current Directions in Psychology Science*, 16(5), 240–244.

von Hippel, W. and Dunlop, S. (2005). Aging, inhibition, and social inappropriateness. *Psychology and Aging*, 20(3), 519–523.

von Hippel, W., Silver, L. A. and Lynch, M. E. (2000). Stereotyping against your will: The role of inhibitory ability in stereotyping and prejudice among the elderly. *Personality and Social Psychology Bulletin*, 26, 523–532.

Vygotsky, L. (1960). *The Development of Higher Mental Functions*. Moscow: Ozdatel'stvo Akademii Pedagogicheskikh Nauk.

Vygotsky, L. (1978). *Mind in Society: The Development of Higher Psychological Processes*. Cambridge, MA: Harvard University Press.

Wakerley, J., Clarke, G. and Summerlee, A. J. S. (1994). Milk ejection and its control. In E. Knobil and Neill, J. (ed.), *The Physiology of Reproduction*, 2283–2321. New York: Raven Press.

Wales, K. (1996). *Personal Pronouns in Present-day English*. Cambridge: Cambridge Univerity Press.

Ward, M. (1971). *Them Children: A Study in Language Learning*. New York: Holt, Rinehart & Winston.

Watkins, K. E., Strafella, A. P. and Paus, T. (2002). Seeing and hearing speech excites the motor system involved in speech production. *Neuropsychologia*, 41, 989–994.

Weber, K. and Indefrey, P. (2009). Syntactic priming in German-English bilinguals during sentence comprehension. *NeuroImage*, 46, 1164–1172.

Weisner, T. (1982). Sibling interdependence and child caretaking: A cross cultural view. In M. Lamb and Sutton-Smith, B. (eds), *Sibling Relationships: The Nature and Significance Across the Lifespan*, 305–327. Hillsdale, NJ: Lawrence Erlbaum.

Werker, J. and McLeod, P. J. (1989). Infant preference for both male and female infant-directed-talk: A developmental study of attentional and affective responses. *Canadian Journal of Psychology*, 43, 230–246.

Wertsch, J. (1986). *Vygotsky and the Social Formation of Mind*. Cambridge, MA: Harvard University Press.

Whitehurst, G., Ironsmith, M. and Goldfein, M. (1974). Selective imitation of the passive construction. *Journal of Experimental Child Psychology*, 17(2), 288–302.

Whiting, B. (Ed). (1963). *Six Cultures: Studies of Child Rearing*. New York and London: John Wiley and Sons, Inc.

Whiting, J. (1941). *Becoming a Kwoma: Teaching and Learning in a New Guinea Tribe*. New Haven, CT: Yale University Press.

Whittemore, R. and Beverly, E. (1989). Trust in the Mandinka way: The cultural context of sibling care. In P. Zukow-Goldring (ed.), *Sibling Interaction Across Cultures: Theoretical and Methodological Issues*, 26–49. New York: Springer-Velag.

Wideman, C. and Murphy, H. (1986). The pathological effects of limited feeding in vasopressin-deficient animals. *Bulletin of Psychonomic Society*, 24, 225–228.

Wideman, C. and Murphy, H. (1990). Vasopressin, maternal behavior, and pup well-being. *Current Psychology*, 9(3), 285–295.

Widstrom, A., Wahlberg, V., Matthiesen, A. S., Eneroth, P., Uvnäs-Moberg, K., and Werner, S. (1990). Short-term effects of early suckling and touch of the nipple on maternal behavior. *Early Human Development*, 21(3), 153–163.

Wiesenfeld, A. R., Malatesta C. Z., Whitman, PB., Grannose, C. and Vile, R. (1985). Psychophysiological response or breast- and bottle-feeding mothers to their infants' signals. *Psychophysiology*, 22, 79–85.

Williams, J., Waiter, G., Gilchrist, A., Perret, D., Murray, A. and Whiten, A. (2006). Neural mechanisms of imitation and 'mirror neuron' functioning in autism spectrum disorder. *Neuropsychologia*, 44, 610–621.

Wilson, S. and Iacoboni, M. (2006). Neural responses to non-native phonemes varying in producibility: Evidence for the sensorimotor nature of speech perception. *NeuroImage*, 33, 316–325.

Wilson, S., Saygun, A. P., Sereno, M. I. and Iacoboni, M. (2004). Listening to speech activates motor areas involved in speech production. *Nature Neuroscience*, 7, 701–702.

Wise, L., Sutton, J. A. and Gibbons, P. D. (1975). Decrement in Stroop interference time with age. *Perceptual and Motor Skills*, 41, 149–150.

Wise, R. (1982). Neuroleptics and operant behavior: The anhedonia hypothesis. *Behavioral Brain Sciences*, 5, 39–87.

Wolff, P. (1969). The natural history of crying and other vocalizations in early infancy. In B. Foss (ed.), *Determinants of Infant Behavior* (Vol. 4). London: Methuen.

Wootton, A. (2002). Interactional contrasts between typically developing children and those with autism, Asperger's Syndrome, and pragmatic development. *Issues in Applied Linguistics*, 13(2), 133–159.

Young, L., Nilsen, R., Waymire, K. G., MacGregor, G. R. and Insel, T. (1999). Increased affiliative response to vasopressin in mice expressing the vasopressin receptor from a monogamous vole. *Nature*, 400, 766–768.

Young, L. and Wang, Z. (2004). The neurobiology of pair bonding. *Nature Neuroscience*, 7, 1048–1054.

Young, L. J. (1999). Oxytocin and vasopressin receptors and species typical behaviors. *Hormonal Behavior*, 36, 212–221.

Yurgulun-Todd, D. (2002). Inside the teenage brain. *Frontline* Retrieved September 20, 2007, from http://www.pbs.org/wgbh/pages/frontline/shows/teenbrain/

Zahed, S., Prudom, S. L., Snowdon, C. L., Ziegler, T. E. (2007). Male parenting and response to infant stimuli in the common marmoset (Callithrix jacchus). *American Journal of Primatology*, 69, 1–15.

Zukow, P. (1989). Siblings as effective socializing agents: Evidence from Mexico. In P. Zukow (ed.), *Sibling Interaction Across Cultures*, 79–105. New York: Springer-Verlag.

Index

CPSIA information can be obtained at www.ICGtesting.com
Printed in the USA
BVOW03*0113130214

344338BV00004B/6/P